Fin de Millénaire Budapest

Globalization and Community

Dennis R. Judd, Series Editor

Fin de Millénaire Budapest

Metamorphoses of Urban Life

Judit Bodnár

Globalization and Community / Volume 8
University of Minnesota Press
Minneapolis • London

MINNESOTA

Published with assistance from the Margaret S. Harding Memorial Endowment honoring the first director of the University of Minnesota Press.

The University of Minnesota Press gratefully acknowledges permission to reprint the following. An earlier version of chapter 3 originally appeared as "'He That Hath to Him Shall Be Given': Housing Privatization in Budapest after State Socialism," *International Journal for Urban and Regional Research* 20, no. 4 (1996): 616–36. An earlier version of chapter 5 appeared as "Assembling the Square: Social Transformation in Public Space and the Broken Mirage of the Second Economy in Postsocialist Budapest," *Slavic Review* 57, no. 3 (fall 1998): 489–515.

Published by the University of Minnesota Press
111 Third Avenue South, Suite 290
Minneapolis, MN 55401-2520
http://www.upress.umn.edu

Library of Congress Cataloging-in-Publication Data

Bodnár, Judit, 1963–
    Fin de millénaire Budapest : metamorphoses of urban life / Judit Bodnár.
      p. cm. — (Globalization and community ; v. 8)
    Includes bibliographical references and index.
    ISBN 0-8166-3584-6 (hard : alk. paper) — ISBN 0-8166-3585-4 (pbk. : alk. paper)
    1. Budapest (Hungary)—Social conditions. 2. Cities and towns—Europe, Eastern. 3. Post-communism. 4. Globalization. I. Title. II. Series.
HN420.5.B8 B63 2001
306'.09439'12—dc21

                                    00-009538

The University of Minnesota is an equal-opportunity educator and employer.

11 10 09 08 07 06 05 04 03 02 01   10 9 8 7 6 5 4 3 2 1

Contents

Acknowledgments

This book began as my dissertation research, which was made possible by grants from the Research Support Scheme of the Central European University and from OTKA, the National Science Research Fund of Hungary (under code F 7111). The project received further financial and intellectual stimuli, for which I am grateful, when I was a MacArthur Postdoctoral Fellow in the Globalization Project of the Chicago Humanities Institute at the University of Chicago and acquired its final shape in a very pleasant urban environment when I was the resident sociologist of GUST, the Ghent Urban Studies Team at the University of Ghent, Belgium.

I am also grateful to a number of people in Budapest without whose assistance this work would not have been possible. I am especially indebted to József Hegedűs and Iván Tosics at the Metropolitan Research Institute in Budapest for their unreciprocated support and for their allowing me access to their unique data on housing privatization. I thank Virág Molnár, whose intelligent research assistance helped me learn more about art movie theaters. Tivadar Ruzsányi and Béla Nagy of Mű-hely Kft. generously provided me with materials on Moscow Square.

Jenő Jedlóczki lent me invaluable assistance with some of the better-looking illustrations, for which I am very grateful. I am also grateful to Chris Chase-Dunn, Susan Gal, David Harvey, and Iván Szelényi for their comments that greatly helped the writing and publication of this book. Finally, without József Böröcz's insistence and supportive criticism, this book would not have been written. I sincerely thank him.

1

Posted

Socialism, Modernity, State

Time has accelerated in postsocialist Budapest. City dwellers are losing their points of reference; the cityscape's secure signposts are disappearing at a speed not experienced before. People are learning new codes, from the overhaul of all telephone numbers to the renaming of some basic points of orientation, especially of the official kind, including the names of the municipal authorities as well as some streets. Recurring tourists from the "West" may lament the rise in prices and the number of car thefts; they are relieved nevertheless as they feel more at home than before. Their image of the world order, which state socialism temporarily muddied, is apparently clearing again. Budapest—or, to be more precise, those parts of Budapest the tourists see and take to stand for the whole—is dressed up in garments that are more and more similar to those in west European, North American, or, in some respects, even "non-Western" cities. This is conveniently explained by the collapse of socialism.

Meanwhile, in western Europe and North America, scholarly and media talk is about "urban renaissance" and "renewal," and even an overall "urban restructuring" in the West. The transformation of east-central European cities is taking place on the ruins of state socialism.[1] Does this mean that the revival of Prague, Cracow, or Budapest can be assumed independent or incomparably different from the renewal of Western (inner) cities? Theoretical considerations urge, and empirical observations compel, the idea that the recent social and economic transformation of east-central Europe is part of global restructuring. Seen from this angle—the view one obtains when looking at, and through, Budapest—the east-central European experience of coming out of socialism provides an exciting, fresh view of the general farewell to modernity that is a main concern of "Western"

1

scholarship today. The recent post–state socialist "Great Transformation" of east-central Europe is but the end of the most systematic social enterprise of modernization accompanied by an attempt to approximate a very specific, collective-consumption-based notion of social justice through state redistribution. The ideology of socialism and its now largely extinct, Soviet-type version fit very well into the context of a modernity that arches from Ford's Model T to fascism. The closing of the century that saw the decline of state socialism, along with socialist ideals, in east-central Europe witnessed a general disillusionment with the possibility of collective emancipation in the "West" as well. "Is it not this single, central fact which . . . sets apart the two *fin-de-siècles*?" asks Beilharz (1994: 105) while arguing for a fundamental similarity with regard to fears and doubts concerning the modernist project in the two periods.

The contemporary central European transformation suggests a conspicuous parallel with the beginning of the history of capitalism. Some authors claim that the ongoing process can be grasped as the "simulation" of the Great Transformation and of the original accumulation of capital. In a sociohistorical context marked by an endemic lack of mobilizable capital, resources have been withdrawn from one sector, the state, and moved into another, the private, in the course of what has come to be known as privatization. In the east of Europe, this is the second process of this kind—a frenzy of "catching up" through state policies aimed at reshaping accumulation patterns by inducing large-scale property change. The first one took place, following Preobrazhensky's ideas, in the early period of the building of the Soviet state. The "socialist original accumulation" raised investment funds for the industrial/state sector at the expense of the agrarian/private sector and also nationalized—that is, forcibly moved from private hands to state ownership and bureaucratic management—all production assets along with some important means of consumption, such as housing and urban space. It is argued that, in an ironic reversal of history, the current privatization rearranges the ownership of those very assets. In spite of its elegance and accessibility, the simple parallel between socialist and postsocialist original accumulation works in some important ways against a better understanding of the current transformation. By placing a strong, consistent emphasis on discontinuities, on beginnings—a characteristic predisposition of all nonadvanced regions experiencing radical social change and wishing to forget or overcome the past—this vision of change partially blurs the view we need in order to perform a proper comparative-historical analysis, to see state socialism as a part of European modernity and to see its transformation within the global restructuring of late modernity.

The dynamiting of the Pruitt Igoe Apartments in St. Louis in 1972 signaled the end of modern architecture for Charles Jencks (1984).[2] Deyan Sudjic (1993) adds that this was the death not simply of modern architecture but of a particular type of modern architecture: social housing. A shift took place against public housing at that time, architecture aside. In the United States, 550,000 homes were built with government aid in 1976. By 1981, the number dropped to half that, and was around 100,000 in 1985. In Britain, house construction by local authorities fell from 300,000 a year to a mere third of that in 1977, and to 15,000 in 1989 (Sudjic, 1993: 191). Sudjic notes, "With a remarkable degree of unanimity, governments in America, Britain and France decided that the policies of the post-war consensus on housing had been disastrously misguided" (191). Now, what is comparative urban analysis to make of the curious fact that public housing construction came to a virtual standstill in Budapest in the early 1980s—that is, still in the state socialist period of the city's history, and almost at the same time as the collapse of public housing as a political project in the "West"? Is this a mere coincidence? In whatever way we read this temporal correspondence, the end of public housing construction certainly meant the death of modern socialist architecture—and much more.

Studying state socialist sites after the collapse of state socialism places the interpreter in a controversial position. On the one hand, the epoch has suddenly acquired a historical dimension: there is a general sense of relief in its becoming the "past." Processes may gain more coherence and directionality; now it will be easier to speak the language of scholarly wisdom retrospectively. On the other hand, a new edge of the comparative problem has emerged. There is a danger that we may attribute the disappearance of some taken-for-granted conditions of urban life entirely to the withdrawal of state socialism instead of seeing some more broadly contextual, in fact outright global, dimensions of their vanishing.

Globalization and Its Challenges

The collapse of state socialism provides a little-examined expression of the process of globalization. This does not imply that the separate logic of state socialism is finally dissolved in a unified homogenizing process of world capitalism. First, consensus has not been quite established that state socialism represented a distinct logic within the world-system. In fact, serious arguments could be and have been made that, in important ways, it did not (e.g., Böröcz, 1992, 1999; Chase-Dunn, 1981, 1982; Wallerstein, 1999). Second, the unified process of world capitalism homogenizes and differentiates as well. In fact, the question of globalization gains a completely different angle if it is seen as a new phase of uneven development, which has not made the world's societies alike.

There is an intimate relationship between globalization and transformations of urban space: cities serve as the nexus nodes of global society (see, inter alia, Knight and Gappert, 1989). The surface of the emerging global society of cities is very uneven, however. The global cities—New York, London, Tokyo—are not necessarily more directly linked to the world economy than the rest; it is the constellation of the particular production and consumption sites they accommodate that places them into a coordinating and power position in the hierarchy of cities (Sassen, 1991). The cities in the next, shall we say, almost-global layer are engaged in increasing competition to occupy regionally significant positions, for however short a while. Budapest is the only city in Hungary, and among the very few in east-central Europe, that has a chance of emerging as a new regional hub of the new service economy.

Centers and peripheries have not disappeared but multiplied in the world-system; their nexuses are less and less arranged according to national boundaries. Signs of imperfection in the developmental process even among the "advanced" countries have become visible recently. The reinstatement of the periphery into the center is a most important theoretical contribution of contemporary analyses of the process of globalization. A powerful expression of the paradoxes of the process is the current reemergence in the inner parts of North American cities of presumably long-forgotten diseases, such as tuberculosis—which used to be called all across fin de siècle Europe, ominously for our subject matter, the *morbus hungaricus* (Hungarian disease).

Some write about "third-worlding at home" (Koptiuch, 1991), others discover the "Brazilianization" of Britain (Massey, 1988), but the most common conceptualizations of this dualization of the "advanced" world are the notions of "advanced marginality" and the "dual city." Drawing on an analysis of New York, Mollenkopf and Castells (1991), for instance, define the dual city as "the dichotomy we observe between the nodal segments of the space of globally interconnected flows and the fragmented and powerless locales of social communities" (417). Urban dualism is not a novelty; what is new is its location in the center. Earlier, the sociological "tale of two cities" was specifically about the "colonial city," as told in Abu-Lughod's (1965) seminal piece. Now, due to the homogenization of urban space and the convergence between certain elements of cities in the center and on the periphery, the metropole assumes some characteristics of the colonial city, argues King (1990). Others see this process merely as a resigned recognition of the ever-present dualism of modernity: it evinces, after Baudelaire, the *ephemeral* whose other half is the eternal and immutable (Beilharz, 1994). The advanced world has found its "other" in itself. The new importance of the city, it seems, lies in its being the privileged space of this dualism.

Sociology's early interest in the city is explained by the view that considered it as a synecdoche of modern development—the *part* that illuminates the great forces of the *whole* of modern society in an intensive form. The city, or at least some cities, is still used in a similar way. As Mollenkopf and Castells (1991) take New York City as a laboratory, they claim to follow Saul Bellow in insisting that "what is barely hinted in other cities is condensed and enlarged in New York" (5). Observing New York, we gain sight of the "forces affecting the globe" (5). Although hardly any twentieth-century visitor to Manhattan Island would deny Bellow's claim, certainly not all cities are likely to be affected by these global forces in the same manner. The *other* point about globalization is precisely that all cities do not become completely similar to one another; some of their elements do converge but others diverge, sometimes wildly, which is why urbanism exhibits more diversity than ever, creating intricately linked, very complex systems. Analyses of "global" or "world cities" cannot aim to represent the whole. The metaphor of the dual city certainly captures the selective transnationalization of cultures. The "third-worlding" experience of New York is, however, still quite different from life in Calcutta, and the "Brazilianization" of British cities cannot be assumed to be the master pattern for Rio or for the "Balkanization" of Budapest. These cities are not incomparable either. The task for comparative urban analysis is to decipher the similarities and differences in a historically grounded comparative framework.

Recent developments in communications and transportation technology, the economic reorganization of the world, globalization, and the attendant "time-space compression" (Harvey, 1989a) suggest to the careless observer that nothing remains unreported. Yet reporting in the media is extremely, and increasingly, selective, and the soaring amount of information does not necessarily make us wiser. Social scholarship is not immune to these processes either. When "new" phenomena emerge, especially in the intellectually non-pattern-setting parts of the world, there is practically neither time nor intellectual space for deliberation, appreciation of complexity, categorization, and naming; simplified, shorthand solutions are often all too easily invoked as proxies for careful understanding. The structures of representation created in this way assume, then, a quasi-real life of their own. In the new round of time-space compression, "the time horizons of both private and public decision-making have shrunk" (Harvey, 1989a: 147).

This increases the responsibility of interpreters both in the centers and on the peripheries. One of my aims in this volume is to revisit some of those instant conceptual imports of social scholarship while looking at, and reinterpreting, a Hungarian urban context.

There is no general solution as to how to deal with the intellectual challenges of globalization. The commonplace formula of "the devil in the details" is more applicable than ever; in our temporally and spatially compressed world we talk in headlines and distrust grand narratives—to a large extent because they require commitment and because they eat up our time. Although, as Mills (1959) insists, a sociological question is always comparative by definition, reading much of what passes for sociology one cannot but emphasize the importance of a refined comparative strategy. That is *not* merely insisting on *difference* in the sea of globalization understood as homogenization; the core of a careful comparative strategy is locating both similarities and differences at the right places and tracing their boundaries with great precision. Analytic features of different cities or urban social phenomena may in general look very similar, yet analysis of their histories and connectedness to other elements of the context makes an enormous interpretive difference.

Every place is unique—a unique constellation of features that it shares with other places. With this book, I also invite the reader to consider the possibility that, beyond accounting for variation, the case of Budapest is instructive for us in our attempt to make sense of *our*—Western—experience in a changing world. This is so, first, because some of the structural conditions that set a city like Budapest apart from the "Western" urban experience—relative levels of profits and remuneration of labor—are *historical* facts. It is in their nature to increase and decrease in a rather erratic, unpredictable fashion so that—who knows?—maybe the experience of a semiperipheral almost-global city like Budapest may turn out to be the image of the future of at least some "Western" locales. After all, in the only ground-level street scene in the seminal dystopian cinematic statement of future urbanity, *Blade Runner,* where the vernacular of supposed twenty-first-century L.A.—described as a creole between Spanish and Japanese—is heard, it is in fact Hungarian spoken with a heavy English accent.

Second, careful attention to the transformation of a city like Budapest is instructive because postsocialism offers a context in which many of the widely documented effects of globalization may be observed in a clearer, more pronounced form: they are more sudden and, hence, less mediated. The process is taking place (1) amid radical political changes and a rarely questioned political rhetoric of the "free market" and foreign capital involvement, (2) during a severe fiscal crisis of the state, and (3) against the backdrop of what had constituted the *differentia specifica* of state socialism, termed retrospectively the "premature welfare state" by institutionalist economist János Kornai (1997).

Changes in the structure of the Hungarian state's finances are significant. Between 1989 and 1993, government expenditure as a proportion of the gross domestic product remained relatively constant in Hungary, but, because the country experienced a 21 percent decline in GDP during this period, government spending dropped significantly in real terms (Campbell, 1996).[3] Due to inflation and resistance to severe cutbacks in social programs, revenues declined faster than expenditures, creating serious budget deficits in most postsocialist countries. The withering away of the "premature welfare state" is quite drastic; in 1990, Hungary's ratio of debt service to exports was among the highest in the world (Campbell, 1996), and international organizations, most notably the International Monetary Fund, have been pressing for welfare cuts while the destruction of the life conditions of the most underprivileged of these populations due to the current economic depression make these expenses more needed than ever. Although the above-noted processes have some specifically postsocialist peculiarities, they are not unique to that context. Acknowledgment of this global link can make our thinking less provincial, East and West.

This volume is not about the process of globalization per se. It looks at metamorphoses of city life and addresses global implications as important components of the causal factors affecting any urban transformation after state socialism. How far can we take a parallel between the well-documented North American and west European processes of urban restructuring and the postsocialist urban transformation(s)? Is the east-central European departure from state socialism merely a local version of the overall "Western" departure from high modernity? Is the "chaotic" and "disorderly" nature of the "transition" not merely the sign of a different order? These are some of the more general questions that organize this study. Raising them implies also gaining some angle on the more general question of whether state socialism "produced a space of its own" (Lefebvre, 1991: 54), which many observers have tended to answer reluctantly and perhaps in imprecise, often overly general terms.

The City in (the) Transformation

The study of postsocialist urban change addresses an aspect of the contemporary central European transformation that has not been at the center of sociological inquiries: in contrast to analyses of new democratic politics, the "market transition debate," or the notion of elite change, the transformation of the state socialist city has received little attention. This is despite the history of social scholarship since the mid-nineteenth century, which suggests that the study of urban space can reveal fine layers of social change not reflected in more grandiose considerations.

There is no need to convince anyone who has observed the collapse of state socialism about the generic importance of the urban as space of representation (Lefebvre, 1991). Despite the painful lack of resources available to the new city governments, street names were quickly changed, and public statues of political origins and signification that were suddenly undesirable were the first elements of the state socialist status quo removed after the collapse. However, it is less obvious how, below the surface, the built environment and everyday life, with its dictum of "programmed consumption" (Lefebvre, 1991), accommodates large-scale social change in its own manner. How is it that the physical hardware of the city mediates, confines, and enables economic and political processes? Urban space has an increasingly visible character, but that ought not be confused with transparence. Its layers can be excavated only through a properly comparative and historical research strategy.

The current material in any society is a mound of historical sediment, and it is impossible to understand Budapest today without paying attention to the numerous layers of its relevant past. Attempting to interpret the current transformation would also be futile without a consideration of the analytic tradition that summarizes the several-centuries-long reign of urban capitalism worldwide. Thus the space of the postsocialist city reveals itself only if we illuminate simultaneously the historical silhouettes of the state socialist city and the contours of capitalist cities. In the text to follow, I keep this constantly in mind. The intellectual strategy appropriate for this purpose could be labeled an *implicitly comparative* approach: while I focus on only one "case"—Budapest—in my analysis I aim to expose, and explore the implications of, the conceptual transferences from social scholarship elsewhere (notably, in the "West"). My narrative position, that of an interpreter—a citizen of Budapest speaking analytically about her city in the American and west European academic context—virtually precludes anything but an implicitly comparative approach.

Needless to say, this study is intended to address scholarly audiences beyond a small circle of "East European" area specialists: the study of the city after state socialism is theoretically essential for urban studies and, by implication, for sociological theorizing in general. The detailed descriptions of Budapest's transformation presented in the ensuing pages ought not mislead the reader: this study operates precisely in the creative tension that arises from writing about unique processes on the ground with the generic theoretical implications in mind. This tension is of course also present when "Western" empirical social phenomena are described and then placed in a generic interpretative framework; what is different here is that, due partly to the region's semiperipheral position, partly to its recent state socialist past, and partly to many other cultural factors, "Western" scholarship has a tendency to place the social experiences of the societies "east of the Elbe" in a remote and dark corner, attention to which needs to be explained with some auxiliary argument. In this book I aim quite resolutely to subvert that arrangement.

At the conception of the field of urban sociology, the city assumed a special significance as an object of inquiry. It was the locus of modernity—the site of a new division of labor for Durkheim, of a specific mode of production for Marx, of the objective spirit for Simmel, and the basis for a new type of human association in the oeuvre of Weber and Tönnies.[4] The city has since largely lost this particular theoretical reference. Searching for a proper subject matter for the field amid the "crisis of urban sociology," Castells identified the theoretical relevance of the "urban" as the site of collective consumption orchestrated by the state. Castells's interpretation of the urban makes the state socialist experience particularly interesting. If *state* socialism made a difference in the urban context, that difference resided mainly in the sphere of collective consumption. A retrospective view of this change from state socialism to post–state socialism is thus informative, and indeed compelling, for general urban theory.

This volume examines the transformation of urban space in Budapest after the collapse of state socialism. Urban scholarship has established that the highly restricted private ownership of urban land and the role of the state in the planning, financing, construction, and distribution of housing translates into differences between "capitalist" and "socialist" cities (see, inter alia, French and Hamilton, 1979; Szelényi, 1993). Consequently, one of the focuses of any analysis of the postsocialist city should be the relationship between property change and the use of urban space. I examine the decline of what had constituted the *differentia specifica* of state socialist urban phenomena—the housing landlordism of the state—culminating in the current process of the privatization of formerly state-owned housing. However, I go beyond the analysis of property change and the state; I subvert the common narrow interpretation of privatization by taking it seriously as the leitmotiv of postsocialist urban change and as a thoroughly social phenomenon with different meanings. The privatization of formerly public goods includes the privatization of public space and, ultimately, of the city. But privatization also scrutinizes the notion of the collective—goods, public, and citizenship. Privatization taken seriously extends the analysis back in time and allows one to see its origins in the late state socialist period. Consumer socialism, also referred to more plastically in Hungary as Frigidaire socialism, in a sense prepared the soil for large-scale privatization. Essentially, it meant individual strategies of tempered consumption on a massive scale that centered on the home, the holiday house, and the car. In a highly politicized interpretation, Frigidaire socialism is often seen as a resistance strategy to the public, state-controlled, realm. From a more general point of view, this small-scale privatization of collective goods was indeed a sociocultural overture, an introduction to the large-scale privatization of collective goods broadly understood that has taken place since the regime change.

As in the Great Transformation—that from feudalism to capitalism—the urban context is transformed through the creation of *enclosures* of former common space: "pieces of common land are," indeed, "converted into private property."[5] This transformation might even be truer to the essence of the notion of enclosures: whereas precapitalist common lands were, clearly, "not common in the absolute sense,"[6] state socialist urban space is moving today from widely universalistic access under state ownership and normative control to more and more fragmented, and hence decidedly particularistic, patterns. The liberating aspects of the widening possibilities for the particularistic use of urban space, the turning inward of urban lives, and the concomitant losses of the declining significance of public goods and public space leave ambiguous markings on the recent metamorphosis of urban life.

Plan of Work

This book is about urban change in Budapest, yet readers will not find discussions of some aspects of urban life. I make no claim to comprehensiveness. The book reads more as a collection of short essays than as an encyclopedic monograph. It is one interpretation of recent changes, yet suggestive of other readings and future alternatives, and aims to reveal some of the background of the extreme durability and fragility of collective life as lived in the city.

Chapter 2 considers a fundamental theoretical and methodological problem in the treatment of east-central European state socialist urban development: how to analyze these cities in a general framework that, by definition, compares them with other cases. The chapter tries to disentangle the bundle of differences assumed under the socialist-capitalist dichotomy and delineates the possibilities of a meaningful, comparative understanding of postsocialist urban phenomena mentioned in this chapter. Finally, chapter 2 presents the theoretical outlines of a comparative strategy based on Karl Polanyi's schemes of integration that has been widely used to relate capitalist and state socialist economies. This frames the "market transition debate" examined in chapter 3. The analysis of the privatization of formerly state-owned housing, a process that demolishes the material basis of state socialist housing arrangements, contributes to an understanding of the interplay of redistributive and market elements and demonstrates how their intricate new constellation produces often grave, qualitatively new inequalities.

Property change is a fundamental force behind the transformation of the use of urban space—a grand site of which is the renewed inner city. Chapter 4 provides a brief account of the main themes of urban restructuring and some accompanying processes in the global context. Then gentrification—a component of urban restructuring—is examined as a local process focusing on the supposed differences between the North American and west European contexts. The chapter proceeds to analyze inner-city renewal in Budapest by counterposing a state socialist urban revitalization project in an inner-city district to the recent "renovation" of downtown. Gentrification, tenure conversion, and functional conversion are treated as variations on the theme of uneven urban development.

"The form of social space is encounter, assembly, simultaneity," writes Lefebvre (1991: 101). Chapter 5 examines a particular place in this regard: one of Budapest's busiest public places, Moscow Square, as it gathers "crowds, products, acts and symbols," and assembles them according to the new order of the city. The experience of the market through the filter of the socialist second economy is counterposed to the new image of the market as condensed in the analysis of market flows in the square. The chapter documents a segment of the urban transformation *in* public space.

Chapters 6 and 7 turn attention to the transformation *of* public space. Chapter 6 compares two new genres of public space in Budapest that are both intimately connected to globalization. Malls as sites of new shopping and public culture are counterposed to the globalization of the most popular art form as shown in the emergence of the Art Movie Network. Chapter 7 relates recent debates concerning the decline or relocation of public space to urban restructuring and its concomitant processes. The urban texture is put under a severe test of endurance because of (1) the strengthening of private enclosures, (2) increasing social polarization, and (3) the emergence of a more heterogeneous citizenry. These tensions pose a challenge to the idea of urban public space. The declining significance of public space and the new philosophy of semipublic space, combined with the effects of increasing marginality and heterogeneity, make it ever more difficult to find some sort of unity amid diversity that may ultimately enhance the fragmentation of urban space. Yet, even if I recount losses associated with the current fragmentation of urban space, my treatment of the theme should read more as an attempt to meditate on the historically conditioned dialectics of unity and difference, of fragmentation and democratization—democratization that goes beyond the introduction of democratic political institutions following state socialism.

Fragmentation is connected with the wild diversity of life in contemporary cities. Globalization seems a tangible everyday experience, because fragments of urban life can be conceived as similar here and there. The expansion of opportunities in the social imagination builds on these fragments. This is why "more persons in more parts of the world consider a wider set of possible lives than ever before," writes Arjun Appadurai (1996: 55). Even though there is a limit on individually constructing possible lives that could always be elsewhere, the global expansion of the social horizon, along with its fragmentation, contributes to making life less "solid" than earlier. In central Europe many connect this phenomenon with the political changes that are always disorienting, but the present condition goes beyond that. Life has become precarious East and West. Yet it still has local genealogy. This book attempts to disentangle this globally connected central European path to our present precariousness.

2

Constructing Difference

Western versus Non-Western, Capitalist versus Socialist Urban Logic

The cities of east-central Europe have stirred little sentiment in the history of urban studies. They attracted some attention when they became socialist, but their debut on the theoretical stages of urban sociology was somewhat feeble even then. A certain conceptual uneasiness has lingered around them ever since because their simultaneously east-central European *and* socialist character made it impossible to disentangle the two. Their differences from "Western" models were widely noted, and this begged for some explanation; their similarities tended to be overlooked or belittled. Difference was explained mainly by reference either to state socialism or to peculiar patterns of historical development in the region. Neither procedure offers, however, a solid theoretical framework that could accommodate comparisons with capitalist and "Western" cities comfortably while recognizing differences within the "east-central European socialist model."

The uneasiness of sympathetic Western observers on the left to relate to state socialism can be explained only partly by the actual features of socialism as it existed or the epistemological and psychological position in which intellectuals often find themselves when witnessing the materialization of a utopia that is necessarily deformed and elevates the original idea to even more utopian levels. Another part of the Western observers' uneasiness came from a conflation of differences: state socialist phenomena occurred in parts of the world they did not, sometimes did not even want to, know well. This left them with little but stereotypes. What they saw was different but not strikingly—sometimes only a shabbier version of what was familiar to them. In their vision, some socialist cities looked as if they were secondhand Parisian cityscapes of sorts, with less glamour, less extravagance, poorer and worse kept. Was that "secondhandness" an inherent feature of state socialism, a consequence of central or east European "culture," or a symptom of unqualified backwardness and poverty?

This chapter is on writing about east-central European socialist cities—especially Budapest—but it is not only about that. In attempting to identify the challenges and most common traps in analyzing socialist urban phenomena in a broad sociological framework, I will also specify some of the difficulties that point beyond the study of state socialism. This should help uncover some fundamental problems that arise when researchers encounter experience that is "different" from the determining, original collective social experience codified in sociology, urban or any other kind. What is the cognitive location of social phenomena that are situated physically in east-central Europe and under state socialism? Are they variations within "our" world—the denotation of what such highly marked notions as "the West" or "Europe" stand for—or do they constitute a different order? Are they kind of like "us" or more like some "other"?

I will analyze three types of approaches that this question has produced. One exaggerates the distinctiveness of socialism, the second ignores it and fits a merely quantitative difference in a universal, unilinear pattern of development, and the third explains socialist urban phenomena away as continuations of patterns *always* qualitatively different from those of the West. These are ideal-typical intellectual traps, and falling into them is, while understandable, avoidable. One need only keep the delicate balance by proceeding along all three dimensions, as I demonstrate in a few examples later. My aim in this chapter is neither to render a comprehensive treatment of state socialist urban issues nor to secure an obligatory niche of a couple of pages in textbooks for state socialist cities; it is merely to isolate the most typical slips of the comparative mind that can be mitigated only by more properly specified comparative intellectual schemes. Conflating comparative dimensions is a strategy that has led to very real misconceptions in both lay and scholarly discourses and has not died with the removal of the qualifier *socialist* from the denotation of the region. The recognition of this is vital. Only then will the outside observer not be surprised to see that contemporary Moscow is different from, say, Budapest or Sofia, in spite of all being "post-Communist," and that a walk in Budapest has not become the same as one in Vienna, only dirtier.

Socialist versus Capitalist Urban Logic

This intellectual journey begins with the Marxist critical urban analysis of the 1970s. In that context, it was common to posit a radical conceptual break between capitalism and state socialism, thus attributing any observed difference to that distinction. The difference of socialism was assumed to be so overwhelming that it excluded—or, rather, subsumed—the consideration of other kinds of difference. This is a problem, as Manuel Castells (1979) points out, because "to designate a social formation as 'socialist' does not elucidate its relation to space and, very often, it tends to divert research, which takes refuge in a series of ideological dichotomies tending to present the obverse side of the capitalist logic, instead of showing the real processes that are developing in the new social forms" (64).

In *The Urban Question,* Castells (1979) addresses the unblessed effects of a dichotomized perspective in social science. Yet his "general framework for the analysis of the role of the urban problematic" (1978: 13) leaves no room for socialist urban phenomena, as the urban, for him, is inseparably linked to the dynamic of the capitalist mode of production. Theoretically, socialist urban phenomena would be connected to the socialist mode of production—an animal defined reactively and rather elusively as the "obverse side of the capitalist logic." The laxness of this definition re-creates the capitalist-socialist dichotomy with full vigor. Castells attempts to include state socialist cities within his overall logic of the urban inextricable from capitalism by claiming that the capitalist mode of production, although subdued for the moment, is still present in state socialism. Nevertheless, Castells concludes correctly that similar-looking urban phenomena may have very different meanings under capitalism and socialism. Unfortunately, there is very little elaboration to this latter point in Castells's work, and only a little more on the *differentia specifica* of urbanization in socialist countries. The primacy of the political and its independence from the economic determine the distinctive logic of the socialist urban, whose specific content may vary according to the party line, the ideology of individual socialist states (Castells, 1979). But the socialist city becomes invariably the incarnation of political will—that of the state, the party, and the planner.

Differences in the relationship between the political and economic spheres under capitalism and state socialism offer an important starting point for comparisons. What complicates the issue is the equivalence set up so easily in this line of thinking between "the political" and the state. One of the most common characteristics of analyses of the socialist urban is that both socialist planners and the Western evaluators of their achievements have assumed the socialist state to be omnipotent.[1]

It is certainly true that in the beginning, "socialism seemed to hold out the possibility of doing everything that the bourgeois state wanted to do but could not" (Harvey, 1989c: 196). This formula captured the prevailing sentiment of leftist and enlightened liberal modernizers, the expectations of people whose professional role in the long-term transformation of the built environment needs legitimation from collective rationality backed up by the state. However, viewing socialism and the socialist city as enacting the propositions of the socialist classics, or as the incarnation of some abstract political will—that is, of the loudly self-announced will of the party state—cannot in itself capture, let alone explain, socialist urban phenomena. This view shields important variations in the power, interests, and methods of the socialist party state to subdue society; it also, ultimately, denies complexity to the state socialist experience. The path from the primacy of the political to the materialization of party will is all too easy for a serious descriptive analysis.[2] This would also leave no room for actors to maneuver, creating a grossly overdetermined political field, a caricature of the "totalitarianism" portrayal of state socialism. The informalization and metaphorization of socialist party state power, as observed at least for post-1968 Hungary (Böröcz, 1999), contradicts this depiction forcefully.

David Harvey (1978) identifies the limits to the interpretation of the urban process in a noncapitalist environment clearly by claiming that the "urban has a specific meaning under the capitalist mode of production which cannot be carried out without the radical transformation of meaning (and of reality) into other social contexts" (101). Instead of an *exclusive* interpretation of this passage, which would see only the exclusion of socialist urbanization from the dominant theoretical framework, a less restrictive understanding of both Castells and Harvey would suggest no more than the idea that any analysis of the urban needs to be contextualized: it requires a properly theorized and historicized notion of the social formation in which the urban is situated. And the urban question is tied historically and intellectually to capitalism.

It is important to remember the background to these restrictive interpretations of the urban process. When discussing the need to "unmask" class exploitation behind the facade of urban sociology—itself an ideology—Castells directs his criticism mostly against urban sociology in the manner of both Wirth and the representatives of urban ecology. Overall, both Castells and Harvey react to notions of urban sociology whose "central problem . . . is to discover the forms of social action and organization that typically emerge in relatively permanent, compact settlements of large numbers of heterogeneous individuals" (Wirth, 1938: 9). Sterile, ahistorical, and apolitical as this and similar images of the study of cities are, they signal the success of the compartmentalizing tendency of modernity in the social sciences. The urban process or urban problems can be discussed as if "the urban" were an independent discipline—similarly to some interpretations of the sociology of aging, industry, agriculture, small groups, and so on—a subject matter with only limited relevance to larger social, economic, or political issues, or to the particular context. More is missing from such analyses than class content—that omission, however, is crucial for a Marxist critique. So, again, only in a more restrictive sense, "we are being told that the concept of 'urban' is indissolubly linked to capitalism," as Szelényi (1981: 173) voices a consensual opinion. On a more permissive note, the reader is being told only that the urban is indissolubly linked to a (set of) historically specific social formation(s), capitalism being quite certainly one—but perhaps not necessarily the only one—of those.

Elsewhere, Castells designates socialism as different from capitalism. In his *City, Class and Power* (1978), where the similarity of urban problems in socialist cities to those in capitalist ones necessitates the definition of capitalism as a different (from socialism) cause leading to similar results, he writes:

> We do not use the term "capitalism" to describe a historical reality which would be immutable and directly determined by profit in all social occurrences. We make reference rather to a particular social matrix, economic, political, ideological, which is determined *in the last analysis* by an organisation of social relationships founded on the separation of the worker from the means of production and on the appropriation of the surplus value by the only holders of the means of production. (27–28)

Because of the absence of a historically rather specific subject—the appropriator as the private individual—from this formula, most theoreticians of socialism would see no difficulty in applying it to state socialism; it is difficult to think of a more thorough appropriator of surplus value than the socialist state. The real question is what happens to it after it has been taken away from its direct producer, and it is concerning possible interpretations of the apparent redistributive activities of the socialist state that opinions vary.

Castells's treatment of socialist urbanization is replete with exciting and intelligent tensions; by unmasking urbanism as an ideology, he makes it more embedded in the social context, but he leaves socialist cities out of the analysis. Although he gives us the sketches of a leftist critique of state socialism by eliminating double standards, he surprisingly insists on constructing socialist urban phenomena as fundamentally different from capitalist. His approach to the city as the site of collective consumption ultimately orchestrated by the state (1976, 1978) could have been used to justify extending urban analysis to socialist cities—or, rather, to transform it in such a way that it could address the specific historical form state socialist urbanism represented. If state socialism made a difference at all, it mostly concerned the means of collective consumption in the city. This analytic opportunity was left unexploited.

Unified Urban Logic

Social ecology takes a rather easy way out of the socialist-capitalist dichotomy; "socialist urbanization" fits easily into the grand scheme of a universal urban development. In spite of the long—manifest or latent—influence of the ecological paradigm on North American and west European sociology (Gottdiener and Feagin, 1988) and the grand streamlined analytic opportunities that this approach offers, social ecology is not represented widely in the urban literature on socialist cities written in the "West."[3] It is an important clue regarding the politics of paradigm choice that versions of human ecology have been more influential in urban analyses written in the state socialist countries themselves. An understandable reaction to the widespread "Western" practice of exoticizing everything socialist and the official Soviet line pronouncing a complete break with the past (that is, capitalism), this approach finds common traces in a very general notion of development—thus emphasizing historical continuity and similarity with the West. For this reason, it can work to deploy the important agenda of legitimating claims of identity constructions painted to be similar to, and inching toward, the "West." A desire for distinctions within what is treated otherwise as an undifferentiated Soviet bloc—by both the "West" and the "East"—is also among the motivating forces behind this selective application of likeness between the West and individual state socialist countries.

Hungarian social geographer György Enyedi argues that urban development consists of different stages in accordance with some universally applicable stages of socioeconomic development. These stages cannot be skipped and are essentially independent of the socioeconomic system (Enyedi, 1988). Thus he states that socialist urbanization "expressed the general rules of modern urbanisation and continuity of European urbanisation" (Enyedi, 1992: 875). This may be true, but the demonstration of similarities is based entirely on a narrow definition of urbanization as the development of the urban network.

The east-central European replica of the "West," however, has some specific features that are the result of "belated and distorted" development, the latter of which is coded to signify the passing, inconvenient phenomenon of state socialism. The "distortion" it has effected is the prolongation of the rural-urban dichotomy, so the difference between east-central European socialist and west European capitalist urban development is, again, reduced to a mere temporal delay in an otherwise inevitable, universal process. According to Enyedi (1992), state socialism also hindered the development of the urban middle class and promoted proletarianization instead. An important point could have been made here, had Enyedi defined proletarianization with reference to separation from the means of production, which, not having been uncommon in west European city development, could have actually added to the number of carefully counted resemblances between "East" and "West." Enyedi, however, refers to issues of class formation only in the narrow sense of *less* autonomy and freedom and *more* state control for individuals. This is a very typical and clear statement of the unilinear developmental model offered in modernization theory (for a critical overview see, among others, Portes, 1974) with a characteristically east-central European, frustrated-compensatory slant. The difference is merely quantitative; the region has only somewhat less of the same substance. Students well versed in various versions of political discourse concerning cosmopolitan versus indigenous development may know that insistence on quantitative difference is a double-edged sword. Regions compared with the "West" are bound to appear inferior, but relief is always gained from their possibility of "catching up with the West."

This treatment of socialist urbanization has the clear advantage of breaking down the socialist-capitalist dichotomy. It also colors the Cold War notion of undifferentiated oppression by the omnipotent state in urban planning and management. Socialist urbanization is counterposed to "private urbanization," that is, the persistent survival of "traditional burghers," the social locus of "urban" (modern) values characterized by similar motivations and goal-setting mechanisms to those found among the citizenry of the more advanced half of Europe. All-European urban—that is, modern—attitudes have always lingered, even if in a suppressed form, in this region. This implies also that east-central Europe should have dissolved in the general model of urbanization in a smooth transition after the collapse of state socialism.

Overcoming the socialist-capitalist dichotomy in this manner is not without difficulties. One cannot help noticing the political stake involved in the vehement emphasis on similarities and the continuity with west European development—a predisposition that was very understandable and sometimes even a brave gesture under state socialism but by no means unique to the period. The entire history of modern central Europe has been characterized by this mixture of serious scholarship, wishful thinking, and intentional or unintentional political statement making. It is also clear that there are serious limits to the comparative horizon thus opened. An additional source of relief from this "catching up" anxiety is found in the fact that the borderline of fundamental similarity with the West is drawn mercilessly on the eastern frontier of central Europe. The refreshing experience of sameness does not concern urban processes east of a central European "us," such as the Balkans, with their purportedly immutable traditions of "egalitarian peasant societies" (Enyedi, 1992: 879).

In a similar vein, but without referring to the human ecology framework, Ray Pahl (1977) establishes a theoretical link between capitalist and socialist cities on a neo-Weberian basis. He argues that the urban features of advanced societies may not be entirely due to the capitalist mode of production. He attributes them instead to more general trends such as technological development and the increasing role of the state in the sphere of collective consumption and urban planning. The state, endowed with considerable autonomy, acts in the interest of some bureaucratically defined national goal. Thus, tied to bureaucratic management and technology, urban systems may exhibit striking resemblances across different types of societies. The focus of the comparison thus shifts from differences between the capitalist and the socialist urban sphere to possible similarities. Once a unified framework for the comparison is established, state socialist urban management appears not as something essentially different from its capitalist counterpart but merely as less of the same substance. The frequently noted, and very visible, wide discrepancies between ideals and reality are results of the specific inadequacies of state planning; the socialist state simply "lacks the necessary technical knowledge and political independence" (Pahl, 1977: 55). Pahl bridges the socialist-capitalist dichotomy, but does so in a way that all differences converge on the relative technological backwardness and lesser bureaucratic efficiency of the socialist state. The qualitative distinction between capitalist and socialist urban phenomena is dissolved in mere quantitative differences, and, again, socialism as a final result assumes the whole history of central and east European development.

Historical Continuity of Idiosyncratic Eastern Features

A third approach reverses the structure of causal argumentation. It sees socialism as radically different and separate from capitalist, Western, development. Explaining the differences in the development of socialist cities builds on an assumption of persistent historical continuity. Phenomena discovered under state socialism are but the culmination of the peculiar development of non-Western regions. Pointing to the historical roots of the socialist city as the locus of state control operating through an overwhelming bu-reaucratic machinery marked by limited consumption and a severe lack of personal freedom results in milder and compartmentalized versions of a dichotomous Cold War discourse. The latter's central idea, totalitarian-ism, presupposed a straight line leading from traditional Oriental despo-tism to the Soviet model. Communist totalitarianism gave form to Oriental despotism—only intensified by modern police technology. As such, it was alien to Western civilization and democracy (Pietz, 1988). This historical continuity is what István Rév (1984) warns us about while criticizing the treatment of the seventeenth-century east-central European (Prussian-type) urban and regional system as the prefiguration of socialist urban and regional management by virtue of a common element of the lack of urban autonomy.

The political overtones of the argument are evident. This may be the reason it is rare to find scholars pursuing any version of Oriental despotism in analyses of their own countries unless it is specifically directed toward the Communist oppressors.[4] Grzegorz Weclawowicz (1996) analyzes state so-cialist Polish society and space from a postsocialist point of view. He identi-fies the most typical features of socialist cities—such as the predominance of working-class populations, their dependence on central-government or-gans for resources, and the uniformity of the urban landscape—and con-cludes that "Polish cities have conformed to these generalizations to vary-ing degree, while maintaining to some degree a national and European character" (73). In a brief reference to Russia and the Soviet Union, the re-gion figures in the following way:

> The non-totalitarian tendencies in Russian history were evident
> only in very short periods; otherwise there has been an authoritari-
> an style of government and an expansionist policy. In the case of
> Germany, . . . the 'drift towards the east' and fascism have not been
> the main characteristics of German history. (182)

The ease of the causal jump from despotic traditions to Communist re-gimes increases as we move eastward. Traditions of thought along the lines of "Oriental despotism" fit well with finding an equivalence via strong state bureaucracy between, for example, the ancient Mandarin organization of space and the spatial policies of socialist Vietnam (Nguyên, 1984). Nguyên also cautions us about creating linearity and causality retrospectively in his-torical processes.

It is certainly true that the history of east-central European develop-ment does not allow the establishment of so strong a link between the city and either the economic or the social/political aspects of the transition from feudalism to capitalism as suggested in urban theory—which usually builds on west European experience. In the eastern part of the continent, the correlation between urban development and capital accumulation has been weaker than in western Europe. Urbanization of the scale and speed of the process experienced in western Europe had not taken place in east-central Europe even by the beginning of the century (Berend, 1971). Also, east European cities played a much smaller role in the production of gesellschaft-type relationships or civil society (Rév, 1984; Szelényi, 1981). Although these historical differences must be noted, they also leave enormous space for detailed historical and causal analyses of change.

Combinations

All of the approaches considered so far, while usually mixing different comparative elements, are dominated by one type of comparative logic. The theories discussed below take the uniqueness of either state socialism or east-central European development less as a fixed starting point while finding difference that may not be due to belated development. Kennedy and Smith (1989) start from the world-system perspective and incorporate the examination of socialist urban development into their global comparative framework. They place the east-central European region into a context—whose references are not limited to western Europe—that east-central Europeans are very reluctant to apply. The uniqueness of the socialist experience largely evaporates: within a broader capitalist systemic logic, socialist east-central Europe is shown to be similar to other semiperipheral regions. World-system analysis, which usually deals with a globally rather homogeneous notion of "dependent urbanization," is forced to be precise and elaborate on some neglected issues of the semiperiphery. The role of the state is, as it were, the *differentia specifica* of the semiperiphery. With the state as the principal owner of the means of production and intricately involved in development, socialist east-central Europe fits the semiperipheral model even more closely than its capitalist predecessor. By setting up their analytic framework with an eye on the state, Kennedy and Smith are also able to distinguish socialist urbanization from dependent urbanization. State socialist cities are not characterized by overurbanization; with the exception of Hungary, they do not exhibit urban primacy; and inequalities of urban consumption are less striking. A state-centered world-system perspective lifts the socialist city out of its theoretical isolation, a move that is most welcome. However, partly as a logical consequence of its macro-orientation, the approach does not distinguish socialist urbanization from other semiperipheral models as markedly in many ways, although Kennedy and Smith argue its distinctiveness from dependent urban development very convincingly.

Iván Szelényi (1981) also opens up theoretical space to analyze the socialist urban meaningfully by loosening the causal link between capitalism and urbanism: "The 'urban' is at least a relatively distinct phenomenon analytically, as much producing capitalism as it is its product" (174). In the theoretical niche thus gained, Szelényi (1993) argues for the difference of socialist urbanization: "Urbanization in socialist Eastern Europe followed a different path from what one might anticipate if this region had followed a Western trajectory of development after the Second World War" (41). He also raises a fundamental problem: How much of the distinct character of the socialist system of regional and urban management is due to the specificities of state socialism, and to what extent is it an idiosyncratic consequence of pre–state socialist east-central European development? This is a crucial point, because the role and meaning of the city, as mentioned regarding approaches stressing historical continuity, were somewhat different under east-central European semiperipheral capitalism from those in the west European countries of core capitalism, and, as we have also seen, that fact has hardly been acknowledged by Western Marxist analyses. All difference, which is always defined as divergence from advanced west European or North American societies, is assumed under the label of socialism.

Jiří Musil (1980) also acknowledges the necessity of accounting for difference. He proposes a three-component explanatory model. Because he relies on this strategy in the context of a comparison of urban development within socialist eastern Europe, he distinguishes the "permanent, common features" of socialist urbanization, stemming from socialism; "specific features" of urbanization due to inherited differences in settlement structure, demographic situation, and so on; and, third, differences resulting from "different phases of industrialization and urbanization" (148). This comparative strategy cannot be fully exploited because it is limited to comparisons within the socialist bloc, and the analysis is confined to the development of national settlement systems where the element most emphasized is the goal-fulfilling strategies of urban and regional planners.

All the theories discussed so far as combining elements of different comparative logics seem to follow a particular strategy: secondary dimensions are allowed to enter a dominant systematic approach without fundamentally changing the theoretical setup.[5] This highlights an important point: different approaches may be predisposed to incorporating difference to varying degrees, thus the implications of transgressing their one-dimensionality may not be the same. Naturally, disciplinary tensions also influence the constraints upon, and possibilities of, the construction of more-accommodating approaches. A historical study may be alert to generalizations, whereas a world-system analysis may gain only by incorporating historical considerations in a controlled form. There is a certain fit between the comparative sensitivity of an approach and the particular question it studies. An approach that takes Wirth's classic definition of the city based on size, density, and heterogeneity may have difficulty accounting for urban phenomena that deviate from the original early-twentieth-century American pattern. As Ulf Hannerz (1980) argues, "Brave attempts, such as Wirth's, to formulate a common urban pattern have in the end supplied straw men rather than lasting paradigm" (98). Hannerz, approaching the problem from anthropology, finds such a framework particularly constraining; he constructs an alternative approach that attempts to deconstruct the urban-rural dichotomy so hastily established by any Wirthian analysis. He breaks down the role inventory of the modern Western city into five domains—household and kinship, provisioning, recreation, neighborhood, and traffic—and by considering relationships among them, includes in his analysis of the city relationships that would not be "typically urban" in Wirth's view and hence would be relegated to the "traditional" city. Hannerz re-creates the meaning of the city to accommodate variation in the analysis. Reconstructions of urban meaning along similar lines may include a dense description of east-central European socialist cities compared with other urban experience. This is, no doubt, an important step, but the analysis may still fall short of compelling theoretical explanations of similarities and differences.

A comparative strategy is not a substitute for suitable theoretical approaches; rather, it serves as a constant check on the generality of theoretical statements. The three-component comparative strategy that I will demonstrate cannot explain east-central European urban development, it can only help us to avoid the typical slips of the comparative mind. First, the region has certainly exhibited peculiarities compared with the western part of Europe. The meanings of the classical concepts of sociology become less pure, somewhat blurred in this context. As Tridib Banerjee (1993) argues in a different non-Western context, "The paradoxes and contradictions in the landscape, if noticed at all, are treated as the signs of an interim stage, of transitional urbanism" (77), ultimately to be resolved along the lines of well-known and documented Western patterns. These I treat as symptoms of qualitative differences, rather than passing disturbances, failures, or inadequacies in a universally valid system. This should not be taken to imply, however, that every society and culture is unique and thus incomparable. One should not be discouraged by the subtle dialectic of the comparative method, as expressed by Evans-Pritchard for social anthropology: "There's only one method . . . —the comparative method—and that is impossible" (quoted in Peacock, 1986: 76).

Second, certain features can be accounted for by socialism, broadly speaking, such as the effect of the elimination of private property, the predominance of state ownership, and the central, bureaucratic management of the economy, resulting in an enormous concentration of capital in the "hands" of the state. Finally, it would not be sensible to pretend that quantitative comparisons cannot be valid. Some characteristics of east-central European socialist cities can surely be explained by reference to differences in the level of development mostly manifested in the level of balanced wealth. This strategy does not necessarily imply a unilinear development with compulsory phases; it only makes space for compartmentalized quantitative comparisons along common dimensions.

My aim is not to present a theory of state socialist urbanization, but to account for some of the perceived differences between east-central European socialist and other types of urban phenomena by combining all three comparative dimensions. I will identify features that were perceived as belonging to the "socialist city," that marked it off from cities under capitalist trajectories of development. A careful application of comparative strategies will demonstrate how a bundle of differences came to be swept under the all-encompassing socialist qualifier.

Underurbanization and Double Dwellers

Underurbanization is a widely noted characteristic feature of socialist urbanization.[6] The term was coined in a comparative triangle: the "overurbanization" of developing countries is contrasted to socialist "underurbanization," and advanced industrial countries are assumed to exhibit balanced urbanization, which became the yardstick. "Under-urbanization simply means that under this pattern of industrialization-urbanization, the growth of the population falls behind the growth of urban industrial and tertiary sector jobs" (Szelényi, 1993: 49). The definition of urbanization elsewhere includes references to the growth of infrastructural investment as well (Konrád and Szelényi, 1977). In this framework, under "proper" urbanization, the growth of the urban population does not lag behind the growth of industrial jobs, and infrastructural changes keep up with industrial growth. In developing societies, urban growth is faster than that of industry, and infrastructural development lags behind population growth, producing crowded cities with worn-out services.

The peculiarity of socialist (extensive) industrialization (a feature of the 1950s and 1960s in east-central Europe) is that industrial growth occurs with slower population growth and low infrastructural investment. The imperative of industrial growth has its roots in socialist ideology, but it can also be seen in a more global context as a development strategy of the semiperipheral state and, in a socialism-capitalism contrast, as the requirement for the socialist bloc's ability to engage in the arms race of the Cold War. Infrastructural investment is not only unproductive, it is costly as well. Thus preventing unbalanced urbanization—let alone eliminating regional inequalities—is also expensive. The semiperipheral socialist state may lack some resources, but it is still strong vis-à-vis its own population: to avoid overcrowding, it is in a convenient position to place administrative restrictions on cityward migration. The imbalance between infrastructural investment and industrial growth itself is not a specifically socialist phenomenon—it is typical of all the other than advanced industrial part of the world. What is a unique result of specific features of the semiperipheral socialist state is the separation of industrial growth and urban population growth. In the long run, it may very well indicate merely the state's ability to insert a time lag between industrial growth and population growth.

As a social consequence of the process, a large part of the cost of industrialization is shifted to the countryside. There is a sharp increase in the number of people who are employed in urban industries while living in rural areas. This is not the classical pattern of suburbanization, however. Some of these people are daily commuters from villages and towns near the capital, whereas others board in workers' hostels in Budapest during the week and travel hours to see their families on the weekends. This category of "commuters" or "rural working class" gives a special class content to the rural-urban dichotomy under state socialism insofar as these workers comprise an underprivileged working class compared to their urban counterparts (Szelényi, 1981). Translating the Hungarian term, *kétlaki,* used to refer to people whose way of life is marked by a bifurcated residential arrangement, I will call them *double dwellers.* This term captures their dual position explicitly and is not meant to imply that they have followed a path of complete proletarianization or have cut every productive (income-earning) relationship with the countryside. They feel at home (or alien) in both contexts. The double dwellers' in-between way of life is that of the disadvantaged. Urban residence, "the right to the city," thus becomes a privilege in a special state socialist sense. It is not the logic of capital, the takeover of the inner city by businesses, and the exile of the working class to the *banlieue* (Lefebvre, 1972) that deprives laborers of the advantages of city life, but the socialist state's policy. It underprivileges urban infrastructural development and still favors urban vis-à-vis rural in the conservative sense of making urban residence an estatelike privilege. From a different perspective, double dwelling can be portrayed as a highly flexible multiple-source income-earning strategy. With the majority of a wide spectrum of Hungarian agricultural produce having been supplied by families whose members were engaged part- or full-time in typically urban forms of economic activity, double dwelling has served as a powerful element in combined survival strategies.

Double dwelling is not entirely new to east-central European societies. Industrialization in the cities in the nineteenth and twentieth centuries attracted large numbers of migrants from the countryside. Some of them did not completely become part of the urban working class; they preserved their double dwellings and double income-earning strategies for a long time, living as industrial wage laborers during most of the year and returning to their villages for the agricultural season. For women, who were only very moderately employed in industry prior to state socialist industrialization, domestic service was the alternative, often combined with agricultural wage labor during the summer months. These women preserved their double-dweller status until they got married and retired to their villages (Gyáni, 1983). These phenomena mirror a specific feature of east-central European development: early industrialization took place with a greater retentive force of agriculture and rural residence than elsewhere due to labor-intensive (or poorly mechanized) production (Berend and Ránki, 1974).

Double dwelling was also part of a distinctive form of Hungarian urban development described historically by Ferenc Erdei (1974). The agricultural town *(mezőváros)*, a rather old type of settlement, was economically based on agricultural production—land cultivation or animal husbandry—which took place outside the borders of the town, on scattered farms whose owners had their main residences in town. They would leave town to take care of their farms and then return to carry on their lives as urban residents. In spite of their double dwelling, Erdei considers them not as peasants but as a specific form of bourgeoisie: "Although people sometimes work in solitude and live and work under simple conditions, they breathe city air, since their isolation is temporary" (187). The dichotomy of town and country, which is not a relationship of two legally circumscribed entities with no permeability between them but whose functional hierarchy gives

this permeability an estatelike sense of exclusion, became the general clas-
sificatory principle of modern European societies (Erdei, 1974). According
to Erdei, the agricultural town transcended this dichotomy in its relationship to its hinterland. In a somewhat Marxist manner, Erdei envisioned the
elimination of the "class struggle" between city and country through the universal extension of urban privileges, the main vehicle of which would be the
agricultural town. The double dwelling that developed during socialist industrialization is an ironic reversal of the developmental potential of Erdei's
idiosyncratic bourgeoisie; the phenomenon of state socialist double dwelling did not decrease the estatelike separation of town and country. This
situation, however, which could be seen as begetting an underprivileged
working class, also provided some double dwellers with the possibility of
engaging actively in market-oriented small-plot agricultural production
with the opening up of an alternative economic space, the second economy.
Some of these families may have actually experienced a sort of "peasant
embourgeoisement" (Szelényi, 1988)—a peculiar form of social mobility.

Double dwelling emerged as a reaction to a structural feature of extensive industrialization, labor shortage, the specific form of which was
made possible by low transportation costs (a state socialist attribute), the
lack of available housing in cities (a widespread urban phenomenon mixed
with state socialist ideological reasons), and a specifically state socialist administrative push. Double dwelling can be seen largely as the result of the
twin processes of state socialist industrialization and underurbanization,
and thus as a specific feature of state socialism. On the other hand, if the
focus is shifted from the administrative, migration-restricting role of the socialist state, one can also see the greater retentive force of agriculture and
the thereby emerging combined income-earning strategies that have historically accompanied east-central European industrialization, making it
somewhat different from other semiperipheral developments (Kennedy
and Smith, 1989), not so much in terms of double income-earning strategies, which are not uncommon outside of socialist east-central Europe, but
in terms of their relative success. With one foot securely planted in the state
sector, double dwellers could have the opportunity to make more out of
their combined strategy than mere survival and to contribute to the economic advancement of their households. Here the description fits the
Hungarian case most closely; the availability and economic attractiveness
of this double income-earning scenario was nowhere as great. Underurbanization and double dwelling, while characteristic features of socialist
urbanization, were more typical in some areas than in others. For example,
even though commuting required a relatively dense network of roads and

railways—which were largely inherited from the past—the former GDR, with the exceptionally good transportation system around its cities, did not exhibit the kind of double dwelling typical of Hungary.[7] In spite of the homogenizing tendencies of the state socialist system, there was great variation among the socialist cities. Historical continuity, features of underdevelopment, and the special effects of state socialism are all intertwined in the montage of "socialist urbanization."

Uniformity of the Socialist City

A distinctive feature of the socialist city, numerous analyses suggest, is that it is less urban (Szelényi, 1993) than the nonsocialist city, or, on a more disparaging note, it has a sense of outright uniformity and boredom.[8] There is some evidence implying the possible dissociation of dullness from socialism. In the case of Budapest, historian John Lukacs (1988) notes that for A. Nicolson, the British consul-general to Budapest at the end of the nineteenth century, "the four years he spent in Hungary 'were four years of boredom'" (65)—which would support some sort of historical continuity in this respect. Lukacs, however, dismisses the diplomat's opinion on the basis of Nicolson's personal bias against Hungarians. More to the point, Böröcz (1996) notes how Budapest was described in tourist guidebooks to Europe published in the United States in 1877 as featuring churches and public buildings "of no particular interest," whereas an edition published twenty years later allowed that "some of the new public buildings are elegant in their way" (23). Yet a generation later, the 1924 edition of the same publication went on to suggest, in striking contrast, that Budapest's "picture at sunset is one of the most striking in Europe" and that "it is not only the most considerable city of Hungary, but is probably to be numbered among the four most beautiful capitals of Europe" (23). A word of caution is thus in order: these "Western" observers' aesthetic judgments about east-central European cityscapes appear to be greatly unstable.

We can see that this is particularly so if we consider the proclivity of east-central European cultures during the state socialist period toward complex, often ironic, informal, and hidden institutional arrangements. The cultural scene in most state socialist capitals of almost the entire socialist period has been described by insider participants as featuring a colorful palette of fully, semi-, or nonpublic performances.[9] A possible a priori objection to taking at face value the notion of the topos of the monotony of the socialist city noted by "Western" observers would be that some of that must be attributed to foreign observers' lack of subtle keys to the culture's complexities.[10] What appears as dullness to some may in fact be exciting complexity along different cultural codes.[11] The influence of a lesser degree of commercialization should not be understated either: difference and diversity can be accentuated or even initiated effectively by the market.

A striking visual experience often described by Western visitors, uniformity is manifested mostly in the monotony of urban architecture and street furniture—monuments and central-square kiosks (Church, 1979). Street names are repetitive, shops have functional names with no personal references (French and Hamilton, 1979), services are uniform and standardized, and even a sympathetic guidebook writer observes that in socialist cities gift shopping is a bore (Kane, 1968). With a small jump, observers often conclude that "it may well be that these reflect the uniformity of socialist consciousness pervading the new societies of Eastern Europe" (French and Hamilton, 1979: 15). The ideological-political component of urban processes is usually overemphasized; the quest for equity orders the development of urban space expressed in the uninhibited intervention of planners not restricted by rents. This and the undifferentiated land, labor, and transport costs are seen to result in the homogeneity of the urban environment (Hamilton, 1979).

The housing estate has become the symbol of new socialist urban development and uniformity. It represents the purest form of socialist town planning, architecture, and social policy; socialism's most tangible contribution to the city. It is well-known that these projects are not unique architectural markers of state socialism; the Grands Ensembles of Paris look very much like an average housing estate in east-central Europe from the 1970s. If there was anything special about socialist housing estates, it was their class composition: they were not pockets of poverty or concentrations of the urban underclass. The average class position of their dwellers was higher than in similar projects in nonsocialist countries (Szelényi, 1983). There was a time—now forgotten by many—when, due to very limited housing construction and the deterioration of the old housing stock, the modernness and neatness of newly built prefabs were popular among educated middle-income people.

Another phenomenon that is widely accepted as a result of the specificities of socialism is the lack, or at least smaller degree, of social segregation. Again, there are several levels and modes of explanation, among which voluntaristic ideological ones dominate. For example, "Planners in socialist societies should be attempting to create uniform residential areas according to Marxist-Leninist principles to eliminate social segregation" (Hamilton and Burnett, 1979: 290). The uniformity of apartments does increase the chances of a random distribution of dwellers by social class, and of preventing their segregation, but only when availability is not restricted by rents.[12] Nevertheless, even areas outside of the newly built housing estates of socialist cities tend to be less segregated than their Western, especially North American, counterparts. Historical reasons connect this phenomenon to specific features of east-central European development.

Historically, the spatial distanciation of social classes becomes more marked with the weakening of the elements of status-oriented society and with the advent of modern class society.[13] When the invisible control of status or estate position loosens over where one's place is, where one belongs, the emphasis on residential spatial distance becomes stronger: "A society compensates for blurred social distinctions by clear spatial ones" (Sommer, 1969: 23). Segregation becomes important when privileged classes develop "bad conscience" about displaying wealth amid poverty and a sense of fear about the proximity of lower classes. From a different angle, residential segregation is more than symbolic when the market economy assigns different income groups to different locations; it becomes inherent in the capitalist use of space (Harvey, 1973). East-central European societies did not experience a clear transition from feudalism to capitalism; their modernity has always been mellowed by estatelike features (see Böröcz, 1997; Márkus, 1971; Tóth, 1991).

The built environment also has an impact on the social composition of areas and buildings, as we have seen in the example of housing estates. Far from advocating any spatial determinism, the built environment may place constraints on patterns of social cohabitation. A certain type of apartment building—the popularity of which reached its peak around the end of the nineteenth century—is partly responsible for the fact that the physical proximity of wealth and poverty has historically been part of inner-city experience in most east-central European cities. Housing is organized into a combination of vertical and horizontal hierarchies, with the most well-to-do tenants occupying second- and third-floor facade apartments, while the more humble units of the upper floors and the ones facing the poorly lit inner yard accommodate people from the lower classes (see Figure 2.1). The horizontal segregation of the units is enhanced by a second staircase, commonly called the servants' stairs, that connects the apartments facing the inner yard. True, the classical tenement building, with its vertical hierarchy, is an integral part of the modern Parisian cityscape (Texier, 1852), but increased horizontal hierarchy and sometimes the nestedness of several inner yards opening into one another seem to be specifically central European.[14] Another particularly central European characteristic of these tenement buildings is the shabbier look one finds as one goes beyond the richly ornamented facades. During the fin de siècle construction boom in Budapest, a series of tenement buildings was erected on the Great Ring in the city's haste to "catch up with the West." These houses clearly imitated Parisian and Viennese predecessors. Their ornamented facades looked rather similar indeed, but the real differences opened up for the visitor after he or she entered one of these buildings (Hanák, 1984). First the marble covering became artificial, then a large group of people appeared whose existence was inconsistent even with *artificial* marble. The facades hid the misery of the densely populated, poorly lit inner yards.

The less-secure economic position of the east-central European ruling classes can easily be traced in the interior details of even higher-class buildings. The meager means of the east-central European aristocracy and bourgeoisie facilitated the intermingling of social classes. Even the owners of urban palaces built for representative purposes sometimes could not afford displays of undisturbed wealth; their dwellings had to be joined by visibly lower-class tenement buildings occupying the same plots to provide resources for the maintenance of the big houses. The coexistence of various social groups within the same building is unusual only with regard to U.S. cities; it is definitely not a rarity in European cities, yet there was something peculiar about the visual and social experience of tenement houses in socialist east-central Europe. A higher degree of social mixing took place against the background of generally dilapidated scenery; status and class distinctions were limited largely to the interior of the apartments. Even the scattered instances of renovation did not bring radical changes in the social composition of tenants.[15] What changed the situation was the slow takeoff of new construction, especially of cooperatively or privately owned buildings.

The homogeneity and relatively low levels of social segregation in socialist cities, which are usually associated with the impact of socialism, cannot be fully explained as entirely socialist products, as historically specific east-central European features, or as merely results of underdevelopment. These three types of reasoning are inextricably intervowen. The difficulty of their separation, however, should not collapse into the great dichotomy of socialism versus capitalism.[16]

The Method of Mirrored Comparison

One of the most original and influential comparative strategies for describing state socialism builds on Karl Polanyi's forms of economic integration. Polanyi's (1957) "mosaic typology" posits three basic types of social relations—reciprocity, redistribution, and exchange—as constitutive of any

Figure 2.1. Inner yard of a typical turn-of-the-century apartment building in Budapest. Photograph by author.

concrete arrangement of economic integration. Specific socioeconomic regimes display various configurations of the three; differences are due mainly to which of the three is dominant. The institutional framework of any given economy is designed to support the dominant mode of integration and provides the system with stability.

Harvey (1973) relies on Polanyi's scheme to construct a theory of urbanism. Linking the modes of economic integration and the concept of surplus in the urban space economy dissects the capitalism/urbanism equivalence and enables a doubly comparative approach. It provides for temporal comparisons, thereby deciphering the origins and history of urbanism, and allows a sensitive comparative analysis of variations within the contemporary capitalist space economy. "Urbanism as a way of life comprises all three modes of economic integration as well as the societal forms with which each is associated" (283). This interpretative mechanism—although not applied explicitly to the comparison of capitalist and state socialist cities—provides a key link to an analysis of state socialist and post–state socialist cities.

Making that step is the main purpose of Szelényi's theory of state socialism. György Konrád and Iván Szelényi together (1979) and Szelényi (1978) on his own have built on Polanyi's original suggestion that state socialism is a social formation in which elements of redistribution and market exchange are integrated under the overwhelming logic of state redistribution. This is different from capitalism, where market exchange is the dominant integrating force and redistribution plays a subordinate role. With the two systems thus defined, "mirrored comparison" becomes possible. As David Stark (1986) has summarized this method, whereas in market economies state redistribution tends to act to temper the whims of the market and the inequalities the market creates, under state socialism market mechanisms work to correct the inequalities produced by the state. This proposition inspired the "market transition debate," which I discuss in chapter 3. Polanyi's reconfigured typology opened up refreshing possibilities in the heavily ideological context of the analysis of state socialism. Focusing on small, relatively circumscribed elements of large systems renders more grounded comparisons conceivable. However, I will also show in chapter 5 that the proper contextualization of these elements is of utmost interpretative significance.

As a reaction to the reification of the study of the urban as an independent phenomenon and an independent discipline, urban sociology expanded its focus to embrace broader issues and other fields of inquiry. The "new urban sociology" needs another extension of its boundaries to examine reflexively the historically specific origins of the field and to incorporate historically specific, non-Western, noncapitalist, and noncore urban experiences in their own right. The politically fueled necessity to explain east-central European socialist experience could not help being influenced by the easy dichotomy of capitalism-socialism and the ideological overtones of the project. State socialism has collapsed, the dichotomy has disintegrated, but it survives uncannily in some analyses of "post-Communist" societies. The problem of how to theorize east-central European cities as different from, and similar to, their west European counterparts comes back with full vigor.

True, state socialism did not vanish without traces. Today's east-central European capitalist cities awaiting new theorization are also postsocialist, and the intellectual challenge to account for the difference state socialism made, or could have made, still prevails. Finding a meaningful, nontransitory place for east-central European postsocialist cities would be a good test of the new sensibility of the "newest" urban sociology.

3

"He That Hath to Him Shall Be Given"

Inequalities of Housing Privatization

On September 15, 1993, Mr. K. became the happy owner of a small villa in the Buda hills. Just three years earlier he had risked a sum that would have bought him a new stereo and put a down payment on the inner-city apartment he had rented from the district government for some thirty years. As the new owner, he immediately let it to a multinational corporation that was establishing its first office in east-central Europe. And with the rent payments in hard currency, he was able to purchase the villa.

Mrs. J., widow of a foundryman and former tenant, purchased her place at roughly the same price in a prefab high-rise on the outskirts of Pest. Maintenance costs rose and consumed most of her pension. She found the prospects of her new ownership daunting. On the same September day when Mr. K. bought his villa, she also made a resolution: she walked to the district government office and requested that the government buy back her apartment and reinstate her as a tenant. (The request was refused.)

This chapter provides background to these parallel stories and seeks to explain how, despite their contrast, they represent characteristic trajectories of the postsocialist housing transition. Housing privatization is the main element of the transition in the urban context; it demolishes the material basis of state socialist housing arrangements and signals the end of the state's role as dominant landlord—a peculiarity of state socialist urban phenomena. This is the reason I discuss housing before other aspects of urban transformation. Also, housing is still the most important site and the geographic center of urban practices, although other factors that condition people's ability to use urban space—their work, income, culture, and gender—can be equally vital.

Ownership change, in the way it has been accomplished, polarizes the chances of former tenants. This is so because housing privatization is marked by continuity with state socialist urban arrangements, and the process itself is such that is bound to increase housing inequalities. To substantiate the argument, in this chapter I (1) relate housing privatization to the transition debate, (2) provide a brief narrative of the process in Budapest, and (3) scrutinize the relationship between privatization and inequality in housing by examining quantitative evidence from a detailed Budapest housing survey.

Theories of PostSocialist Transition and Their Implications for Housing Privatization

Theorizing on the social consequences of ongoing transition and the nature of the process has been shaped by what has come to be known as the theory of market transition. In his influential 1989 article by that title, Victor Nee proposes that the opening up of an alternative economic space—the "market"—in the redistributive system of state socialism lessens the significance and efficacy of redistributive power. Arguing that the introduction of market reforms in the otherwise state socialist context of rural mainland China diversifies economic opportunities and practices and offers opportunities to groups systematically disadvantaged under state socialism, Nee concludes that social inequalities are reduced.

Later, inspired by more recent evidence, Nee (1991) qualified his original statement. Data from rural China show that after the initial decrease, inequalities were increasing again with the advent of further market reforms. Nee acknowledges that under "partial market reforms," the conflation of redistributive and market power may temporarily modify the dominant trend of the reduction of social inequalities. His analysis suggests a modest increase in income inequalities. This result, however, does not question the overall validity of the theory of market transition: Nee finds no evidence that newly emerging market coordination perceptibly widens inequalities.

Nee's reformulated theory contains the problematic notion of "partial market reform." How can we decide whether "the transformative shift has taken place" (Nee, 1989: 679)? How do we decide whether the economy of any given former state socialist society should be considered as marketlike, operating within the main logic of redistribution, or merely as a "less developed market"? Ákos Róna-Tas (1994) points out that Nee's qualification of the market transition thesis through the introduction of "partial market reforms" makes the argument immune to falsification: any further empirical finding can support either the main theory or its qualified version.

Another problem has to do with the way market transition theory links distinct conceptual levels. In its core stands a highly abstract image of *power* as it becomes "mediated more by transactive exchanges and less by administrative fiat" (Nee, 1991: 267). Elsewhere, the conceptual effort then addresses itself to *"social* inequalities" (Nee, 1991), whereas the empirical analysis is confined to *income* inequalities. The latter is of real importance as an indication of changes during the transition, namely, the increasing significance of income in determining inequalities. Yet benefits in kind—particularly access to provisions of housing and other human services—are a very characteristic form of income in all redistributive economies, as well as in a great variety of market-dominated economic systems.

No doubt, the quality and quantity of in-kind benefits—as well as all forms of monetary allowances—declined during the transformation of central Europe. This was due partly to the withering away of the socialist state and partly to the fiscal crisis of the postsocialist state. Inequalities in kind have, however, shown no sign of complete disappearance, and it is extremely unlikely that they will vanish in the foreseeable future. State benefits—including housing—can be assumed neither absent nor constant. Thus transformations of inequalities in kind should be one of the key tests of the theory. This chapter is, among other things, a contribution to the market transition debate, focusing on an aspect of inequalities hitherto unexamined in the context of this debate—housing property.

Nee's evidence (which comes exclusively from rural China) is clearly insufficient to serve as a basis for a general theory of the transition from plan to market. His work is nevertheless relevant for my purposes. Market transition theory has shaped sociological discourse on the transition from state socialism profoundly. It has set the tone for analyzing and evaluating the process and has identified the significant issues out of the variety of events taking place.[1] It raises the question of "who benefits" in a particular way and provides a framework to answer it. The thesis also contains a strong suggestion about the workings of social inequalities. Furthermore, market transition theory is important for theoretical-historical reasons. Most of its current propositions are extensions of earlier debates that had initially drawn on evidence from the housing sphere.

The market transition debate builds on Iván Szelényi's classical Polanyian formulation of the comparative logic of market and redistributive mechanisms under state socialism. The foundations of both Polanyi's and Szelényi's theories are discussed in chapter 2. Analyzing housing allocation in Hungary, Szelényi concluded that the principal structures of inequality were created by socialist redistribution itself (Szelényi and Konrád, 1969), whereas the expansion of market transactions vis-à-vis state redistribution tended to decrease inequalities (Szelényi, 1978, 1983). The distribution of public housing systematically favored wealthier and better-educated people, while it was in the opening up of the housing market that the disadvantaged could seek alternative opportunities. Data drawn during and in the immediate aftermath of the introduction of the late 1960s Hungarian economic reforms under state socialism support Szelényi's "mirrored comparison."

Almost twenty years after it was originally advanced, the validity of Szelényi's thesis was challenged on empirical grounds. Hungarian sociologists József Hegedűs (1987) and Iván Tosics (1987) found from a housing survey in Hungary during the first half of the 1980s that both mechanisms produced inequalities, and they claimed that market inequalities were of greater magnitude than redistributive ones. Hegedűs and Tosics's argument in fact does not dissipate the broader appeal of Szelényi's theory; once a temporal dimension of historical change is introduced, their contradiction dissolves. Also, Szelényi qualified his position in the meantime: he made it clear that market mechanisms are not inherently more egalitarian than redistributive ones; they act so only as secondary mechanisms and can lose this capacity with their expansion (Manchin and Szelényi, 1987). Hegedűs and Tosics's empirical analysis clearly demonstrates this possibility coming true.

Temporality is a key aspect of the problem. The method of "mirrored comparison" is formulated to compare two static systems. Brilliant as its fundamental theoretical theme—Polanyi's typology of integration—may be, it does not provide a clear concept of change. The dynamism of the state socialist transformation cracks the "mirrored image." It is an intriguing and challenging task to conceptualize social transition from one system to the other and operationalize the turning point. A tacit recognition of this problem lingers in nearly all studies on the transition but is rarely addressed directly.

In a welcome exception, Róna-Tas (1994) develops a distinction between the *erosion* of socialist economies and the *transition* to the market. The basis of the demarcation is not necessarily the size of the private sector; rather, it is the potential for private sector development determined by the attitude of the state. "During the erosion, the socialist state either fights the private sector or makes concessions it considers temporary" (Róna-Tas, 1994: 47). In Róna-Tas's theory, the transition begins when the "state makes a credible commitment to create the legal institutions of a market economy that are intended to be permanent" (47).[2] Introducing stages into the original Polanyian argument can reconcile the seemingly contradictory findings. Inequalities of the redistributive system may in fact be balanced out by the expansion of the market during early market reforms, as shown by Szelényi in the late 1960s. Hegedűs and Tosics's examination of the housing regime of the mid-1980s demonstrated very well how quickly formerly privileged groups adjusted to the opportunities given by the expansion of the housing market, which led to interference between redistributive and market-based inequalities.

Market transition theory in its initial formulation treats the conceptual step from an analysis of inequalities under state socialism to the inequality-generating effects of the transition from state socialism as unproblematic. Its revision senses the importance of distinguishing between stages of the transition but ends up twisting the theory in a way that contradicts Szelényi's argument: inequalities increase due to the incompleteness of market reforms, not because of their advanced stage (Nee, 1991). Nee's notion of "partial market reforms" could be classified as falling under the period of the erosion of state socialism, and Róna-Tas's (1994) contrary findings, according to which market transition increases income inequalities, are also in line with the conceptual scheme because they stand for the period of the transition. Lacking even the minimal capital to access the formerly "advantageous" market, the poor become even more disprivileged among the new circumstances than before. The "secondary inequality-producing mechanism" of state socialism starts displaying characteristics that very much resemble those of the "primary mechanism" under capitalism. In their search for tools to correct the inequalities of the market, postsocialist societies have no recourse other than the possible welfare functions of the born-again capitalist state.

When the market becomes the basis of economic and social integration coexisting with redistributive and reciprocal elements, it happens in a way particular to the context. Continuity is the underlying theme in the notion of "path dependence" borrowed from transaction cost economics by David Stark (1992) to mark economic transformations in east-central Europe. Stark sharpens the argument for the institutional background of "transferring ownership rights of productive assets held by the state" (23) and shows that previous and currently existing institutional settings constrain and orient the course of action taken in the process of transformation and influence the results of those actions. Path dependence is more than mere insistence on continuity; its reference to institutional inertia and the high initial costs of change is more pronounced.

József Böröcz (1993), in his analysis of property change in Hungary, defines the main element of path dependence in prolonged informality from the last period of state socialism. Informality shapes the "paradoxical task of the simulation of private property in the absence of previous accumulation of capital" (105). Endre Sik (1994) works with a similar network-based notion of path dependence. He identifies as a main characteristic of the transition to market economy the survival of "'communism-distorted' market behavior and capital" (68)—the result of a nationwide subculture and dense personal network that socialized people into the socialist second economy.

Chris Pickvance (1994) also presents a compelling path-dependence argument in his comparison of the origins and nature of Hungarian and Russian tenants' organizations and movements. The particularities of state socialism and its erosion in the two countries certainly had an impact on the formation of citizen groups during the transition, resulting in very different types of collective action: smoother and more cooperative relationship with the authorities in Budapest; more radical, less co-opted, and more individualistically inclined collective actions in Moscow.

This analysis examines the privatization of formerly state-owned apartments and the inequalities emerging from that process. To summarize the specific expectations developed from a generic overview of the theoretical arguments so far, housing privatization signals that the state had made a credible commitment to the transformation of the system. The transition to a different housing logic is, however, path dependent. The radical extension of the realm of private housing property is accomplished through the selling out of formerly state-owned apartments to sitting tenants by "drawing on" noneconomic assets (Böröcz, 1993) accumulated under the redistributive (in)justice of state socialist housing allocation. Economic resources are also drawn on in the process insofar as cash payments are required for housing privatization (Böröcz, 1993).

I hope to contribute to the market transition debate by showing that at this stage it is misdirected and unproductive to focus on whether markets or redistributive mechanisms are more egalitarian. It is not necessary that increasing inequality be experienced *either* because of the survival of state socialism *or* because of market reforms. It is also possible that growing and polarizing inequality is a *combined* effect of the legacy of state socialism and the logic of the market.

History of Housing Privatization

The transformation of the state rental housing sector started well before the collapse of state socialism in Hungary. The sale of state-owned apartments to sitting tenants in fact first became legally possible as early as 1969. However, privatization did not grow from a mere legal possibility into a social issue before the institutionalized transition at the end of 1980s. With a single act in 1990—placed in the context of a general law determining the obligations and powers of local governments—property rights shifted from the state to the local governments.[3] The latter gained full control of the disposition of rental units, including setting rent levels and sale prices. According to the Hungarian Central Statistical Office (KSH, 1993), this affected 22 percent of the households nationwide and 52 percent of those in Budapest—the entire state rental sector at the time. Until 1989, property change could take place only on the basis of some kind of collective action: tenants of more than 50 percent of the apartments in a building had to commit themselves in order for purchases to be allowed. This restriction was removed in 1989. Privatization of housing by the sitting tenant gained real momentum. In the subsequent three years, about 35 percent of the previous rental units were transferred to private hands in Budapest.

Were it not open to local government intervention at two points, the process could be considered almost automatic. The tenant submitted a written request to the local government expressing intention to buy the apartment. This claim could be denied only if the house was listed as nonsalable because it was classified as a piece of architectural heritage, selected for renovation, or claimed restricted by the local government for some other specific reason.[4] If the local government consented to sell the property, the price of the unit was determined and presented to the tenant, who had the option to agree or disagree with the terms and conditions and either sign or refuse the sales contract, which provided him or her with formal property rights, sealed through the issuance of a real estate title.

The selling price was determined by the property's "market value," which was assessed by a third-party expert whose services were arranged and paid for by the housing administration. By state guidelines, from which deviations were possible, the price of a unit in an older building that had not been renovated in the preceding fifteen years was 15 percent of the market value; a unit renovated in the past five years could go for up to 40 percent of that value. The down payment could be as little as 10 percent of this sum, with the rest having to be paid in the next thirty-five years at an interest rate of 3 percent. The 3 percent fixed interest rate was of course a form of intense state subsidy, a remnant of state socialist times; because of inflation, current mortgage interest rates would not drop below 25 percent. In the case of instant total payment, a further 40 percent of the balance beyond down payment was to be discounted. According to these regulations, in 1992 a fifty-square-meter apartment in the prestigious but dilapidated

District I of the city would be appraised at Ft 1.6 million (U.S.$20,000 at the current exchange rate).[5] It would be offered to the tenant for 15 percent of this price. He or she would have to put down 10 percent, which would amount to Ft 24,000 (U.S.$300) with the rest to be paid over a period of thirty years in payments of roughly Ft 800 (U.S.$10) a month. On the rental market, the same unit could be leased for between Ft 13,000 and Ft 25,000 (U.S.$162 to $312) a month.

The gap between the required investment necessary to privatize the household and the "gain," or the market value of the unit, provided a rather strong incentive to buy. This incentive was further increased by the uncertainty of the future. In the sea of political changes and high inflation, tenants were losing their sense of stability. Fear of rent increases and the curtailment of their quasi-owner status gripped them with all due reason.[6] Although it did not become part of any official housing policy, the program of the major opposition party (among others) to the first democratically elected government planned the "reduction of former distributive advantages," including the abolition of inheritance rights and moderate but consistent rent increases.

Despite these remarkable incentives to buy, there are two main reasons tenants may still have opted not to privatize. One is the belief that the state "would not leave them on their own": rents would not increase dramatically for political reasons, and the state-landlord's right of eviction would be as elusive as before. The other reason is a well-substantiated fear of having to assume not only rights, but also certain responsibilities. Because the socialist state had been a singularly sloppy landlord, deferred maintenance was estimated as high as Ft 100 billion (U.S.$1.25 billion) in the Budapest rental sector in 1990 (Hegedűs et al., 1993). This would require an investment from some of the households approximating the actual market value of their units. In spite of the "rationality" of this fear, it was usually suppressed: the possible collapse of a house never seems imminent enough.

The practice of housing privatization was questioned from two sides. The growing annoyance of a group of would-be owners was channeled into political concern with the extension of privatization: Why couldn't everyone have a private right to a "piece of the national wealth"?[7] Critics from the opposite side warned that selling out the property of local governments may make any social housing policy infeasible.

In the summer of 1993, a new law was formulated in response to both criticisms. The law went into effect in January 1994. It guaranteed the right to privatization for an extended group of tenants while making the conditions of doing so less favorable than before. The upper limit of the sale price of apartments was maximized at 50 percent of the "market price." Immediate cash payment no longer produced an additional 40 percent reduction in price. The down payment was still 10 percent of the selling price, but the length of the installment plan had been reduced from thirty-five to twenty-five years. The 3 percent fixed annual interest rate was abolished; instead, no interest is paid in the first six years, and subsequently the mortgage carries the current interest rate of the National Bank. So, not only did the tenant of my previous example need to make a bigger initial financial effort (Ft 80,000, or U.S.$800),[8] but paying the mortgage—at least triple that under the old regulations—required a more solid economic situation in the long run.

In exchange for the increase in prices, the right of tenants to buy their apartments was now almost guaranteed, and the power of local governments to restrict purchases had been severely curtailed. The new law also made it clear that the privatization of housing was merely a transitory legal institution: in five years, tenants would not be eligible to purchase their apartments. This signaled the possibility of the survival of the rental sector under the management of local governments. According to the new legislation, local governments were obliged to recycle the income from privatization sales—of which, until 1994, they had had unrestricted use—into their remaining rental sector, in the form of either new construction or renovation or the elimination of what was left of the shared tenancies, an institution introduced in the 1950s. Furthermore, the districts lost half of their revenues drawn from sales through housing privatization to the city government.

These regulations projected a set of intended consequences, but the unintended consequences were just as important. The anticipation of the changes made public in July 1993 and introduced in January 1994 generated quite a bit of movement on the housing market. The local governments opened their "final sales" in order to reduce their expected losses. In the downtown area of District VII—which had not been on the forefront of privatization before—regulations were passed quickly in order to give buyers extra benefits if a deal was made before the end of the year and if payment was received in cash. Other districts followed suit. At this point even the most hesitant local governments started to advertise in the papers, looking for liquidators to hire for massive privatization. Local governments rushed sales also for fear of being obliged to accept compensation vouchers as payment with hardly any restrictions.[9]

In setting up the regulations this way, the law spread the burden of the politically motivated compensation scheme among various levels of government and made advance assessment of that spread almost impossible. The local governments were thus prone to experiencing anxiety about the compensation-based form of housing privatization, because (1) the volatility of the exchange value of compensation vouchers forced them to participate in a financial process with highly unpredictable outcomes and could force them to swallow enormous losses, in essence channeling additional portions of privatization revenues from the local to the central government; and (2) successful participation required expertise in complex financial operations rarely found in the local governments, particularly in the smaller and poorer districts.

In this climate, many local governments perceived the new regulation—which installed the right of the city to determine the use of the privatization revenue of the district—as a curtailment of their freedom to dispose of their own property. This feature of the law was challenged on a constitutional basis. In November 1994, the Constitutional Court threw out this section of the law and granted local governments the right to the free disposal of their income from privatization, but only the part from non-housing-related (commercial space) sales.[10]

Inequalities of Housing Privatization

In order to identify systematic inequalities in the process of housing privatization, I will examine three aspects of it: (1) the institutional-legal context as it sets the framework for privatization; (2) "grassroots" tenants' movements that shape the process, as we will see, along the lines of inequalities delineated by the institutional structure; and (3) survey data contrasting individual decisions with the institutional possibilities to determine whether property change occurs unequally and, if so, whether this unequal process is based on inherited inequalities from the state socialist period.

The process of housing privatization displays undisguised, inherent inequalities. The regulations themselves lead to differential advantages. The calculation of prices hardly reflects quality, and the housing stock ready for privatization comes in many different forms. Except for taking into account the time of the last full renovation of the building, characteristics such as location within the city and a unit's location within a building and quality of amenities are almost completely disregarded. This leads to absurd monetary equivalences between a prefab apartment on the outskirts of the city and a villa in the Buda hills. The insensitivity of prices to quality was particularly striking in the last days of the state socialist regime.

The price appraisals of local governments almost always underestimate market prices,[11] and a maximum of 25 percent variation (i.e., 15 percent versus 40 percent, depending on the time of the last renovation) in an already suppressed price does not make much of a difference. Due to the legendary negligence of the state-landlord, very few buildings were renovated in the five years preceding the new regulations, so that only a small portion of the would-be privatized apartments are eligible to be privatized at 40 percent. Meanwhile, everything redone more than fifteen years ago is sold for 15 percent of the estimated market value, notwithstanding the enormous variation within that large group; a building rehabilitated fifteen years ago competes with one whose renovation was forced by—or postponed indefinitely in spite of—the damage suffered during the siege of the city in World War II. In 1990, of all the units owned by local governments, one-fifth had been constructed in the nineteenth century—and one-half before World War II (KSH, 1993).

Furthermore, the process of privatization has been accompanied by disparities among districts from the very beginning. Before the collapse of state socialism, the district councils used the legal possibility of privatizing apartments very selectively; privatization had taken place only where sufficiently powerful tenants had voiced their demands loudly enough. Prior to 1990, more than half of the "council apartments" had been designated for sale by the local councils in the most pleasant areas of Budapest, such as Districts I and II on the Buda side, and the proportion had been only slightly lower in the two other "good" districts of Buda—XI and XII. Meanwhile, the proportion was around 10 percent in the predominantly working-class outer districts of Pest.

"Social movements" of tenants played a part in shaping the process of privatization. Local governments proved more cooperative with claims filed from sites of greater potential monetary gain. Tenants, in turn, adjusted very quickly to the new, smoother local conditions of property change and the absurdly homogeneous prices in a differentiated urban setting. No potentially privatizable storage or laundry room could pass unnoticed by vigilant tenants in Districts I, II, and XII of Buda and District V (Budapest's administrative and commercial center) of Pest. The actual rates of privatization meticulously reflected the initial inequalities: between 1990 and 1993, the rate of privatization—27.7 percent for all of Budapest—was more than 40 percent in most of these areas and in District XI, which rapidly caught up with them; it was almost 40 percent in districts II, III, and XII, while sagging well below 10 percent on the outskirts of Pest (see Table 3.1).[12]

When these figures are examined in the context of the market value of

Table 3.1

Council-owned housing stock and housing privatization in Budapest, by districts, January 1, 1990, to December 31, 1992 (housing units and %)

District	Stock, January 1, 1990 no.	Privatized in 1990 no.	Privatized in 1990 %	Stock, December 31, 1990 no.	Privatized in 1991 no.	Privatized in 1991 %	Stock, December 31, 1991 no.	Privatized in 1992 no.	Privatized in 1992 %	Stock, December 31, 1992 no.	Percentage change, 1990 to 1993
I	10,838	1,308	12.1	9,530	2,414	25.3	7,116	1,504	21.1	5,612	48.2
II	16,977	2,900	17.1	14,077	1,966	14.0	12,111	2,719	22.5	9,392	44.7
III	24,229	3,960	16.3	20,269	4,391	21.7	15,878	850	5.4	15,028	38.0
IV	21,044	107	0.5	20,937	73	0.3	20,864	915	4.4	19,949	5.2
V	18,655	973	5.2	17,682	3,845	21.7	13,837	3,455	25.0	10,382	44.3
VI	25,834	496	1.9	25,338	2,424	9.6	22,914	2,703	11.8	20,211	21.8
VII	35,780	1,720	4.8	34,060	3,312	9.7	30,748	732	2.4	30,016	16.1
VIII	36,365	761	2.1	35,604	2,255	6.3	33,349	1,481	4.4	31,868	12.4
IX	28,701	878	3.1	27,823	4,455	16.0	23,368	3,488	14.9	19,880	30.7
X	19,772	217	1.1	19,555	896	4.6	18,659	1,795	9.6	16,864	14.7
XI	30,207	3,066	10.1	27,141	5,391	19.9	21,750	11,897	54.7	9,853	67.4
XII	12,396	1,727	13.9	10,669	2,877	27.0	7,792	770	9.9	7,022	43.4
XIII	39,076	2,517	6.4	36,559	6,530	17.9	30,029	6,050	20.1	23,979	38.6

Table 3.1 (continued)

District	Stock, January 1, 1990 no.	Privatized in 1990 no.	%	Stock, December 31, 1990 no.	Privatized in 1991 no.	%	Stock, December 31, 1991 no.	Privatized in 1992 no.	%	Stock, December 31, 1992 no.	Percentage change, 1990 to 1993
XIV	33,468	656	2.0	32,812	1,675	5.1	31,137	1,785	5.7	29,352	12.3
XV	16,239	169	1.0	16,070	727	4.5	15,343	1,628	10.6	13,715	15.5
XVI	1,806	39	2.2	1,767	26	1.5	1,741	0	0.0	1,741	3.6
XVII	4,338	60	1.4	4,278	94	2.2	4,184	445	10.6	3,739	13.8
XVIII	8,220	39	0.5	8,181	295	3.6	7,886	382	4.8	7,504	8.7
XIX	12,495	81	0.6	12,414	673	5.4	11,741	1,869	15.9	9,872	21.0
XX	9,115	301	3.3	8,814	730	8.3	8,084	1,183	14.6	6,901	24.3
XXI	11,604	114	1.0	11,490	1,354	11.8	10,136	481	4.7	9,655	16.8
XXII	3,761	67	1.8	3,694	588	15.9	3,106	1,150	37.0	1,956	48.0
Total	420,920	22,156	5.3	398,764	46,991	11.8	351,773	47,282	13.4	304,491	27.7

housing by districts (see Figures 3.1a, 3.1b, and 3.1c), one finds a strikingly strong relationship between housing privatization rates and average housing price by square meter.[13] The relationship is strongest in the case of early privatization: the most valuable units were the first to go (Figure 3.1a).[14] Because of the above-outlined changes in regulations over time, this suggests that the units that were bought first (located in the most expensive districts) were also relatively the least expensive to buy.

Inequalities within the public housing sector display a similar spatial pattern to that of the exit from there. Between 1989 and 1992, the local governments of only the two most homogeneously wealthy and resourceful districts of the Buda side invested more into their housing stock than they received as rent (KSH, 1993).[15] Due to the nature of the changes, it is understandable that local governments should neglect their housing stock now more than before, yet it is certainly remarkable that spatial differences should display the same kind of unequal pattern.

The institutional context of privatization is very selectively conducive to property change. I now turn to survey data to examine how people act to use these possibilities, what background factors affect decisions to privatize, and who has advantages in becoming a home owner.

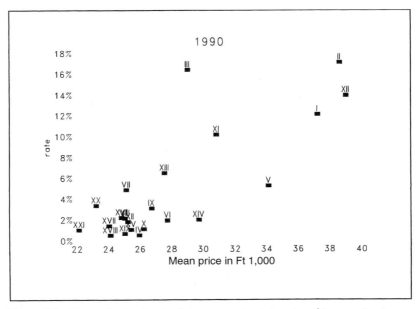

Figure 3.1a. Rates of privatization by mean real estate prices (thousands of forints per square meter) for Budapest districts, 1990. Source: Calculations from *Ingatlanpiac.*

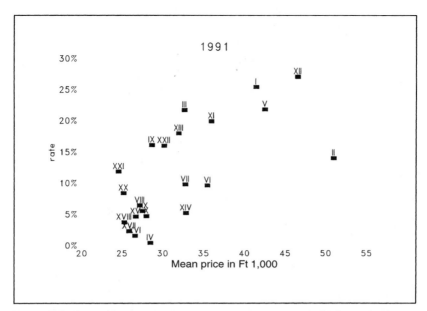

Figure 3.1b. Rates of privatization by mean real estate prices (thousands of forints per square meter) for Budapest districts, 1991. Source: Calculations from *Ingatlanpiac.*

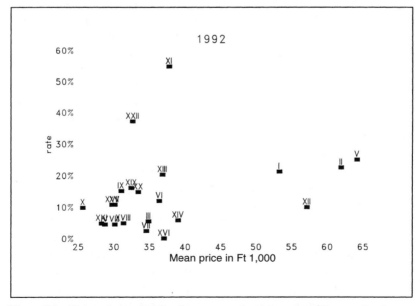

Figure 3.1c. Rates of privatization by mean real estate prices (thousands of forints per square meter) for Budapest districts, 1992. Source: Calculations from *Ingatlanpiac.*

Data and Methods

This analysis uses survey data collected by the Metropolitan Research Institute in Budapest. The representative sample was drawn from Budapest households living in state-owned rental housing in January 1990. The thousand interviews on which this analysis is based were carried out at the same addresses two years later, in January 1992. Only 5 percent of the apartments had changed occupants in the meantime, whereas there was ownership change in 20 percent of them. This figure reflects a citywide trend: this two-year period generally witnessed massive privatization, during which approximately 17 percent of the Budapest rental sector was sold (Table 3.1).

The dependent variable is based on the status of the apartment as reported by the respondents.[16] It captures different stages of the privatization process, ranging from "not even considering the purchase of one's tenement" to "having completed the legal process of ownership transfer." I made an attempt to reflect those various steps in the dependent variable. In the first model, only the units completely "privatized" by January 1992 were considered. Drawing the dividing line this way, the model represents as "privatized" only 18.3 percent of the flats.

A second model enlarges the "privatized" category, incorporating those tenants who have shown evidence of their intention and means to privatize, received consent from the district government, and are most likely to have completed the process since the time of the survey. With this coding, 23 percent of the sample is grouped under private ownership.

A third model examines the sampled households where the idea of purchasing the tenement was rejected or had not yet been considered. Some 38 percent of households were in this "nonprivatization" scenario.[17] The predictor variables describe the social background of the household. (For details, see the appendix to this volume.)

Locational advantages are important, although they are more difficult to grasp and quantify than in the North American context. Spatial segregation of social groups is not uncommon in the city, but socially and ethnically homogeneous areas are few, small, and difficult to identify (Csanádi and Ladányi, 1987). Such variation is poorly reflected in the larger spatial categories of districts, but I decided nonetheless to use districts as proxies for locational advantages. On the one hand, it is my contention that recent spatial rearrangements point in the direction of the internal homogenization of neighborhoods and the sharpening of the demarcation lines among them. On the other, most housing advertisements start with district location, and newspapers group the ads on that basis. District location has emerged as the most commonly used and accepted category, by both sellers and buyers, to describe the quality of places and assess their value, thereby forcefully inducing other than discursive homogenization on the district level. Therefore, I included average housing prices by districts for 1991—reported by the Capital City Fiscal Office on the basis of registered housing sales[18]—as rough signals for locational advantages.

Results

A higher-education diploma gives a direct advantage in the process of privatization, whereas other components of better socioeconomic situation have an indirect effect on it (as shown in my path model, presented in Figure A.1a in the appendix). It is housing quality that directly influences ownership change. Contrary to my expectations, top managerial position bears no significance with respect to housing quality or privatization decisions. The overwhelming majority of this group has relocated into the private sector by now; others have never lived in public housing.

Housing quality is influenced by educational background and income. Higher educational attainment increasingly adds to the odds of a family's living in a unit with full amenities. More education, again, is increasingly important in shaping the internal quality of the unit, together with income. Education is still significant with respect to the look of the building, but a higher-education diploma loses its additional effect, and income does not bear an effect on outer quality, either. This suggests that higher income marks the family interior rather than the appearance of the building where they live. Most public housing is in dilapidated tenement buildings, the rehabilitation of which requires major collective effort. Housing mobility is still low, and high income may not be high enough to be translated into a better outer appearance. The meager means of Budapest city dwellers could induce only a meager version of gentrification: they could not upgrade whole neighborhoods, only their apartments, which, along with other factors, produced a striking cohabitation of abundance and poverty within the same buildings.

Floor space is, again, progressively influenced by the level of education and income. Furthermore, family size has a strong effect on apartment size, which is not mediated through income.[19] In contrast to other proxies of quality, the average price of a unit of housing space by district does not seem to be very much tied to social and economic characteristics of the household; only university diploma produces a weak effect on location. Better-priced locations do, in turn, have a head start in privatizing. The scale of amenities bears no significant effect on privatization, nor does size. The net gain from privatization is enhanced by size, but only in case of better quality.

People occupying good-quality apartments in good-quality buildings have an advantage in becoming owners of their units.

Educated people show a statistically significant higher log odds of being among those who purchase their apartments. A less restrictive interpretation of the dependent variable, which includes the well-substantiated intention to privatize in addition to complete privatization (as shown in my second model; see Figure A.1b in the appendix), eliminates the direct effect of higher education on the odds of becoming an owner. The market-assigned value of district location does not lose its significance. Housing quality still predicts ownership change. The overall fit of the model to the data somewhat loosens with the extension of the category of "privatized" (see Table 3.2). Late or later privatizers are less affected in their decision by quality and, therefore, by the anticipated gain. At this point, the best of the housing supply is already gone; one can only make less profitable decisions, but one feels more pressed to make them.

The third model focuses on those who completely refrained from or are locked out of property change (see Figure A.1c in the appendix). In analyzing the relationship between my indicators and the odds of being a "non-privatizer," the model produces a very good fit (see Table 3.2). The odds of remaining a tenant are influenced only by the second layer of variables: none of the background characteristics bears direct relevance. Better external condition of the building decreases the odds of not purchasing the unit, and so does better location. Housing interior, which is influential in determining ownership change, does not produce a reverse significant effect on the lack of privatization. The amenities of the unit do not appear to influence a family's chances of becoming owners, but do affect the family's possibility of remaining tenants. The odds that a household living in an apartment equipped with full amenities will stay in public housing are more than one-third smaller than for those lacking basic comforts.

Housing privatization is an unequal process. Some become owners, others remain tenants. Sitting in potentially valuable units predestines tenants to become owners. Wealthy and, above all, educated people had better housing at the beginning of the privatization wave, and they have the lead in privatization. Time matters: early privatizers gain more. For latecomers, the gap between their costs and the market potential of their units declines. They become owners of worse-quality dwellings, and the consequences of deferred maintenance are increasingly transferred to them. The capital-intensive task represented by full renovation of a ninety-year-old building or a high-rise prefab, the prospect of which frightens even its architect, is beyond the means of most households. Thus, like the acts of a true monarch, privatization arbitrarily transfers wealth to some and burden to others.

Conclusions

The results reported above are in line with findings of similar studies. They support Hegedűs and Tosics's general argument about the inequalities of the privatization process (see Hegedűs et al., 1993). In a later study, Hegedűs and Tosics (1994) make it even more explicit that during the first two years of privatization, the quantifiable monetary gain of former tenants was distributed very unequally. The process favored the upper echelon of the housing stock—the most valuable units—even more so than was the case with rent subsidy before. Property change also occurred much faster in the upper 20 percent of privatized apartments, based on the estimated value of the units. This, the authors conclude, leads to polarization.

The approach presented here differs from Hegedűs and Tosics's on both theoretical and methodological grounds. I place the analysis in the context of the "market transition" debate and ask the main questions from a "midrange" theoretical angle. Both models examine who privatizes on the basis of similar background variables. My path model, however, does not utilize the monetary value of expected gain, nor does it rely on variables pertaining to a rational choice approach (e.g., anticipation of rent increase). My findings suggest that the assumption of rational monetary calculation on the part of all tenants is not necessary to describe the process as it unfolds under path dependence. A systematic account for the historically inherited constraints is capable of controlling for a large number of predictor variables and produces a statistically equally or more plausible solution than one produced through reliance on the rational choice assumption.

Although circumstances, evaluations, and explanations vary, analysts of other cities seem to agree that the consequences of housing privatization are highly selective, and the lower end of the market requires inventive housing policies (Musil, 1995; Pichler-Milanovich, 1994). Daniell and Struyk's (1994) analysis of housing privatization in Moscow, where a similarly rigorous survey was undertaken, indicates that there, too, the most valuable housing is the first to go, and intellectuals and directors are the most eager to become owners, but their financial situation does not have much effect on their decision. Daniell and Struyk hypothesize heightened disparity in quality between privatized buildings and state-owned ones; however, the peculiar nature of the Russian privatization process, being free of charge, may make a difference in how and to what extent polarization will take place. The inequalities of state socialism may be finalized, and later widened

Table 3.2

Logit path model for housing privatization in Budapest, 1990–92

Dependent variables	FAMINC	KOMFORT	Quality inside	Quality outside	Floor space	Location	Privatized (complete)	Privatized (initiated)	NOT PRIV
n	896	896	881	891	888	896	871	871	871
Independent variables									
Head of household									
Age	254.3*	-.016	.004	-.006	-.167	-.093	-.038	-.015	-.004
Age squared	-4.4**	-.000	.000	-.000	-.003	.000	.000	.000	.000
Top manager	11131.3***	-.079	.198	.104	7.670	.914	.697	.634	.004
Full-time in the labor force	8151.3***	-.236	.145	.045	2.762	.751	-.044	.013	-.105
Education									
Elementary	1215.2	1.434***	.313**	.319**	9.308***	-1.165	.755	.087	-.387
High school	5252.6**	2.068***	.535***	.469***	12.618***	-.418	.838	.133	-.212
College	7098.5***	2.324***	.722***	.407**	20.532***	-.422	1.401*	.555	-.648
University	11085.6***	2.688***	.672***	.340*	25.533***	2.055*	1.181*	.530	-.647
Female-headed household	-5150.1***	.330	-.079	.003	2.051	.716	.221	.266	-.032

Table 3.2 (continued)

Independent variables (continued)	FAMINC	KOMFORT	Quality inside	Quality outside	Floor space	Location	Privatized (complete)	Privatized (initiated)	NOT PRIV
Number of persons in household	3349.0***	.175	.006	.023	5.923***	-.096	.069	.108	-.093
KOMFORT							.826	.736	-.965***
Quality inside							.300*	.236	-.044
Quality outside							.423**	.451***	-.352***
Floor space (m^2)							.006	.008	.002
Total family income		.000***	.000***	.000	.000***	.000	.000	.000	-.000
District		126.8(11)					.042**	.045**	-.067***
Model chi²(d.f.)							101.1(16)	100.6(16)	127.0(16)
Model R^2	.365		.122	.035	.301	.049			

* $p < .05$; ** $p < .01$; *** $p < .001$.

by the market, but at least institutional intervention in the process may not contribute to the unequal nature of it. The longer history of a more intensive state landlordism can introduce other differences with the Hungarian experience (Pickvance, 1994).

Today's privatization of formerly state-owned dwellings is the principal means of urban restructuring in the postsocialist context. Its course and outcome are, however, very much shaped by the state socialist "housing regime" and by the unequal distribution of services it had created. Previous institutional constellations provide the process with resources and place constraints on it. The institutional-legal context of housing privatization allows for very unequal access to the gains of privatization. Tenants use this to their own benefit in full. Recognition of privatization opportunities, quick reactions to legal changes, and, first of all, a good starting position explain new housing inequalities and unequal urban privileges. This aspect of the transformation of state socialism has thus been marked by "path dependence"—similar to the arguments of Stark, Böröcz, Sik, and Pickvance noted above.

Continuity prevails in the distribution of privileges; these results show that those favored by the ancien régime are doing quite well.[20] Intellectuals were privileged in the state socialist allocation of housing, and they seem to enjoy the real benefits of privatization. In the initial stage, intellectuals have an additional advantage in capitalizing on their very unequal state socialist heritage, which is another sign of how well they have adjusted to the workings of the market (Manchin and Szelényi, 1987). This analysis also demonstrates again that the general implications of the theory of market transition concerning the market as a force decreasing inequalities do not hold anymore. The advancement of market mechanisms, except for the very early stages, increases social inequalities, and by the time of housing transformation, markets have certainly lost their emancipatory ability. To be precise, *alternatives* have this ability—and those happened to be market mechanisms at a certain historical conjuncture. There is, however, basis for criticism concerning both Polanyi's original scheme and its transmogrification into the "mirrored comparison." Polanyi (1944) recognized that the "self-regulating market" was only a transient moment in the history of capitalism. However, he did not take the expanding dynamism of the system into full consideration, and his optimism concerning the self-corrective capacities of market-integrated systems proved immature, as István Mészáros (1995) points out. This optimism—which has been directly reproduced in the method of "mirrored comparison"—becomes extremely important in the market transition debate. Is it really the nature of every market-dominated system that state redistribution works as the market's corrective mechanism and nothing else? What is the specific institutional mechanism that ascertains this mutually corrective relationship between state and markets and assures that no other constellation emerges? It is difficult to exclude a priori the possibility that alleviating without contributing to enhancing the system of inequalities produced by the market is not all the capitalist state does. In fact, Mollenkopf and Castells (1991) argue for a different—but, like my subject matter, also semiperipheral—context, very clearly that "in the Latin American model of urban development, the state perpetuates and reinforces the segmentation of the society" (410). Similar doubts could also be raised for state socialism. The relationship of market and redistribution as presented in the model may have been a specificity of a certain period of state socialism and, on the reverse, that of west European welfare states.

In Budapest's housing sector, recent property change accentuates and, with the joint forces of the market and the law, finalizes differences created by the peculiarities of state socialist urban phenomena. Those who have had, or may have, the possibility of converting their respective legacies of state socialism into monetary gains on the real estate market freer from restrictions than before appear to be in the most advantageous position.

Some of them may eventually emerge as members of a new rentier class, as Mr. K. managed to "capitalize" his state socialist legacy and made his own transition. Fates, however, are not necessarily sealed along the dividing line between owners and tenants. Ownership itself does not place one on the side of those who successfully and profitably adjust to broader urban changes, as Mrs. J.'s story suggests. She bought herself the freedom to pay for future renovation and maintenance in a house constructed with low-creativity technological solutions in an age that had no respect for individual solutions or for energy-conscious designs. Privatization, while placing some in the ownership of great wealth, traps others in their very private misery and despair.

4

Inner City Doubly Renewed

Global Phenomenon, Local Accents

Postsocialist Budapest is undergoing a very selective renewal. The inner city is being "revived," as analysts and investors say, equating life with the movement of capital. Some see "gentrification in the inner city . . . proceeding along easily recognizable Western lines" (Kovács, 1990: 118). Other areas are rapidly deteriorating, creating striking contrasts sometimes in tight spaces. This is a new phase of uneven development on the urban scale. "Unlike that in London or New York prior to the 1970s, Budapest gentrification did not begin as a largely isolated process in the housing market, but came fully fledged in the arteries of global capital following 1989," writes Neil Smith (1996: 174). Did this make it "proceed along easily recognizable Western lines"? Given that urban theory derives these transformations from some structural features of global capitalism—in this case, from uneven development—the apparent similarity of the urban process in the aftermath of state socialism prompts the question. When we look at the double revival of postsocialist inner cities, are we witnessing the same thing, a variant form, or the deceptively similar looking but substantively different outcomes of genuinely different causal mechanisms?[1] In this chapter, I seek to find sociological answers to those questions. I first provide an overview of the themes of urban restructuring and some of its accompanying processes globally, and then look at Budapest in search of similarities and differences. I examine an example of "socialist gentrification" in Budapest, a radical act of urban rehabilitation in an inner-city district during the state socialist period, and analyze the "spontaneous" gentrification of downtown after the collapse of state socialism. My main motive is the uneven development of the city as revealed in the themes of gentrification, housing privatization (which I treat as a case similar to British tenure conversion), and functional conversion, either from residential to commercial or from low-to high-profit use. I begin the analysis with an overview of changes in accumulation and their correlates in residential patterns, specifically gentrification and suburbanization, in the context of the United States and western Europe.

Flexible Accumulation without Social Illusions

Late capitalism has rearranged the sites of production and consumption. The long economic boom that started after World War II was over by the mid-1970s (Harvey, 1987). The project of modernization, with its belief in the earthly advent of efficiency, functionality, and rationality, was out of breath by that time. So was the type of economy in which that enterprise was embedded. *Fordism*, a term used, after Gramsci, to distinguish the mid-century regime of accumulation from the "extensive" pattern of the nineteenth century, expanded the circle of consumers by taking the historical step of incorporating an important sector of the working class, at least in the core countries of global capitalism. A massive "uniform mode of consumption of simplified products" had emerged, as Aglietta (1987: 154) notes. The Fordist mode of consumption was fundamentally isomorphic with the key institution of the labor process—the assembly line. Expansion, as Aglietta's description suggests, was accompanied by standardization, especially of two commodities: housing and the automobile. By the late 1970s, Fordism gave way to new, more flexible capital and labor practices (Harvey, 1987, 1989a). Large-scale assembly-line type of production had shrunk in the pattern-setting countries and moved to the "lower east sides" of the Americas, Asia, and Europe. Production became differentiated, tailored to specific needs and destined to satisfy the consumer's needs for personalized services more than ever.

Received wisdom suggests that today the benefits of standardization are taken for granted, and their novelty value has started to wear off. The consumer seeks distinguished products and services. He or she thinks of him- or herself as a "finding artist"—a Japanese way of the celebration of natural forms and the cultivated gaze that discovers them—who manifests his or her limited creativity in finding the product that suits his or her delicate taste and social position. It is the uninhibited intertwining of economic and aesthetic strategies that defines the sophisticated consumer society of late capitalism.

> Paradoxically, capital has fallen in love with difference: advertising thrives on selling us things that will enhance our uniqueness and

individuality. It's no longer about keeping up with the Joneses, it's about being different from them. From World Music to exotic holidays in Third-World locations, ethnic tv dinners to Peruvian knitted hats, cultural difference *sells*. This is the "difference" of commodity relations, the particular experience of time and space produced by transnational capital. (Rutherford, 1990: 11)

Rutherford is not alone in evaluating the new phase of capitalism in this manner. The only objection to be raised from a historical-comparative perspective is that its temporality is ill calibrated. Coquetry with difference is a birth defect of capital; in itself, it is not new at all. And life has never been entirely about keeping up with the Joneses; it has always been partly about being different from them. It is precisely the tension between the two fundamental tendencies of capital, that between the equalization and differentiation of conditions of development, that makes capitalism go round. Analyses of nineteenth-century modernity, especially of urban modernity, are replete with observations of this tension even for classics of sociology other than Marx. Simmel's description of modern fashion and style moves in the same conceptual space as his observations concerning the leveling and differentiating tendencies of the mature money economy. Fashion and style are assertions of individuality and difference in the face of the overwhelming objectification and homogenization of society, and they are intimately connected with modernity. "Fashion represents nothing more than one of many forms of life by the aid of which we seek to combine in uniform spheres of activity the tendency towards social equalization with the desire for individual differentiation and change" (Simmel, 1971a: 296). The individual seeks distinctions by belonging to a group, by pursuing a style that is shared by some other people as well. Fashion is, thus, about controlled difference. Simmel also notes that the latest fashion by definition affects only the upper classes; as soon as lower classes start copying it, the upper classes abandon it. Consumption that cultivates difference is, thus, hardly unique to post-Fordism. What we see today that is different from the past is that constant change and diversity are perhaps at a more massive scale now. The global system of flexible production renders this possible. The appreciation of the *couleur locale* of commodities and services is all the more ironic in the present world-system, where global strategies of production and extremely complex product chains make locating the origins of products very difficult. The enjoyment of "local" products becomes universally conceivable, irrespective of the distance between the two localities involved: the place of production and the place of consumption.

Today almost every American city has its own Little Italy, China- or Koreatown, and Greek, Polish, German, Indian, and other ethnic neighborhoods. This originally ethnic matrix, an outcome of the migration patterns of preceding periods, is very effectively reinterpreted as consumptive diversity. Global commercialization makes ethnic diversity universal, massive, and independent from time and space. It shapes difference according to its own requirements by making it just appropriately exotic, one-dimensional, and controlled, thus mass-consumable. Diversity becomes sterile: it loses some flavor, smell, and color—but it sells.

Today's economic restructuring rearranges the economic base of urbanization and the hierarchy of cities. The sectoral composition of the labor force has changed considerably in the past two decades. Total U.S. manufacturing employment declined by 10 percent between 1979 and 1985, while service employment increased by almost the same proportion (Sassen, 1990: 467). The change was even sharper in the now leading producer service cities, such as, in the United States, New York, Los Angeles, and Boston (Sassen, 1990: 467). As an example of uneven development within the most advanced countries, change was similarly drastic in, for instance, North Dakota, where the significance of agriculture and (buffalo) hunting has passed to the extent that nowadays the state is inhabited mostly by widows (Margolis, 1995). New service companies recruit people at the top and the bottom: highly qualified professionals entrusted with uniquely responsible tasks and unskilled laborers who perform mostly temporary, repetitious jobs. At the same time, the logic of flexible accumulation informalizes economic actors, the majority of whom are inner-city minorities (Sassen, 1990). The consolidation of the informal economy, whose participants are outside of regulation concerning health, safety, minimum wage, and so on, signals a break in the social contract between workers and employers that has been in effect more or less since the end of World War II. The working class in the "classical" sense is disappearing: it has become fragmented, with some becoming permanently unemployed and the entrepreneurial spirit awakening in others. Selective "embourgeoisement" is taking place within the ranks of the former working class.

The new logic of accumulation shapes the city. Urban restructuring has consequences for the housing sphere, along with the disproportionate concentration of the poor and ethnic minorities in the inner cities and the consolidation of an underclass. The simultaneous disappearance of manufacturing jobs and the increased presence of advanced service sector employees translate into a twofold change in the urban texture: the decay of the housing stock and the emergence of colonies of conspicuous consumption in formerly poverty-stricken areas. Industrial sites are rapidly disappearing from the cityscapes of the advanced world. Some adjust flexibly to the new circumstances, and others go through adjustment in a different way, living on with a new identity and function: they become loft apartments (Zukin, 1982) or hotels. The inner city "revives." New services in need of business density and communications infrastructure tend to open their offices in inner cities. International finance, entertainment, fashion, and advertising industries, as well as some branches of high-tech research, pornography, and tourism, all have taken a renewed interest in the old business districts, driving out more traditional crafts, the turnover and profit margins of which are usually much lower. Real estate prices and rents are creeping up, tumult emerges on the way to downtown.

The residential housing market takes part in the general process of the revitalization of the profit rate. Groups of the middle class start moving into certain inner-city neighborhoods that had not been cultivated earlier by "their kind." Their relocation is accompanied by radical changes in the housing stock and the character of these neighborhoods. The process is then labeled *gentrification*—a term coined by Ruth Glass (1964)—and the word quickly finds its way into the social sciences and the popular media. The consensual definition of the process is the "rehabilitation of working-class and derelict housing and the consequent transformation of the area into a middle-class neighborhood" (Smith and Williams, 1986: 1). To be sure, gentrification does not take place in all inner-city areas with derelict housing; "derelictness" is a necessary but not sufficient condition for gentrification. It is the good potential of those derelict houses that appeals to capital and the newcomers. Recycling old housing should be seen against the general process of standardization and the decline of the quality of workmanship in construction. In a context where most housing features eight-foot ceilings and prefab construction, old brownstones do offer a reasonably desirable variety even if located in not so "good" neighborhoods.

Neighborhood "revitalization" can take on many forms: the gentrification of lower-status residential areas, the conversion of lofts abandoned by capital into apartments, and tenure conversion are only three important institutional varieties. All these processes are usually, the last one especially often, conflated and assumed under the heading "gentrification." Common to all is the sudden in-migration of capital—be it individual residential, developers', or any other type of business capital. It is accompanied by the replacement or, from the bottom-up perspective, forceful displacement of the residential population.

Urban renewal is embedded in postmodern architecture and urban design, which "broadly signify a break with the modernist idea that planning and development should focus on large-scale, metropolitan-wide, technologically rational and efficient urban *plans,* backed by absolutely no-frills architecture" (Harvey, 1989a: 66). The term *planning* is used less and less frequently, as are the phrases *slum clearance* and *construction of social housing.* Charles Jencks (1984) argues that urban design and architecture, finally rid of the rhetoric of social reforms, became uninhibitedly market oriented. It is not necessary that the planner should assign various functions and social groups to various neighborhoods anymore; the market can be trusted to take care of that. This new order of things lifts the obstacles to the homogenization of neighborhoods and the exclusion of areas with higher concentrations of resources. Segregation on the other end of the income scale is usually an involuntary consequence. Gentrification at first seems to disturb this order, but, once it has gained momentum, it homogenizes the scene with considerable zest. In this sense gentrification is but an urban variation on the theme of the tension capital embodies, that between equalization and differentiation.

Gentrification has received much attention, both in professional circles and in the media. As Smith and Williams (1986) complain, its importance has grown out of proportion, at the expense of more comprehensive and theoretically driven analyses of economic restructuring and the city. A most common feature of treating gentrification is the haste with which prophecies of urban sociology projecting the decline of downtowns and the inevitable suburbanization of the city are declared to be challenged by gentrification and neighborhood revitalization.[2] A closer look shows that gentrification did not reverse these processes. In fact, gentrification and suburbanization are not mutually exclusive. They are both part of the larger scheme of uneven urban development (Smith, 1996). The kind of partial success achieved by the middle class in suburbanization can be very informative for gentrification, a later landscaping activity by a later middle class, most often referred to as "the new middle class." Although, as Smith (1987) argues, the emergence of a new middle class does not explain the phenomenon of gentrification completely, the two are nevertheless connected.

The Self-Defeating Victory of Suburbanization

Lewis Mumford (1961) examines the history and transformation of the meaning of the suburban way of life. The suburb has served, throughout most of its long history, as a spatial and class-based retreat from the disorderly big city, and as such it was clearly an upper-class privilege in its early days. In its earlier days yet, even 150 years ago, living outside the town walls signified destitution, exclusion, and physical sqaulor (Jackson, 1985). The aristocratic country home, however, has always been an object of envy to the middle class and the main status symbol of its most ambitious people. It became available to them once a major redistribution of wealth and certain technological changes in construction and transportation rendered that possible. The process gained momentum after World War II, and the suburban way of life became a standard form of middle-class living.

The massification of the suburb resulted in a mode of life very far from the original desire for space and creative environment, a new synthesis of nature and civilization. Instead, "the [suburban] part became the substitute for the whole" (Mumford, 1961: 495), an entire universe of a transitory existence where "compulsive play" rules among "childish dwellers." In poorly built row houses, privacy can amount to less than might be found in a well-designed urban tenement building, and, in most suburbs, there are few signs of a modern Jeffersonian town-hall democracy emerging. The urban problems people were escaping did not get solved—perhaps because their solution lies in *both* the *urbs* and the *suburbs*, or because their essence is in the class relations of urban life, which were not changed, only temporarily and spatially reconfigured, in suburbanization. Thus "urban problems" proved difficult merely to leave behind, according to the American tradition of displacing conflicts by continuously expanding the frontier. The result is that "the two modes of life blend into each other; for both in suburb and in metropolis, mass production, mass consumption, and mass recreation produce the same kind of standardized and denatured environment" (Mumford, 1961: 495). This may have been an unconscious politico-economic insight on part of Mumford, nevertheless, it is one of the most important observations about suburbanization in the United States that he made. Suburbanization and urban growth, or suburbanization and gentrification, are twin sides of the process of capitalist urbanization. Gentrification is not the reversal of suburbanization. The legendary boredom of American middle-class suburbs and the visceral reactions most metropolitan citizens display against them are not unrelated to the extreme dangers and "wilderness" of cities.

Although Mumford implies that the massification of any "distinguished" way of life may kill the very distinctiveness of the ideal, he does not conclude mechanistically that this is why the suburb has failed in its contemporary form. He insists that suburbanization, if not seen only as an escape, can benefit from the best traditions of urban design and human cohabitation, such as appropriate zoning and land-use legislation. Witold Rybczynski's (1995) inquiry into the history of suburbanization also refutes any simplistic dichotomy between city and suburb. Rybczynski points out that garden suburbs were not conceived in opposition to the traditional city. Postwar suburbanization, the mass production of housing and urban planning outside of urban areas, was a different case, however. He notes that "the failure of the postwar subdivisions was, paradoxically, a result of their great commercial success" (196).

Gentrification has run a very similar course. Gentrifiers bought into the distinctions of past times, but the aura of a gentrified neighborhood is a far cry from a bustling commercial and residential downtown, with its several social and aesthetic layers to which most citizens can connect. In an ideal situation, attempts at exclusive redefinitions of inner cities are rarely successful. If a few members of the "gentry" come, they have to develop some sensitivity to adjust; if their whole class comes, fear, laziness, and the capital they bring with them overrule the necessity of adjustment. And if all that takes place against the backdrop of the radical dichotomization of suburban and urban life and the lack of the history of cohabitation of different classes, it is bound to be aggressively expansive and to reproduce the frontier experience.

An Atlantic Gap?

"Is there an Atlantic gap in gentrification?" many, mainly European, analysts ask (e.g., Carpenter and Lees, 1995; Hamnett and Randolph, 1986; Lees, 1994; Weesep and Musterd, 1991). There is a consensus that gentrification is a universal phenomenon in the cities of the advanced Western world, although it may vary in its intensity. At the heart of the debate are the causes of the phenomenon. The disagreement was sparked by Neil Smith's (1986) analysis in which he claimed that "what is remarkable about the rent gap is its near universality" (23). The rent gap develops in the context of the cycles of capital investment and disinvestment, when, parallel to the expansion of suburban investments, land value is declining in the inner city and there is a marked difference between capitalized ground rent under current use and potential ground rent that could be obtained under other uses of the location. The spiral dynamic of the process leads to even more complete withdrawal from maintenance responsibilities and to a significant abandonment of inner-city property until the situation is ripe for restructuring, a residential form of which is gentrification. Smith provides a basic politico-economic conceptualization of the emergence of the "opportunity" for changes, and the analysis of the rent gap is firmly embedded in the larger process of urban restructuring.

Yet attention seems to center on the rent gap somewhat removed from its original context (Weesep and Musterd, 1991), and perhaps a hurried dichotomy is constructed between Smith's idea of the rent gap and the value gap explanation of Hamnett and Randolph (1986). The latter hold that the non-American context requires a slightly different analysis. Their main variable, the value gap, is the difference between the potential value of the building in a vacant state and its tenanted investment value. Landlords may not always be able to approximate the latter to the former due to rent regulation by the state and the protected status of tenants; thus selling apartments to owner-occupiers, whose interest is aroused as a conjuncture of other economic factors, may be a more profitable solution. Massive tenure conversion may eventually lead to gentrification.

The difference between the two approaches to the discrepancy of current and potential gain is that instead of adding the role of the state and tenants' rights to the fundamental scheme (as proposed by Smith), Hamnett and Randolph (1986) incorporate these modifying factors into the first level of the explanatory scheme. Smith's description is on a different level of abstraction. Hamnett and Randolph's is a well-argued case study of the transformation of housing in inner London, and a special case of that: tenure conversion. The benefit of the debate is, clearly, the recognition that the context of gentrification does matter (Lees, 1994). One may add that it matters not only whether the context is the United States, the United Kingdom, or continental Europe: the larger context of gentrification and its link to different loci and levels of current restructuring also need to be taken into account. In all fairness, Smith acknowledges variations in the consequences of gentrification in different cities, especially in his later writings (e.g., Smith, 1996). In fact, he gives a good analysis of gentrification in three European cities. The uniqueness of the case of Amsterdam is that "it seemed to retain a mix of social classes in the city," which has to do with "the retention of strong state regulation" (Smith, 1996: 171). In this regard, Hamnett and Randolph could not agree more. But they would stop here; this is what really matters to their analytic purpose. Smith moves on: "The vital question surely is: how long can such ecumenical gentrification co-exist with traditional working-class habitation of the inner city?" (1996: 171). Asking this question is surely vital, but it relegates the difference and Amsterdam's uniqueness to temporality.

The debate on gentrification has taken an interesting route. The process caught attention in England first and was captured in a characteristically British way (Glass, 1964). The term succinctly uses the historic connotations of the concept—a middle position distinct from both the aristocracy and the yeomen. Thus *gentrification* in English subtly refers to the fact that it is not the upper class, with its unshakable self- and financial security and aesthetic judgments, that is the key actor in urban revival, but the aspiring middle class. The class distinctions suggested by the British term seemed to be lost in the American context for a while, only to be brought back into the analysis by critical human geographers (Harvey, 1987; Jager, 1986; Smith, 1986; Williams, 1986). The process emerged in its purest and ideal-typical form in U.S. cities somewhat later, and the ensuing discussion gained such momentum that nowadays, in analyses of gentrification, U.S. examples are the yardstick. Murie (1991) notes that the discussion of gentrification is based too much on a specific ecological image of the city that represents first of all the North American city.

American cities seem to be unique in their exaggeratedness. Urban revival is presented in a more dichotomous way in the American context than elsewhere in the core of the world economy: as a counterpoint to suburbanization, as radical displacement of old inner-city tenants, as complete renewal of the old housing stock. Here the front lines are clearer, the frontier manifests itself in a more pristine form than anywhere else, the distinction between old and new also draws the line between losers and winners unmistakably. Gale (1984) notes that the United States is an exception in the ferociousness of the process even within the English-speaking countries whose revitalization was "more dramatic" than in continental Europe. Smith's (1992) analysis of the transformation of Tompkins Square Park and the accompanying struggles encapsulates this difference in the degree of ferociousness. The arrogance of urban cowboys/gentry is responded to by the natives' chanting, "Die, yuppie scum!" and for the anarchist gang of unemployed working-class kids in London's Docklands the slogan goes, "Mug a yuppie."

Inner-city "revival" is fundamentally linked to the reproduction of capitalism. So, understandably, most of the difference is to be explained by the faster and less inhibited move of capital and the less restricted use of urban land in the American context. There are also more specific reasons behind the fact that, it seems, inner-city revitalization and gentrification have been the starkest in American cities economically, socially, and aesthetically.

Suburbanization has also had a more dramatic effect on American urbanization. The government-supported process was so intensive that it easily swept away wealthy populations and capital from the cores of American cities, which from the outset had been less compressed, less vital, and less attractive for residents and capital than their European counterparts. In stark contrast, the continuity of most European inner cities has never been seriously challenged. Heinritz and Lichtenberger (1986) argue that suburbanization and the "emptying" of cities is not necessarily bound up with the crisis of the central city. If inner-city public services are well maintained, suburbanization—the scale of which has, in certain European areas such as West Germany in the 1970–80s, reached that in the United States—does not lead to the decline of old downtowns. This clearly takes away from the intensity of urban renewal and diminishes tensions accompanying the process.

These continental differences introduce the theme of the level of control exercised by the state in urban development. The structure of housing in the United States has been quite different from that in European countries. In the United States, the home ownership rate was 47 percent in 1900. It reached, after a real takeoff in the 1950s, 65 percent in 1976, and the privately rented sector accounted for most of the rest of housing (Hamnett and Randolph, 1986). Public or quasi-public housing was only 2 percent of the total U.S. housing stock in 1976 (Gale, 1984: 148). In contrast, in 1914 only 10 percent of British housing units were privately owned; the rest were privately rented (Gale, 1984: 148). By 1978, the proportion of private renters fell to 16 percent; 54 percent owned their homes and 30 percent rented public housing (Williams, 1984). In other European countries public housing has also been significant; for example, in Germany it accounts for one-third of total housing. This in itself has a retardant effect on occupancy turnover in Europe. In addition, tenants are more protected against eviction even if they are renting from private landlords. English property law does not make it necessary in the case of tenure conversion to convert the whole building into condominiums; owners and renters can live side by side (Hamnett and Randolph, 1986), with the profound effect of allowing a greater possibility of a mixing of different levels of income, classes, and cultures. State involvement in securing the tenants' position also means that displacement is not as widespread as in American inner cities, thus the process is less antagonistic and the discussion less focused on displacement. Williams (1986) cites British and Australian examples of lower-class residents with long tenancy who actually benefited from the rising prices in their neighborhoods. Gale (1984) notes yet another feature of European inner-city urban architecture and design that also makes their gentrification less striking. The housing stock of European downtowns mostly consists of apartment buildings or apartment blocks, the majority of which were constructed at the end of the nineteenth century or in the early twentieth century. Exterior change is less typical, and, when it happens, it takes place with public aid, because the scale of such projects renders solely individual efforts impossible.

There are differences between North America and Europe in urban revival as there have been differences in the abandonment of inner cities: the process has been less mediated, faster, and more forceful in American cities. But it did not emerge overnight, and, in spite of the opinions of experts in real estate who insist on "degentrification" as the current theme of urban transformation, as discussed by Smith (1996), gentrification is not over. What is over is its fifteen-minute fame, but that was enough to have called attention to a more fundamental process: the merciless move of capital under an increased necessity and the possibility of spatial flexibility, which is in contradiction to human boundedness to place and people. And both capital mobility and human boundedness have racial, cultural, ethnic, gender, and class components. The renewal of the physical environment is hardly a negative phenomenon in itself. It becomes so when the very logic of capital that had pushed poverty and minority existence into the inner cities—where ties based on the spatial proximity of neighborhood relationships are more important for survival than they are in the upper social classes—disrupts these relationships by displacement and makes the life of social groups that do not have many choices unreasonably difficult.

Gentrification in Budapest?

A preliminary reply to this chapter's opening questions can be derived from the above overview of the gentrification debates: that is a cautionary tale about the significance of institutional conditions for recasting global phenomena.[3] By presenting a case from both state socialist urbanism and afterward, I hope to learn more about how the "context of gentrification matters" in general, not only in Budapest.

Although some argue that, in Budapest, "the primary process taking place in the inner city [had been] social and physical downgrading" until the late 1960s (Hegedűs and Tosics, 1991), the similarities with North American cities should not be overstated. Besides the fact that, as Heinritz and Lichtenberger (1986) demonstrate, urban "blight" never reached the same dimensions in continental Europe as in the United States, there are system-specific aspects of the dynamics of investment and disinvestment. In the Stalinist period of 1948 to the early 1960s, the primacy of production in socialist ideology delayed new housing construction everywhere in east-central Europe until political crises and the ensuing liberalization of the system exerted a substantial enough force on politicians and planners to change the dominant policy. Housing received little attention and few resources and, once the decision was made to deploy both in the early 1960s, the overwhelming majority of resources went into the construction of new housing estates. There was a time—the 1960s and 1970s—when this form of housing was extremely popular among the urban middle classes, who also tended to have better access to new housing than other groups (Szelényi and Konrád, 1969). The middle classes flooded the new prefab high-rises regulated by the redistributive policy of the state, and their new life began to resemble in its structure and aesthetics those of suburban middle classes in western Europe. Most of these estates were erected in the outer districts of the city, so their habitants were daily commuters using mass transportation. Their modernness was intoxicating, partly because nothing similar could be experienced in the residential development of older areas. Once the neatness of the new buildings started to wear off and the refurbishing of the neighborhoods was ever more sadly lacking, the new housing estates lost the only attractive feature they had for many tenants and owners.

Meanwhile, precious little money went into the maintenance, let alone the upgrading, of the old, turn-of-the-century housing stock. In spite of that, the strictly understood downtown never lost its prestige completely. Precipitous decline took place in areas whose status had always—that is, well before state socialist times—been ambiguous. Certain parts of inner-city districts next to downtown had been built for speculative purposes and of dubious-quality materials: they became transitory areas right after their completion. In 1935, the average number of inhabitants per room was 2.17 in District VII, 2.25 in VIII, and 2.32 in IX—three typical cases of such ambiguous areas adjacent to downtown (Illyefalvy, 1941: 58). In the two downtown districts—IV and V at that time—and all over Buda, that number was well below 2 (see Figure 4.1).[4] The former areas started to age in terms of both the physical environment and the demographics of their inhabitants in the 1960s. These inner-city, next-to-downtown districts constitute a transitional zone (Szelényi, 1983)—between the city center and the new housing estates—whose social status declines fast. They are squeezed between two more prestigious and resourceful areas, making the ecological model of the east-central European state socialist city somewhat peculiar.[5] Szelényi (1983) observes that the population of the new housing estates came largely from the wealthier and younger families of the areas of transition and notes the similarity of the outward movement of this group to the emergence of slums in Western cities, with the fundamental difference that the centrifugal flows in Budapest were caused by the nonrecognition of the value of central land and, thus, by the state's insensitivity and inability to mobilize resources for its redevelopment. Also, given the "quantitative housing shortage" under state socialism, the idea of renovation—which, in order to improve living conditions, may even decrease the number of

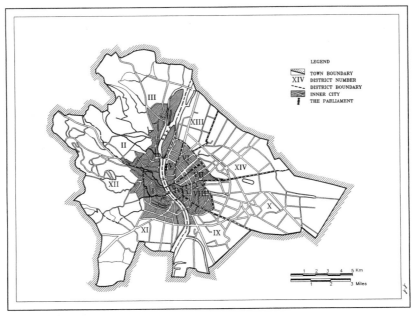

Figure 4.1. Districts and zones of Budapest, 1941. Source: Illyefalvi (1941).

apartments—seemed untenable, it would not have solved the "problem" as articulated by the housing policies of the socialist state.

Suburbanization had not been very significant in the Budapest metropolitan area until the 1970s. When it started to gain momentum, it did not happen because of people's preference to leave the city but because of limited access to urban residences. The latter was restricted by housing prices and, more important, by regulations that required new migrants to show proof of at least five years of Budapest domicile and a stable job in order to qualify for public housing, which at the time constituted the majority of Budapest housing. As a result, the villages and small towns of the surrounding Pest county started to grow, displaying a combination of sprawls of bungalows, typical rural family housing on microplots, and eleven-story prefab tenement buildings in a new, haphazard landscape with very low infrastructural investment. Social and economic distinctions were manifest in this "unregulated" expansion: following the traditional dividing line between Pest and Buda, ceteris paribus, the more prestigious and wealthier families tended to settle in the villages of the Buda side.

The inner city did not decline and suburbanization did not proceed as quickly as these processes took place in the western part of Europe. Nevertheless, the rehabilitation of the transitional zone became an issue by the end of the 1970s. Private builders had very limited access to these inner-city neighborhoods due to building codes and zoning. The rehabilitation project became overwhelmingly the business of the state, the single major landlord in the area. The original idea was a comprehensive redevelopment of these areas, and the pockets in which it started showed the same disastrous effects as slum clearance projects in the United States or western Europe, mediated only by a strong socialist welfare state. A bizarre advantage of the resource poverty of the state is that it can reduce some of the radicalism of grand cityscaping activity: as slum clearance projects ran out of money, there came a renewed interest in more "conservative" approaches. The most visible and largest-scale product of "regulated gentrification" (Cséfalvay and Pomázi, 1990) was the renovation of Block 15 in the middle of District VII, or Elizabethtown. I will address this case in more detail.

This area is characterized "by high building density, dilapidated buildings and an environment which led to the aging of the local population and the increase of an inappropriately living (lumpen) stratum" reads the report of the local council in the 1980s (quoted in Balás and Hegedűs, 1990).[6] The aim of the rehabilitation project was "first to mitigate ongoing social tension, then to eliminate it." The concept, which was originally accepted by the Municipal Council of Budapest in 1978, immediately got caught in a fiery debate between those who promoted the creation of a large number of small apartments and those who insisted on size and quality. Block 15 was the only location where the latter group gained some ground and, as a result, the new design broke up small units, cut back on the number of one-room apartments radically, and quadrupled the proportion of units with at least three rooms. The project had severe financial problems from the beginning, so two houses on the block were sold to the Ministry of Defense, and the idea of incorporating office space in the originally residential project emerged as "the most efficient solution" (Balás and Hegedűs, 1990).

Tenants had to be relocated during the construction work. They were offered other public housing on a new housing estate or in older parts of the city, with the condition that they pay for any value gap. The renovated apartments were allocated through two channels: (1) the Rehabilitation Management Office, which selected new tenants from the district, mostly from tenement buildings awaiting renovation; and (2) the local council or the City Council of Budapest, which chose from among those on the waiting list without any official or publicly known criteria.

As a survey by the Budapest-based Metropolitan Research Institute demonstrates, it was mostly older families with relatively high incomes who gained access to housing through the Rehabilitation Office. Meanwhile, the central selection mechanism favored young professional families who had the access and skills to use the redistributive process to their benefit (Balás and Hegedűs, 1990). Both channels excluded families with very low incomes—usually, those at the bottom did not even bother to apply—and the "lumpen" elements (a proxy almost completely for Gypsies in the district vocabulary). As an overall result of the renewal process, the social status of the block rose, but demographic rejuvenation was not so obvious given the extremely high proportion of pensioners in the area.

The rents of the new apartments went up, but not as steeply as the quality of the buildings. On the average, rents in the block amounted to 11 percent of household income—with utilities, 28 percent—whereas the national averages were 6 percent and 14 percent, respectively (Balás and Hegedűs, 1990).[7] Rent and maintenance could be a heavy burden: one in seven families spent at least half of their income on housing (Balás and Hegedűs, 1990). The dominant mood among the new tenants was disenchantment; although the project achieved its main objectives, it was a thankless enterprise overall. The report concludes that new tenants got the maximum amount of subsidy from the state-landlord in spite of relatively high rents in the renovated block. However, these privileges were not available to everyone; they were conditioned on the ability to pay an "admission fee." The discontent of those who managed to do so—a surprise to the researchers—shows the limitation of these projects. Tenants were justly unhappy because the contractors left them with much minor repair work to be done. Their rents were in the highest category of public housing, and they made comparisons with those few apartments that belonged to the same category but were better located, usually in the greenbelt of Buda. A restricted introduction of market elements into the state redistribution of housing can be very misleading: the tenants of Block 15 had the impression that subsidized housing on the Buda hills would have been available to them. Their complaints about the environment, the quality of air, the lack of green areas, security problems in the neighborhood, and the behavior of the tenants outside the block illustrate some of the obstacles to promoting new middle-class life in the inner city.

This particular design was very generous with green in the inner-city context for Budapest, however. A main objective was to alleviate the traditional high density of inner-city tenement buildings, so some of the poorly lit sections in the inner yards were turned into a park with several playgrounds. The original idea was to link the new park area to the outside, to create a big passagelike quasi-public space accessible to everyone. The first and last act of the Tenants' Committee was, then, to lock the gates on the block and thus semiprivatize the park inside. Still, the park is a constant source of bitter complaints by the tenants. As one noted: "The park used to be so nice, but it lasted only for two years. Now kids from the neighboring houses destroy everything and there is no one in charge of the park. Public order has broken down completely." Others think that the area and the nearby square—a site of constant clashes with the lower-status population of the neighborhood—was still "fine and in order as long as the Communists were in power. Since they left, no one has collected the trash in the park."[8] The lack of means and concern for maintaining public space certainly adds to the tension that accompanies the insertion of this pocket of higher social status into the general depression of the district. The contrast would not be so overwhelming now had the rehabilitation process, of which the renovation of Block 15 was to be only the first step, to be followed gradually by other blocks in the district, not come to a halt. This explains some of the discontent of the tenants, for whom the benefits of their new units and the expensive landscaping would increase if the rest of the neighborhood were better kept. Now they see the neighboring streets beyond control.

Some see Block 15 as a case of "socialist gentrification" (Cséfalvay and Pomázi, 1990) and suggest that state involvement led to vast injustices. It certainly re-created familiar patterns of spatial injustice. Yet that was not because the project was financed and controlled by the state instead of a more "spontaneous" market. The only just solution, assuming that all the former tenants were in desperate need of housing subsidy, would have been the complete return of former tenants to their renovated units. This would not have been a realistic suggestion amid the urban housing shortage and given the growing importance of market elements in the otherwise redistributive system of housing. The housing allocation system of late state socialism was such that an initial decree of apartment allocation by the local council was usually followed by a series of exchanges in which value and quality carried definite monetary equivalence (Bodnár and Böröcz, 1998). A subsidy of this kind would have met serious opposition by the more and more calculative middle classes. Even more important is that this solution would have been in stark contrast with the idea of making the area "more orderly" (by displacing disorderly tenants)—a principal objective of the project and a major source of injustice.

"Socialist gentrification" seems to have produced results that are strikingly similar to gentrification under capitalism in very general terms: the social status of the area has risen with improvements in the condition of the housing stock, and the new tenants have become increasingly aware of their environment and its tensions. However, the similarities end there. The newcomers are not predominantly "yuppies"; they are older-than-average, sometimes poor people, and many had lived in the neighborhood for a long time. The process had its built-in injustices; nevertheless, it was more moderated and less radical than any textbook case of gentrification known from western Europe or the United States. This is not to praise the local government or state socialist urban management per se; rather, it is to show the inherent limitations of every "renewal" in which the renewal of the physical structure cannot be separated from a concept of "social renewal," thus making the endeavor and its evaluation very problematic. The effects of the enormous amount of money and effort that went into the renovation of Block 15 were rather modest. One can only argue that, had it been otherwise, little old retired ladies whose housing costs amount to half of their income would not be sharing a house with neighbors who live on 160 square meters and built a sauna at their own expense. The activities of the Tenants' Committee surely would not have stopped at installing locks on the gates (which have never worked properly anyway). The *social success* of urban renewal programs and gentrification lies in their *partial economic failure.* If the upgrading of the neighborhood is complete both physically and socially, due to the one-dimensional logic of capital, there is more complete displacement and there remains room for fewer social "accidents" of mixing. Urban renewal that is based entirely on a cost-benefit analysis does not allow anything but radical solutions—the transformation most preferable for real estate value. Such "clean" outcomes are bound to please fully only real estate developers; even a well-intentioned and not very socially conscious "gentry" would feel uneasy about moving into a recently "sterilized" environment.

The most interesting similarity between Block 15 and the process commonly described by analysts of gentrification in North America and western Europe is in the choice of the particular area. Although in Budapest the site for renewal was selected by the local government through a process that would be rightly described by comparative analysts of socialism versus capitalism as a quintessentially nonmarket process of bureaucratic allocation, it can be argued that market-based gentrification would have been most likely to take place in a section of Budapest with curiously similar characteristics, perhaps even exactly the same block. State of disrepair, proximity to downtown, social composition, and inability of tenants to finance the neighborhood's renewal would have likely prompted a similar decision. In other words, the transformation of Block 15 revealed the unmistakable logic of the market—embedded in the institutional process of the bureaucratic allocative decision by the local state. The implications of this observation for analytic work on the postsocialist transformation in general are very far-reaching, complicating the streamlined picture of the transformation— a simple move from the state to the market—painted in the transitology literature.

This explanation works, thus, on two levels. First, as indicated earlier, along with significant public housing, there existed a housing market in Hungary at that time, and even the sphere of public housing was thoroughly saturated with calculative practices and monetary transactions. On a general level, there are very serious signs of uneven development under state socialism. These general features make state socialism similar to capitalism, as long as both are painted with broad enough strokes. The existence of a dynamics of urban investment and disinvestment is also similar; the effects of disinvestment in some inner-city areas of Budapest showed slow preparation for some sort of restructuring. This started with the Block 15 project and expanded, later, after the privatization law. On the one hand, this all indicates the universality of the process of urban renewal and gentrification. On the other, the detailed institutional history of investment and disinvestment under state socialism is quite different from its capitalist counterpart. One level of the explanation is the same, the other differs. If we accept that, it also makes sense to make a distinction and claim that the main theme of urban transformation in Budapest is housing privatization that shows more structural similarity with tenure conversion. The residential upgrading of inner-city neighborhoods is not the most characteristic consequence of tenure conversion or housing privatization.

Tenure Conversion

Tenure conversion is a form of urban renewal that produces results similar to gentrification but with a time lag. In the British case, as presented by Hamnett and Randolph (1986), the emergence of a value gap between the tenanted investment value and the vacant possession value of the property prompted landlords to seek a more profitable solution by selling their property. The first component of the gap had a strong upper limit: "Delayed and expensive repairs coupled with controlled rents presented post-war landlords with a poor return on their investment" (132). Vacant possession value increased as a result of a relative shortage of housing in inner London and housing price inflation. Other factors, such as the concentration of well-paid employees in these areas and their desire to live there, combined with the wider availability of mortgage finance, created the possibility for sales to owner-occupiers. "However . . . this 'preference' for ownership is to a large extent a constrained preference, for the potential central-London resident will have to buy his or her accommodation in the absence of a functioning private rental sector, outside of the limited high-rent, short-stay luxury end of the market" (139).

In Budapest the situation became similar after a 1990 law that passed the property rights of public housing to local governments and strengthened their autonomy from the city.[9] The all-encompassing state-landlord became splintered into twenty-two local landlords with declining budgets in a mixed economy. The number of districts increased to twenty-three with the splitting of one of the larger districts later. In this situation, the difference between rent income and maintenance costs, which had always been negative and would have been considered "irrational" on a housing market but escaped such logic in a state socialist system in which the single largest landlord also owned most of the means of production, became revalued. The district-landlord was expected to assume all responsibility for a housing stock where delayed investments created a severe renovation crisis. The fiction of low rents and tenure security quickly evaporated for tenants; although actual measures did not touch their fundamental rights and the rent increases did not move the public sector closer to the prices in the private renting sector, people had an understanding that it was merely a question of time. The situation was ripe for tenure conversion.

The nature of state socialist housing determined the particular institutional form tenure conversion took. The quasi-ownership right of tenants marked the system off from even highly subsidized public housing in other than state socialist countries. No idea of privatization would have been feasible politically except the sale of apartments to sitting tenants at affordable prices. Mortgage financing was so wildly favorable that the possibility of tenure conversion became easily available. Hungarian privatization law allows for a mixed tenure system within a multistory building. In this regard the process is very similar to British flat breakups, as described by Hamnett and Randolph (1986). These authors also comment on another feature that distinguishes the British experience from American condominium conversions and gentrification: inner-London tenure conversion did not involve the renovation of buildings. They interpret the process from an angle usually not even mentioned in the literature: tenure conversion also shifted the responsibility of long-due repairs to the new owner-occupiers.

The latter point is exceedingly relevant for the east-central European context. Although the mayor of Elizabethtown, a firm believer in the beneficial impact that ownership exerts on individual responsibility, insists that "houses are cleaner and repairs have started all over," one should not exaggerate the success of private initiatives to improve the quality of common space in the buildings. These efforts are usually exhausted with the installation of an entry-phone system, as Hamnett and Randolph (1986) also observe was the case in London. Small, four- to six-unit buildings may acquire a new coat of paint inside and outside, but there are few examples of this in the bigger tenement buildings that constitute most of the inner city.

The postsocialist version of tenure conversion has its own defining characteristics as well. Most striking, the process is burdened with vast injustices. These stem partly from the logic of the previous distribution of housing and, it is important to note, do not coalesce along the line of displacement versus gentrification or neighborhood upgrading. In Budapest, tenure conversion includes the conversion of extremely good-quality residential units from rental to ownership, creating an unjust advantage for those already privileged by the socialist state's allocation mechanism (see chapter 3). Tenure conversion in Budapest did not result, thus, in the renewal of inner-city housing or the large-scale circulation of inhabitants. Instead, it created an opportunity for a very selective urban renewal fundamentally orchestrated and performed by commercial users. Aside from downtown, a prime target of these aspirations has been Elizabethtown, probably the only area of Budapest where a real tension has emerged between the current and alternative uses of the neighborhood: its central location mobilized considerable energy to upgrade this derelict part of the city. We should be reminded that it was in the same neighborhood that "socialist gentrification" took place under the control of the local government.

Local Politics of Renewal in Elizabethtown

Before passage of the Housing Act, the details of the housing question caused serious political ruptures in the local governments in the early 1990. The decentralization of public authority in the capital city, although very much in line with the political rhetoric of postsocialist times, may have been a hurried decision. It made citywide coordination extremely difficult, and the decentralization of the heaviest legacy of the state socialist housing system implied the acknowledgment of the possibility of very unequal urban development.[10]

Elizabethtown is, again, an interesting example. The area had, due to its location, potential for development in a more overtly market-oriented use of space, and pockets of renewal had already been created through the use of resources other than those obtained from the local government. Nonetheless, the district has always had a large proportion of apartments without full amenities. As a result, rents, which had not been very sensitive to quality but reflected at least the lack of comfort, were low enough to induce an inflow of poor migrant families from the countryside into the area who were, clearly, more forgiving toward the shortcomings of the housing. The proportion of units without toilets—the tenants of which use shared lavatories located outside the units on each floor—was still around 15 percent. The rent income of Elizabethtown for 1993 from both residential and commercial rentals was about 60 percent that of District V of downtown, which has roughly one-third the number of rentals (KSH, 1994a: 143). In all fairness, it should be noted that rent efficiency was worse in some other districts, such as District VIII of Josephtown or even in sections of District XIII, but other districts do not compare themselves with downtown, nor do they have aspirations to become a financial center second to downtown.

Given these circumstances, it was only logical that the local government of Elizabethtown should try to shift the burden of maintenance and repair to the future owner-occupiers by privatizing the housing stock. Rent increases on a large scale were very desirable—given that in some cases rent income hardly covered the electricity bills for light in the common spaces in the buildings—but that was, clearly, not a realistic idea for the majority of the local population. For the same reason, it would not have been conceivable to expect a complete privatization of the housing sector had the financial conditions of the process been all too favorable. The local government soon realized that it would have to assume some kind of responsibility with regard to social housing in any case. This realization led some to a very critical stance on the privatization of housing that was taking place with full force on the basis of an old 1969 regulation, while awaiting the new housing law. The latter came only in the summer of 1993. By 1993, about 16 percent (five to six thousand units) of all housing was sold to former tenants, and approximately the same number of units were assigned for evaluation and privatization.

The local government was split on the issue and a debate ensued. One group, formed around the mayor of the district, was for all-in privatization. Past experience had shown, they argued, that the local government would not be able to maintain the housing stock, and restricting privatization at that stage would have been a source of social injustice toward the privatizer-to-be. All housing and commercial space should be sold to private owners in the name of justice and "so that the dweller could finally rise from the status of a subject to that of a citizen and bourgeois," as the mayor put it. Even this group held, however, that some of the buildings could and should not be sold, such as those whose price did not reach 75 percent of the ground price and those without full amenities.

The other group, whose leaders were the two vice mayors, had a comprehensive housing proposition that relied on an in-depth background study commissioned from the Metropolitan Research Institute. This group also appealed to social justice, claiming that the ongoing injustice of the privatization process should be stopped. Prices should be raised to approximate market values. This would result in less-hurried decisions by the tenants and, without bringing undeserved wealth to their owners, only those units would be sold that could stand on their own in the market. According to the predictions of the study, as a result of changes in the conditions of privatization, less than a third of the tenants would purchase their units. Others would remain tenants and pay higher rents. The other, more significant part of the income of the local government would come from the radically increased rents of nonresidential spaces, the sale of which this group vehemently opposed. By combining resources from the residential and commercial sectors, the local government could finally assume the responsibility of delayed repairs. This group insisted that, at least theoretically, renovations should be accompanied by only temporary displacements; old tenants should move back to the renovated buildings.

Entrepreneurial and especially foreign investment capital did not play a major part in the latter group's vision of the neighborhood's future. The advocates of this view were in fact rather skeptical about these possibilities. A representative of this faction self-ironically recalled the detailed proposition the local government put together for incoming capital about which "nobody cared." One of the "best investments" was the sale of a potentially valuable vacated and renovated building to a lawyer who already owed the local government a significant amount from another deal. A minor reconstruction plan involved a block adjacent to the Dohány Street Synagogue, the largest one operating in Hungary, and indeed in central Europe, whose extended renovation had created a pocket of renewal in the district. The new plan concerned the back of the same block on Síp Street. It included the architectural heritage building of the National Printing House, which was up for privatization with the condition that the buyer should renovate it. Most of the other old buildings in the block would stay, and a back wing would be demolished to make room for an underground garage serving the hotel and the shopping center—the highlights of the reconstruction project. There were negotiations with Israeli developers, the mayor said, and he added: "Quite logically, right next to the synagogue such a hotel needs to be built which does not clash with religious activities." Unfortunately, the rest of the local government did not even hear about this possible deal.

The mayor's camp imagined the local government more in the position of a night watchman; the market would take care of the housing question and the renewal of the district. The mayor, who had been a company manager in socialist times and a confessed "friend of private property even when the elected body was not," was convinced that only the system of private ownership would "start some healthy process." The central location of the district is a guarantee to business success. Elizabethtown will become an extension of downtown, which has become the City—the financial center—of Budapest. "Residential displacement is a desirable process; people cannot insist on living at the same place all their lives." Furthermore, this group managed to present this scenario as desirable even for those displaced, because they could finally sell their apartments and build houses on the outskirts of the city. The general harmonizing effects of the market thus construed stem from a well-intentioned ignorance about monetary equivalences and a complete disregard for individual preferences and constraints.

Both groups have realized that the income the local government obtained from apartment privatization would not cover the costs of even minimal renovations. They all also admitted that "in the last three years we have not spent a penny on rehabilitation."[11] (In fact, only 5 of their 990 tenement buildings were renovated in 1993; KSH, 1994a: 144.) Having identified the problem, the representatives of the two views came to conflicting conclusions: one would leave the grand-scale restructuring of the neighborhood to entrepreneurial capital, and the other would change the premises of the economic possibilities of the local government by modifying the conditions of current privatization, thus creating a basis for a comprehensive management of space in the district that would incorporate stronger redistributive elements than the ideas the mayor's group tried to promote. The latter would leave only 150 to 180 buildings in the hands of the local government, those that are unsalable due to their condition. It was very telling about the political situation that the groups were not divided along party lines. Both factions enjoyed support among the Free Democrats—the majority party in the district—although the majority sided with the vice mayors, who were also backed by the then-ruling nationalist center-right party, the Hungarian Democratic Forum as well as the then-opposition Young Democrats. Their opposition drew on the support of a minority within the Free Democrats, the Hungarian Socialist Party, the Smallholders, and the Social Democrats. The Socialist Party was represented by its liberal wing; they thought "realistically" or "opportunistically"—depending on the commentator's political preferences—that the welfare state was an "illusion" in this part of the world and the party should focus on the middle classes. Their idea of social justice was to make everyone the owner of his or her apartment, referring to the historical example of land distribution after World War II (Zolnay, 1993).

The main front line between the two groups was the housing issue. Their views generally diverged on the future development of the district. This became manifest in the debate on the only concrete project of urban restructuring: the Madách Passage (see below), an initiative that complicated further the tense situation within the local government. The architect of the project belonged to the local Democratic Forum, so that supporting the project became a cardinal question for the faction. The majority Free Democrats with whom they sided on the issue of housing were strongly opposed to the creation of the passage. However, fearing that the delicate alliance formed over the housing question, the cornerstone of their urban policy, might break, the Free Democrats decided to put aside their criticism of the project. Following a fierce debate in an auditorium filled with passionate tenants, the plan was passed in March 1992, and a ban was introduced on the sale of buildings that were part of the reconstruction project.

The idea of a passage starting at the Town Hall and running into the Great Ring, following Király Street all the way, is a plan that has been re-cycled several times (see Figure 4.2). It emerged first in the last decade of the nineteenth century only to grasp attention again at the turn of the century (Braun, Czike, and Lencsés, 1993). In 1928 a new and less ambitious version came up and was taken so seriously that the architect of two corner houses in Madách Square designed an arch between the two buildings with the intention of making it the opening of the passage. This was erected while the rest of the passage remained merely a plan, in spite of efforts in the 1950s to turn it into an avenue for socialist parades. In 1990, the newly elected body of Elizabethtown's local government rediscovered it in their renewed efforts toward distinction and identity construction. "We wish to build a neighborhood that resembles both the air of past times and also a business, commercial, and cultural district worthy of a world capital," wrote a newspaper that called the project "the Bond Street of Budapest" (Pogány, 1990: 15).

The legitimacy of the project from the point of view of urban plan-ning is to expand the crowded historical downtown in the direction of the Great Ring, a secondary commercial street and important traffic line. There would be a covered shopping arcade running between the Town Hall and the Ring. The plan involves the demolition of 25 blocks of flats and 23 other buildings, which translates into the liquidation of 382 apartments and a further loss of 334 due to reconstruction. A total of 29 new building plots

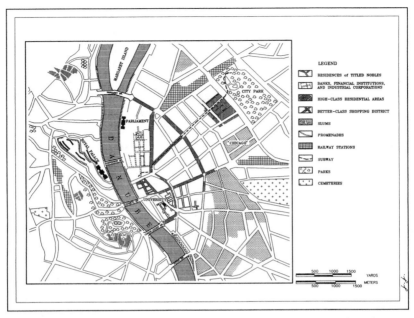

Figure 4.2. Social map of inner-city Budapest, 1943. Source: Beynon (1943).

would be created, and 1,430 apartments would be upgraded and the ground-floor ones would be converted into commercial spaces (Bartók, Pomsár, and Falk, 1993: 24). The tiled passage would accommodate elegant street furniture: benches, statues, candelabra, trees, hedges in containers. An underground garage system would be built under the main line of the passage. One of the weak points of the design within its own premises is that increased car traffic would have to be taken up by two parallel neighboring streets that are narrow and already congested.

This reads like a case of full-fledged gentrification, and has been interpreted as such very correctly even in the *New York Times* (Perlez, 1993), which has taken special note of the "522 apartments demolished" and "over a thousand people replaced." Indeed, the Madách Passage project includes displacement, but, in all fairness, it should be noted also that most of the people to be "displaced" are public tenants and are less vulnerable to mistreatment by their landlord (the local government) than their private counterparts. The law requires that they be provided with new rentals of comparable if not better quality, many of which are located in the same district. Displacement and the disruption of neighborhood ties usually do injustice to the people involved, but if moving mixes with the promise of change for the better in certain respects (level of amenities, more light, and so on), it becomes very difficult for the tenants to resist such proposals unanimously. This is why Neil Smith (1996) has observed "very little resistance or organized opposition to gentrification" in Budapest (180). This he identifies as a distinguishing mark of gentrification in Budapest, and he is perfectly right in terms of an implicit comparison with the United States and western Europe. Resistance is weak when demarcation lines are not very clear, and they cannot always be drawn between the gentrifiers and the displaced. Also, displacement in the classical sense is not always part of the process. Once a person owns his or her apartment, he or she cannot be forced out easily. Condo fees and other maintenance costs are not so high yet, and their collection is not so strongly enforced, that this can happen very frequently.

The Madách Passage plan actually met opposition by architects, local government managers, and ordinary local citizens alike, but not necessarily those directly concerned. Disagreement was more professional than overtly political. The "conservatives" lamented the losses that would disrupt the traditional texture of the neighborhood, such as the demolition of a kosher butchery and a Greek Orthodox chapel and the breakup of an architecturally unique design of nested courtyards (the Gozsdu Courtyard). According to a survey of five hundred families affected by the reconstruction, local people decided to support the plan due to the apparent lack of an alternative and because they were led to believe that incoming entrepreneurial capital would bring enough revenue to renovate houses even in the backyard of the passage (Városkutatás Kft., 1992). Quite a few officials in the local government and on the Madách Passage Committee supported the plan with a humanitarian argument: "The old tenants could finally be moved out to modern apartments with full amenities; many unhealthy units would be liquidated, and the extreme density of the neighborhood would be broken up." They were annoyed by the "conservatives" who were afraid that the old character and atmosphere of the neighborhood would be lost: "Interestingly, the people who live here do not complain about 'losing the old aura'; in their damp apartments there is a rather damp atmosphere." These officials based their optimism on the interest of foreign capital pouring into the neighborhood, which they estimated would ultimately amount to U.S.$62 million. In spite of the fact that the first building of the project, the Madách Trade Center was well under way,[12] even the mayor, who could not imagine any other solution in order to "bring back the old commercial profile of the district" than moving the Madách project ahead, voiced his doubts about "inpouring" foreign capital.

Those critical of the project did not see the financing of the passage as feasible; they also questioned the architectural merits of the design and were pessimistic about its effect on the local population. However, they were very distant in their worries from the local population, who may not have wanted to leave the neighborhood but would certainly have preferred better housing. They were not unaffected by demagogic political rhetoric, either. They were outraged that the rent of a renovated two-room unit would triple, which would be a shocking dynamic in itself but should not be detached from the absolute level of rents, in which case the rent of a renovated apartment would amount to the price of eighty liters of milk or 10.5 percent of the average net wage in Budapest in 1993 (KSH, 1994a: 75). The socially minded liberal supporters of the plan admitted the problem and argued that it should not be solved by postponing rent increases. Special subsidies should be given, instead, to "local" tenants in order to avoid radical population change in the area. Countering this, the "conservatives" asserted uncompromisingly that "it is easy to see that such a measure would be gravely discriminative" (Braun et al., 1993: 24).

Due to the moderate interest of foreign capital, which ultimately proved the skeptics to be right, no sweeping changes have taken place in the district yet. In the meantime, the liberal district government lost the new elections and the socialists won the majority. The first congratulatory telegram for the newly elected mayor came from Mr. Hemingway, a Los Angeles–based businessman. He was not motivated by long-term renovation plans; he would merely have liked to purchase a considerably large piece of commercial space he had been renting from, among others, the government of Elizabethtown. He owns a sweetshop chain that is slowly being turned into Dunkin' Donuts, Pizza Hut, Kentucky Fried Chicken, and an authentic American Californian-Mexican restaurant.

Economic Transformation and Privatization with Illusions

Fundamental changes have taken place in Hungary's economy. These changes in general terms follow economic restructuring documented in the United States and western Europe. Manufacturing has declined and the service sector has grown. As Table 4.1 shows, these processes originated well before the political transformation of the country, which only accelerated these trends. The above-noted changes have been even more pointed in Budapest (Table 4.2). In 1992, the proportion of investments in the nonmaterial sector was 42 percent in Budapest, whereas it varied greatly but never went above 30 percent in the rest of the country. Of all financial investment in Hungary, 73 percent was associated with the capital city (Barta, 1994). The distribution of foreign capital displays similar regional inequalities. In both 1991

Table 4.1

Changes in the sectoral composition of the Hungarian labor force, 1949–90 (%)

	1949	1960	1970	1980	1990
Agriculture	53.8	38.4	24.7	18.9	15.4
Manufacturing	19.4	27.9	36.3	34.0	31.1
Construction	2.2	6.1	7.4	8.1	7.0
Transportation, communications	4.4	6.5	7.3	8.1	8.6
Trade	5.3	6.3	8.0	9.8	11.0
Water management	0.1	0.2	1.2	1.5	1.6
Personal, economic services	3.5	2.5	2.8	4.0	5.6
Health, social, and cultural services	3.7	5.5	7.5	10.3	13.4
Community, administrative, and other services	7.5	6.6	4.9	5.1	6.5

Source: KSH (1992: 44).

and 1992, 58 percent of direct foreign investment was concentrated in Budapest (KSH, 1994b: 69), changing to 55 percent in 1995 and 1996 (KSH, 1997: 44). The city of Budapest, with roughly 2 percent of the total population of east-central Europe, received altogether 30 percent of direct foreign investment arriving in the region, and another 20 percent was directed to the rest of Hungary (Barta, 1994).[13] The composition of foreign capital is rather uneven: 85 percent of it flew to only 5.3 percent of the enterprises in Hungary, the largest ones with funding capital above U.S.$1 million (KSH, 1994b: 67). In 1992, 54 percent of direct foreign investment was located in industrial manufacturing and 20 percent, the second-largest concentration, was in food, beverage, and tobacco manufacturing (KSH, 1994b: 68–69).

Although summary statistics do not indicate a sharp decline in the overall level of manufacturing, they hide severe changes. The transformation of a prime political symbol of state socialism, the Csepel Iron- and Metal Works, is perhaps the most telling. The closing of industrial plants has been a more sensitive social and political issue than any of the new

Table 4.2

Sectoral composition of the labor force in Hungary and Budapest, 1993 (%)

	Hungary	Budapest
Agriculture	8.1	0.8
Manufacturing, mining	30.7	20.2
Construction	4.4	4.7
Trade	8.0	9.2
Hotels and catering	2.0	2.7
Transportation and communications	9.4	10.8
Finance	2.2	3.1
Real estate, rental, business services	3.2	6.5
Public administration and social security	9.5	20.9
Education	10.7	8.3
Health and social services	9.0	8.6
Other community, social, and personal services	2.8	4.2

Source: Calculated from KSH (1994a: 254–55).

governments would have expected, which is a reason there has not been an even sharper decline in the number of industrial employees. The Csepel Iron- and Metal Works was born as Manfred Weiss Works in 1892, when Manfred Weiss, a young and rather successful industrialist, rented some grazing lands in a tiny village on the island of Csepel, south of Budapest. The growth of Weiss Works stands on its own in the history of Hungarian industrialization. It started with a few barracks and 150 workers. By the turn of the century, it employed 900 people, 6,000 in 1913, and 15,000 in 1915, only to redouble by the end of the war (Sz., 1995). The company made shells, ammunition, army canteens, bells, and small coins during World War I, as well as pots and pans, joints, sewing machines, motorcycles, and tractors after the war. During the Depression, 3,200 people lost their jobs, but the world war that followed brought another upswing. In 1948 the factory was nationalized, given the name Csepel Iron- and Metal Works, and changed its profile: according to the preferences of the time, it became the center of steel and machine production. Its old reputation as the locus of active working-class struggle became officially sanctified, and it stood as a symbol of socialist modernization. Following the political and economic changes in 1989, first its bicycle plant was sold to the U.S. company Schwinn. The workers who stayed had higher wages in their new contracts, which also contained a clause renouncing the right to unionization. As of 1995, some of the other factories had been closed down, and others were awaiting privatization. The kindergartens and holiday houses have been sold, and the 142 companies that operate on the territory of the former Csepel Iron- and Metal Works employ 6,000 people altogether. And the number of unemployed is 3,200 again (Sz., 1995).

The wage structures of the country as a whole and of Budapest are both skewed in the direction of dynamic, new services. In 1993, the financial sector and its auxiliary services paid the highest salaries, more than 70 percent higher than the average net wage. The difference increased to 80 percent by 1996 (KSH, 1997: 29). Finance employees earned 46 percent more than the next-highest-paid group, those in the mining sector,[14] and 66 percent more than the also well-paid service employees in real estate and other economic services (KSH, 1994a: 64; 1997: 29). The deconstruction of the finance sector displays even greater similarities. Male white-collar employees made 3.2 times the average gross income in the city, whereas their female counterparts only doubled the average income (KSH, 1997: 29).

Economic life seems to be bustling in Budapest. The city accounts for 44 percent, more than twice its share in terms of population, of all savings in the National Savings Bank (Barta, 1994), and the level of unemployment is by far the lowest in the country. Signs of renewal are not equally spread, even within the city. The symbolic center of the new times is the inner city of Budapest: District V of downtown and pockets of District VII of Elizabethtown and VI of Theresatown. The main theme of the current transformation of the inner city is the functional conversion of a segment of formerly residential space into commercial space and the selective upgrading of commercial buildings.

An accompanying process of urban restructuring in the great cities of the advanced countries is the reevaluation and revalorization of traditional central areas by the communications-intensive branches of the service sector. In Budapest, as in most European cities, there has not been a decline in the economic role of inner cities, so ongoing restructuring merely increases the hunger for centrally located office space. With the liberalization of regulations concerning joint ventures, the influx of foreign capital created a sudden demand for good-quality office space. This led to a sharp increase in rents. In 1990, rents in this category were running higher in Budapest than in downtown Vienna. (It is worth remembering that, in terms of real wages, the differential between these two cities was about five to ten times, to Vienna's advantage.) Around 1993, the increase of commercial rents slowed down and gradually stopped, but the level has not started to decline, in spite of predictions to the contrary (Gerő and Pecze, 1994). Due to the traditionally high building density in the inner city, the very limited availability of building spots, and initial legal difficulties concerning the sale of state-owned office and public buildings, small-scale individual strategies became important in alleviating the pressing demand.

The privatization of formerly state-owned housing, which swept through the better-kept parts of the inner districts (see chapter 3, especially Figures 3.1a, 3.1b, and 3.1c), created an opportunity. The difference between residential dwelling prices and rents on the one hand and commercial prices on the other put pressure on new owners to either sell their new homes or become commercial landlords. Some could not resist the lucrative deal. Many multinational companies started their operations in small apartments in residential buildings. The Hungarian affiliate of the international consulting and accounting firm Price Waterhouse (PW) started its operation in a three-room apartment still furnished with grandma's earthly possessions in District I in Buda. In a year's time, PW moved to a new, air-conditioned office occupying a whole floor in a brand-new, otherwise residential, building in a neighboring street, only to expand to the top floor a year later. Zoning regulations make this kind of functional conversion possible. Only when business use affects the entire building do permits need to be obtained from the city government. Companies would rather avoid the costly and cumbersome process that requires them to build some additional infrastructure. The result is a vivid functional mix in the old and new tenement buildings of the city and increased competition for street parking. (The difference between old turn-of-the-century buildings in the inner city and the ten-story prefab housing estates lies mainly in the scale of the enterprises: the housing estates accommodate mostly shabbier, one-person businesses.)

For this reason, contrary to scholars who see the emergence of a central business district as the most important feature of the changing city (Kovács, 1994), real estate specialists argue that in Budapest the functional dividedness of the central city precludes the formation of a business district (Gerő and Pecze, 1994). The absolute size of office space may be much greater in other inner districts, such as I, XI, or XIII (Figure 4.3), but its concentration comes nowhere near to that in the inner city. The financial center

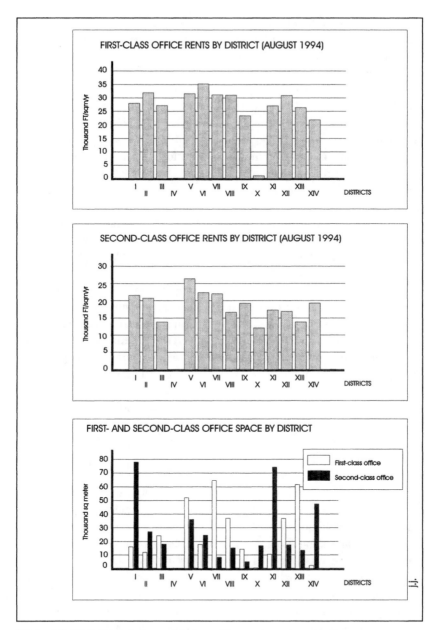

Figure 4.3. First-class and second-class office rents and space. Source: *Ingatlanpiac,* September 8, 1994, 13.

of the capital is undoubtedly located in the very heart of downtown, along only a handful of streets and squares (Figure 4.4). The only outliers are the branches of the National Savings Bank to be found in every district. True, the office building boom, as a result of which sixty-three office buildings were erected between 1990 and 1993, concentrated in two areas: (1) adjacent to District V, between the Small and the Great Rings, and (2) on the outskirts of the inner districts, such as inner Buda and District XIII (Cséfalvay, 1995). In fact, real estate developers see the most profitable investment in building second-class office centers in these less-traditional business areas, because the occupancy rates usually run higher than in the case of more representative, more centrally located, thus more expensive offices, where the turnover of renters happens also to be higher.

Real estate development is a new form of investment among large companies. As the manager of a development and consulting agency for an insurance company recounts, the insurance company invests 15 percent of its savings in real estate, which is 5 percent higher than what is usually permitted by law, and another 15 percent is in enterprises. The company's most profitable form of investment is real estate development, especially office development, but only "if the whole process is in their own hands, from picking the plot to finding the users."[15] (For the same reason, the firm has withdrawn from hotel construction, a very lucrative business a few years earlier; it did not have access to foreign tourist markets.) The company builds with local construction companies that are much cheaper than foreign ones and are the appropriate choice for second-class office buildings. First-class offices accommodate more features of an international style, which require technological solutions and a reputation local constructors may not have. This division of the builders' and designers' market contributes to the differentiation of the inner city.

Charles Jencks (1984) writes that every epoch has its own type of building that indicates the symbolic and financial preferences of the age. The preindustrial epoch found its form of expression in the temple, the church, the palace, the agora, or the city hall; hotels and restaurants are the incarnations of symbolic power today. To expand the list, the characteristic contribution of state socialism came in the form of party headquarters, prefab housing estates, and "houses of culture." Postsocialism's symbolic building, then, could be the office building in the inner city and the multifunctional service center, known as the shopping mall, on the outskirts and in the inner suburbs. The most grandiose examples of the new inner city of Budapest are both located in busy intersections of the Small Ring: the International Trade Center (see Figure 4.5) and the East-West Center.

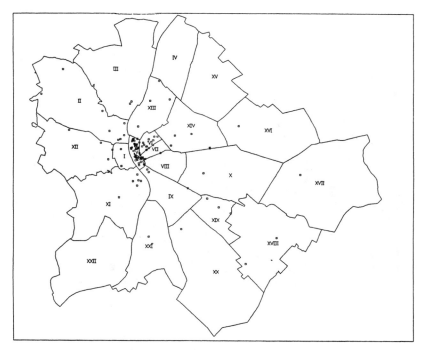

Figure 4.4. Locations of banks, Budapest, 1993.

Both breathe the air of international high-tech postmodern architecture designed by Hungarian architects and built by foreign companies. The buildings rise slightly higher than their surroundings, and the amount of mirror glass, steel, and advanced technology they display weighs heavily on the worn-out, many times adjusted, and much more moderate Budapest inner city. They do not communicate with their environment. The architect of the International Trade Center blames this on the "tasteless" behavior of the international capitalist client, who rejected the original, more outward-looking design, which would have opened the entire street level up toward the street and the neighboring classicist inner yard (György and Durkó, 1993). Nothing challenges the air-conditioned security of the office world in the East-West Center either, but it is at least made public: the representatives of international trade and finance are put into a shop window from which they cannot escape, and they can seem slightly ridiculous in their flying elevators in the eyes of passersby, argues György (in György and Durkó, 1993).[16] In all fairness, it is also possible to find new inner-city shopping centers that display a more respectful attitude toward their environment.

Figure 4.5. The International Trade Center, with the dome of the cathedral in the background. Photograph by author.

Aside from the functional conversion of apartments into offices, there is an increasing differentiation in the inner city determined by more and more homogeneous criteria. The nature of businesses changes. The cobbler, the photographer, the clay-kneading worker, the self-service restaurant, and the small artisans and traders who cannot upgrade their merchandise and spirit of operation to the liking of tourists all take their leave. The new occupants who supplant them are the representatives of very different businesses. What scholars have noted without exception in their treatises of state socialist cities as the "wasteful" use of urban space (e.g., French and Hamilton, 1979; Szelényi, 1993) has vanished into thin air. The self-service restaurant and the Center for East German Culture are upgraded into all-German car showrooms; a travel agency moves into the middle of Women's Fashion only to be replaced by a Honda—in harmonious coexistence with women's clothes. The "golden youth" of the city goes to the Olympic Swimming Pool to play billiards at half past nine, and students and professors can purchase cotton socks in the assembly hall of their university. In the gray orderliness of one of Hungary's longest-standing bureaucratic institutions, the Central Statistical Office, a note advertises cleaned secondhand import clothes. The downtown bookstore closes and is born again as Citibank. The small grocery store, which could never complain about the "stinginess," or the poverty, of its numerous customers, joins the Austrian grocery store chain Julius Meinl, then is shut down amid the protests of local shoppers and to the chagrin of the local government land- lord, who nevertheless has to go with the highest bidder.

Some old businesses stay and glitter even more than before. Gundel, a famous restaurant of the previous fin de siècle located in the generously designed architectural ensemble of City Grove, entered the new era in a somewhat shabby condition. In 1992 it was given a face-lift as a result of a fruitful cooperation between international capital and gastronomical tradi- tions. A famous gourmand and restaurateur carried out the renewal on Ronald Lauder's (from Estée and Lauder) money. As a result, the Gundel re- gained its original glitter.

The Young Artists' Club had been housed in the basement of a once- elegant villa on the spectacular Andrássy Avenue for decades. After 1989, the city sold the building to the managers of the pub that had already been operating there. For a while, the avant-garde interior of the new pub, Made Inn, was still frequented by some of the artists who used to hang out in its predecessor, but they gradually disappeared and gave way to shadier char- acters. A few months later, a hand grenade was thrown into the garden restaurant, the unmistakable signal of organized crime turf wars in Buda- pest. As a final act of breaking with the past, the building is now being turned into a hotel.

Although novelty is appreciated and curiosity prevailed when the first cars appeared in downtown shop windows, local dwellers start finding them more and more "inappropriate." This growing critical mood prompt- ed defensive articles even in a real estate weekly claiming that "Gerbaud [the oldest and most cherished confectionery in the heart of downtown] is staying; it is entirely out of question that it should be replaced for example by a fast-food canteen or a car showroom."[17] Finally, indeed, it was not. It became more expensive than ever and acquired a new, German owner who—the employees hold—is slightly off the profession: he is only a baker, not a confectioner.

Local governments are very receptive to changes that bring in large amounts of capital. Their understanding of the prospects of the aging physi- cal environment and their lack of funds make them so. If they are not threat- ened by immediate displacement, even local habitants see functional con- versions that they may consider "inappropriate" as inevitable necessities in order to save old buildings in their city. The members of the mayor's group in Elizabethtown, even those with preservationist inclinations, placed their faith in foreign companies to buy and revitalize old buildings. "Old buildings will not disappear; if a Westerner comes, he will do complete rehabilitation," the mayor responded confidently to "conservative" concerns. Real estate developers think otherwise. The investment manager of the insurance company mentioned above, after authoritatively stating that "residential construction is not profitable unless it serves the top of wealth," went on to say that "renovating old multistory buildings is even less profitable. Costs are high, it requires skilled labor, and the internal structure of these houses does not allow for efficient economies of space." He was speaking from experience as he sat in a former warehouse, a piece of architectural heritage, that his company renovated. Construction costs ran higher than in the case of new buildings, and the enormous windows, spacious hallways, and high ceilings do not translate into "useful" space, thus into high rents. Only certain prestige investments are exceptions to the rule. Among them, commercial renovations go much deeper and further than residential ones. They are, however, not many and, understandably, only the most well-preserved building stock is chosen for such projects. Only financial institutions, especially large banks, figure prominently in the otherwise short and uneventful history of full rehabilitations in Budapest.

Budapest Bank presents a unique case. It established its stronghold in a former office building in the historical government district, behind the House of Parliament. In a few years it bought out the tenants of the other three buildings on the block, and, by slowly renovating them, created a representative office complex with exclusive facades in all four directions. The Hungarian Foreign Trade Bank did a full refurbishing of the immense nineteenth-century building of the Gentlemen's Casino in the heart of downtown, supplemented by another building on the block. The facade of the building regained its old glamour down to the foundations at enormous cost and effort, including the injection of every other brick with a special insulation material. Interior remodeling also followed the original design but added all the luxury amenities of the time. This, however, is a strict exception.

The built environment has not altered radically with the new times. Some buildings with businesses on the ground floor have been partially "dressed up"; some have been renovated, others got new signs or brass plates. The exteriors of buildings usually acquire a new coating that stops at the first floor of the multistory houses, strictly respecting the lines of ownership (see Figure 4.6). This "ground-floor gentrification" is exhausted in lavish interiors, hardwood portals, refined lights, and new fixtures. Rather typical is the asymmetrical facade of the District I apartment building shown in Figure 4.7. The freshly painted first-floor section accommodated a new

Figure 4.6. Partial gentrification: ground floor exterior refinished. Photograph by author.

Figure 4.7. Partial gentrification: one-half of ground floor exterior refinished. Photograph by author.

gay bar at the time, now a more popular straight yuppie bar rumored to be also connected to organized crime, with extremely well-built private security guards standing around the luxury cars parked ever so casually in the middle of the street during peak business hours. The other wing has housed the local bottle recycling depot for decades.

In the usual streetscape, the glittering of pockets of conspicuous consumption reign semivictorious over the dirty streets and dilapidated buildings. This mixture of wealth and poverty is by no means unique to Budapest or the postsocialist condition. Such coexistence, however, has never been so visible. As mentioned earlier, the typical apartment building prior to the Bauhaus-inspired plans of the interwar period accommodated prestigious and less prestigious social classes by architectural design. The building's ornamented facade would hide the misery of the densely populated, poorly lit inner yard, where tenants of the facade apartments would not need to go in order to access their places. To this carefully circumscribed spatial hierarchy, the partial commercial conversion of apartment buildings and ground-floor gentrification only added a new layer and produced visual examples of the kind seen here in Figures 4.6 and 4.7. Today's fin de millénaire cannot even keep up the facade in the inner city; it would cost too much, require longer-term profitability calculations, and fly against the rampant logic of privatization. Money assimilates only its most immediate environment. This is reflected in the appearance of some truly new social locations in Hungary, concentrated very much in the capital city. Next we take a quick glance at them and how they use the doubly renewed city.

High-Class Spectacle and Middle-Class Fragility in the City

A foreign observer describes the places of representation for new money in Budapest, not very sympathetically, as follows:

> They are everywhere, seated at the expensive cafés along the Danube, making deals in the lobby of the Atrium Hyatt, handing their Mercedes and BMWs to tuxedoed parking attendants. At night they go to places like the Nautilus Nightclub and Restaurant, which is made entirely out of fish tanks, where they have whiskey surrounded by tropical fish that swim under their feet and over their heads, and eat such things as blinis with caviar and octopus Provançale from gold plates. They pay with large-denomination *deutsche marks* and speak English with the waiters, dipping into Hungarian only when it's absolutely necessary, like in the marble toilet where the attendant speaks only the vulgate. (Codrescu, 1994: 290)

Although this depiction should be considered an artistic composite in which certain elements may not come directly from Budapest,[18] this vignette, to the extent that it does reflect the nightlife in Budapest, does provide a sense of the phenomenon that strikes any visitor.[19] The following description will stay on this level; instead of an in-depth analysis of the transformation of social classes, it is intended merely to provide flashes of the social landscape and show the nouveaux riches and the new middle class only insofar as they enter the image of the city.

As happens with every major economic and political change, new fortunes accumulated very swiftly, and a new social and visual component was added to the Budapest cityscape. The entry of the nouveaux riches was most spectacular. This derogatory label is usually reserved for those from among the rapidly enriched who lack cultural capital and make this public. What unites the members of this very diverse group is their conspicuous consumption, which is taking place in a manner not experienced, especially publicly, in the preceding decades. But the public got used to it quickly. In a few years, the novelty of the nouveaux riches faded, and local dwellers and tourists started to notice other, no less visible, groups that gradually grew in their shadow. Aside from the appearance of urban marginality—the beggars and day laborers of Moscow Square and other public spaces—a large segment of the middle class has become impoverished to the extent that their very class identity is threatened. The decline has been the starkest among retired middle-class people.[20] In contrast, urban restructuring has also created its "new middle class." The viability of the new service sector—economic services, nonprofit foundations with the involvement of foreign capital—with its need for qualified professionals (architects, legal consultants, economists, human resource management experts, and so on), has carved out a niche for the new middle class. These people are young, members of a generation that did not have to align themselves with politics under the state socialist regime or overcompensate for this alliance later. They could develop an undisturbed belief in career and professionalism. As one social analyst has observed, they are probably less corrupt than the older generation has been; they prefer unambiguously laid-down rules and "clear" games, whatever the rules are, and they are distanced from politics (Szalai, 1993). They are not necessarily more honest, it is only easiest for them to be so; they are *a*moral. They do not have any nostalgia for the earlier epoch; they feel secure and have no social illusions.

The major source of their self-confidence is the surprise that, so unusually in Hungary, they can live very well on only one job and identify with it. They can afford to be outside the general process of informalization. They can afford to dine out, eat healthy, pick a wine at dinner, keep a Western-made car, join a good fitness club, buy an orchestra ticket at the opera, fly to the United States for a holiday, and start building a condo in Buda. Their appearance in public added a new color to the urban crowd, that of the official look signified by ties, suits, and well-cut overcoats. After the informality of the dress code of the state socialist years, the new middle class brought in a new—at least in scale—and stricter, neoconservative urban look that used to belong to either older or higher-prestige people who were not necessarily seen in public.

Bourdieu (1984) grasps the novelty of the French "new middle class" in its attempt to escape the very act of classification, to defy definite locations, which used to be the privilege of intellectuals. They even occupy newly created positions in the division of labor. Freed in a double sense from class memories that constrain but also form collective defenses against the market, they have a more unmediated relationship with the market: they make perfect consumers. This description is particularly apt for the new Hungarian middle class. Its members are completely unarmed by any kind of collective defense against the market. After the suppressed, petit bourgeois consumerism of late state socialism, which ideologically discouraged consumption but unintentionally and surreptitiously promoted it through the second economy, which could not possibly satisfy the intense demand, postsocialist consumers are left with an unrestrained appetite for earthly goods. This appetite is structured by the market most profitably in the case of the new middle class.

The new middle class is the most important and most unmediated social link to international corporate culture. Its representatives came to be socialized into it as young university or college graduates, but the enthusiasm with which they embraced the shocking novelty of corporate culture has long since subsided. Amid the joy they felt over their new lifestyle, some of the representatives of the new middle class have slowly come to realize that they are not the only masters of their universe. They have realized that, although their suits are made of finer material than their fathers' were and are more fashionably cut, the so-called costume money that replaced "uniform money" is given to them not only with the purpose of avoiding taxation.[21] Time, which used to be in abundance in former state socialist first-economy jobs, has become a scarce commodity. In fact, members of the new middle class hardly have enough time to organize their leisure consumption carefully and manage their lives. Running their households in the old way would be too laborious and timely. But their money and the system of flexible production make mass-produced sophisticated consumption possible for them.

Budapest's new middle class is small and fragile. Its members become vaguely aware of their fragility when they must use mass transportation and mix in with the urban crowd. They cannot afford to build their own castles as the new bourgeoisie does. The vulnerability of the new middle class is here to stay: it is a defining characteristic of the insertion of Budapest into the global economy. In fact, it is increasingly the characteristic of the entire global economy, but risks and the availability of adaptational strategies are still rather stratified. Paradoxically, this may also hold out the possibility of a more integrated urban development by inducing a mediating effect on the extreme polarization and segmentation of the urban public. Their spatial and social fragility forces the members of the new middle class to participate in the city more than they might wish.

The inner city of Budapest has indeed "dressed up"; it has discarded its uniform, which was faded and outgrown but functional.[22] The new outfit has some fashionable accessories, but there is fraying on the new dress that lets the shabby underwear show occasionally.

5

Assembling the Square

Social Transformation in Public Space and the Broken Mirage of the Second Economy

In early December 1994, in the Hungarian weekly *Magyar Narancs,* a new category appeared on the "Page of Records"—a sophisticated guide to the "best" places and services in Budapest: "The Most Unsightly Square in Europe."[1] The award went to Budapest's Moszkva tér (Moscow Square). No other contender for this title has yet been found. On the last pages of his monograph on the current architectural transformation of Budapest, art and media critic Péter György reveals in parentheses how his book was inspired by the sight of this area: "I have been crossing the square every day for ten years, and in the last couple of years I would stop ever more frequently—unable to move on—and fixedly stare at the decay" (György and Durkó, 1993: 184).

Moscow Square has never been a masterpiece of urban design—or even a particularly pleasant place. Yet it had never before assumed this kind of (in)famy in the urban vocabulary either.[2] It is not the mere ugliness of the place that generated its disrepute—by anyone's standards, there are much "uglier" sites in Budapest. Instead, it represents the "disorderly" nature of the new order in a striking way. As such, it is seen as a symptom of the "new" city. Nowhere is the tension more visible and unsettling than between those who traverse the square daily to reach the almost splendid isolation of the Buda suburbs and those who stay, between the citizens who make a short appearance in public and those who depend on the square for their living, whose own reproduction is inseparable from this spot in urban public space.

The uncanny air of the place is not produced by the mere juxtaposition of wealth and poverty. The square, and the meaning of the postsocialist landscape of which it is a central part, needs to be assembled from a multitude of things that obey different orderings. *Longue durée* imprints on the social map of the city, long-practiced instinctive knowledge of it, the architectural heritage of nineteenth-century modernization, the no less distinctive examples of socialist modernization, the ravages of modern wars, the spatial imperatives of transportation technology, the presence of old and new users of the square, memories of full and mandatory employment, and multiple incarnations of the entrepreneurial spirit—all are building blocks in the social meaning of the square. To account for the complexities and to provide some historical background on the elements of what appears today as the chaos of the new public space, I will reconstruct in this chapter, first, a history of the place.

The temporal dimension then changes radically in the next section, where I describe one day in the life of the square. A prominent part of the picture of Moscow Square is commerce in its various manifestations. Small and large, private and state-sponsored, foreign and domestic businesses selling various services and merchandise; lonely vendors, artisans, and undocumented migrants offering their labor power—all bend and twist the physical and social landscape of the square. Some of them may have been around and may have pursued the same activities for a long time. Even they are likely, however, to figure in the picture differently than they did, say, ten years ago. In other words, in both the physical and conceptual landscapes, a considerable shift has occurred. The second, and larger, part of the chapter is devoted to exploring this changing conceptual panorama. Market activities as experienced in the second economy of late state socialism let the market be seen in a uniquely positive light.[3] The mosaic assembled from the forms of commerce seen in the square today shows a very different image of the market and defines the overall meaning of the postsocialist vista.

The notion of *risk* is particularly useful in an examination of these differences in the two landscapes. It appears that the economic sociology of state socialist informality has underemphasized the low-risk nature of its subject. In the last section of this chapter, I place the transformation of Moscow Square within the broader process of the postsocialist change—specifically, the decline of a low-risk economy—and show how the removal of the safety net of guaranteed state socialist first employment has transformed the "market" into a high-risk realm of economic activity. Along with the fiscal crisis of the state, this is a major factor explaining the often noted cruelty of the new urban scene.

A Brief History of Moscow Square

Despite having acquired its name and current layout during state socialism, Moscow Square is one of the few places in Budapest that has not been touched by identity crises, struggles, or renaming campaigns since the collapse of the system. Always a meeting point for different regions of the city, this area developed at the end of the seventeenth century as a clay pit that later became the site of a brick-making factory. At the time the Buda section of the main ring that embraces the inner city was constructed, the "pit" found a civic function. At the end of the nineteenth century, the Buda Athletic Club first opened a skating rink and then later athletic fields and a clubhouse there. The excursion tram lines to the Buda hills ran on the main roads alongside the triangular area. During World War II, the sports fields gave way to tram terminals and bus stops, and the square evolved into one of the busiest traffic centers on the Buda side of the river. Officially anonymous until 1929, the square was first named after Kálmán Széll (a leading financier, and later prime minister, at the turn of the century), then took the name of Stalin briefly following the war.[4] In 1946 it was renamed Moscow Square, the name it has retained ever since. In 1972 Moscow Square found new significance as a traffic center when a major subway station opened there. This addition reinforced its role as the important last inner-city stop for the steadily growing number of suburbanites residing in the Buda hills and valleys. Following the construction of the modernist subway station, a modest effort was made to beautify the square: the traffic pattern was rearranged, tram stops were moved around, and an ornamented well was installed with a couple of benches in the center of the loops made by the tram lines (see Figure 5.1).

Moscow Square serves as a true meeting point. Five areas meet there and contribute their distinctive auras to the "pit": (1) Christinatown (Krisztinaváros), with its traditional population of Catholic bourgeoisie and state officials; (2) the medieval-to-nineteenth-century architectural assemblage and current social mixture of the Castle Hill (Várhegy) area; (3) the petit bourgeois Watertown (Víziváros) of the Danube embankment and the area marked by the Danube, Castle Hill, and Margit Ring—once the quarter of the well-to-do bourgeois and trading strata (Enyedi and Szirmai, 1992: 29); (4) Rose Hill (Rózsadomb), a most prestigious residential neighborhood where the Socialist Party elites lived, partly joining, partly supplanting the wealthy of the 1920s to 1940s; and finally (5) the Buda hills, whose suburbs represent the top of the city geographically and socially. The civic functions of Moscow Square have always lagged behind its importance as a traffic and transit center. Its business potential as the last stop before the hills has never been fully used. The social prestige of the square has never approached that of the neighboring areas: it has always remained a low point on the status map of the Buda side, adding a new dimension to its old

Figure 5.1. Moscow Square before the advent of the underground, around 1950. Photograph courtesy of the Kiscelli Múzeum, Budapest.

name, the pit. The square's lack of prestige has never been as apparent as in the past couple of years, however, when its "unsightliness" has become a source of its celebrity.

The Commercial Spirit and Its Multiple Manifestations: A Day in Moscow Square

The square rises early.[5] Around 5:00 A.M., newspaper booths open, as the first subway trains, trams, and buses begin running, and the main post office on the Buda side on the northwest perimeter of Moscow Square unlocks its doors. The place slowly comes to life as people flow through it on their way to work. Soon a distinct contrast emerges between those who pass through—an enterprise that takes no more than a minute—and those who are apparently there to stay. The stationary gather in the largest contiguous space, the southern corner in front of the metro station. Some perform basic cleaning routines: they look definitely wrinkled, having spent the night at railway stations or in parks. Others just hang around. By 6:30 there are about a hundred men smoking and talking, waiting to be hired for a day or, if lucky, more. Luck comes in pickup trucks, transporting the freshly hired to small jobs at construction and renovation sites, mainly villas for the new elite in the Buda hills. Occasionally, larger companies take casual laborers from the square; a journalist, while on assignment observing the early-morning life of the square, reported being hired to dig ditches for phone lines for the national, then still fully state-owned, phone company, MATÁV. The wage he negotiated upon being hired—about 40 percent below the official rate and naturally without social security or other benefits, turned out to be very loosely binding for his employer and started to drop on the way to the site. At the end of the day, his payment hardly covered his evening meal and beer. Employers mostly offer jobs that do not require skills, but skilled laborers are in demand too.

Most of the "supply" at this brutally simple labor market comes from abroad. M. is a good representative: a citizen of Romania and an ethnic Magyar, he came to Hungary from Transylvania with his neighbor.[6] The two of them define themselves as jacks-of-all-trades. They have built summer pavilions, relaid walls, and painted houses and window frames. When they first came to Hungary for work four years ago, they were hired in Moscow Square for a construction job in the Buda suburbs. They were passed on from one employer to another through the broad interpersonal networks of the family that first employed them. They came in the spring, stayed until cold weather set in, then exchanged the money they had saved for Romanian currency and returned to their village. By the following spring direct correspondence brought results, and they came back to Budapest on the basis of a quasi-contract. Employers like them; they are affordable, reliable, and quick. Their rhetoric, as expressed here by another ethnic Magyar from Transylvania, fits very well with pro-immigration arguments in the United States and elsewhere:

> Hungarians [from Hungary] are mad at us for taking their jobs, but
> we work much better than they do. Try me. I don't visit the local
> pub ten times a day, nor do I eat four times the way Hungarians do.
> I climb up the ladder in the morning, come down only at noon, go
> back in the afternoon and don't come down before evening. (quoted in Fucskó, 1995: 7)

Hungarians in the square call them "smoky-faced,"[7] evoking the imagery of the racial slurs usually reserved for "Gypsy," the only widely used, vigorous ethnic derogation in contemporary Hungarian. This verbal barb merges the meaning of the cultural difference between Magyars living in these two neighboring countries and Transylvania's extreme economic marginalization. The designation of ethnic Magyars as "smoky-faced" shows the persistence of ethnic stereotypes and the elusiveness of historical substance:

anybody can be a "Gypsy." Among the men gathering in search of work in Moscow Square recently there appeared some ethnic Romanians from Romania, as well as Magyars and Roma with varying citizenship, but Transylvanian Magyars still predominate.[8] Common to all of them is that they walk a tightrope when it comes to the law. Hungarian citizens violate tax regulations and rules concerning unemployment compensation. The others are undocumented, mostly seasonal, migrants. Most foreigners have permits to stay for only thirty days. This forces them to leave the country every month to obtain new entry stamps in their passports or to go to the border and acquire the stamps illegally, without stepping out of the country. The legal gaps are filled through bribes to the guards at the going rate of the equivalent of a laborer's two-day wage.

In the later hours of the morning, the gender composition of the square changes. Most of the men have been hired by now or have left to give it another try or to find consolation elsewhere. Only a handful remain. Women step in and the labor market gives way to a merchandise market. A few very frail elderly ladies appear with flower bouquets to sell, to supplement their pensions. They represent the continuity of commercial activities in the square; appearing as they did during the early 1970s, they were the first not-quite-strictly-legal immobile elements against the flow of transit passengers in the square. They have been coming with their bouquets for decades. Sometimes, especially on Sunday afternoons following a day of harvest in the gardens and on the "small plots" on the outskirts of the city, they sell fresh fruits. By now, these women have not only grown older and sadder, they have multiplied and diversified, selling more vegetables, antiques, or anything fashionable at the moment, such as pieces of coral brought from a holiday in Greece. They do not interact with the most vital group of women vendors, who sell fine needlework.

Members of the latter group are much younger, larger, and clearly distinguishable: like most of the men who populated the square two hours earlier, they come from Transylvania (Romania). The women I interviewed are all ethnic Magyars from different villages of one particular county near the town of Cluj (Kolozsvár). They are young and unmarried and complain about the lack of opportunities at home since the land reforms. Transylvanian needlework and folk costumes became very visible at public places in Hungary in the beginning of the 1980s, satisfying the dictates of fashion inspired by the then-emerging movement of urban folklorism. The selling of such handiwork full-time became widespread and regular only after the political changes in central and eastern Europe, which resulted, among many other modifications, in the liberalization of the Romanian passport law. The women of Moscow Square come for a week every month or two. They stay and board with acquaintances, come to Moscow Square or a few other transportation centers or downtown squares after the morning rush hour, and remain until the end of the afternoon rush hour or until they have sold the contents of their identical sturdy plastic bags. Hungarian housewives and tourists buy their embroidered tablecloths, bedspreads, and shirts, which used to be entirely—and are still overwhelmingly—hand-made and usually sell for less than $40 a piece. Transylvanian women— sometimes accompanied by elder men—form a distinct group in the square, recognizable for the uniform folk costumes they wear. They are usually quiet, and chat only among themselves. (The two groups of women vendors can be seen in Figure 5.2.)

On the other side of the subway entrance, another line of women vendors is formed. Their merchandise is different: mostly cheap, low-quality, mass-produced clothes, socks, shoes, and liquor—all of highly dubious origin. One of their most popular and visible items is women's underwear. These peddlers are exclusively Hungarian Roma. They are in a constant struggle with the Transylvanian group for the most precious spots—those closest to the subway entrance. This tension occasionally erupts in outbursts of slurs and violence. Police surveillance is a constant threat for both groups; law and order is enforced once in a while, sometimes not in a strictly legal manner, as evidenced by the women's recounting that police officers may simply pocket the fines.

A few years ago the vendors' row included cigarette vendors, too, selling Third World produced "Western" brand-name cigarettes out of sacks. Vietnamese men used to dominate that business. Now, the Vietnamese appear to have moved into other activities, or, due to the state's stricter enforcement of regulations on cigarettes, relocated to some lower-visibility open-air markets on the Pest side.[9]

The once (in)famous group of cardsharpers—the charmers playing "Now you see it, now you don't" who appeared from one day to the next in the last years of state socialism—also disappeared from the scene because of concentrated police action. So did the stabbings that used to accompany their presence.

Public life has become increasingly active in the square. In the late afternoon, two lines are formed cutting through the middle of the square, seemingly without end. Explanation arrives at 6:00 P.M., when two kettles of soup are carried in, by either the Maltese Charity Service or the uniformed members of the Salvation Army, to serve the needy, some of whom have already spent their day in the square. Others were part of the early morning

Figure 5.2. Two groups of women vendors. Photograph by author.

crowd and have just returned. Marginalized political parties and other organizations often come to canvass support here; it does not require great effort to find an audience of twenty-odd people for anything among the homeless or those standing by. These "inhabitants" of the square provide audiences for the indigenous singers from the Andes who perform the same songs one hears in the streets of west European and North American cities. Young American missionaries have become regular weekend users of the square; they come and turn the volume up high, relying on advanced technology to break the quiet melancholy of Saturday afternoons and the noise of public transport. After one of these occasions an unfinished wooden cross of considerable size—a piece of their paraphernalia—was not removed; for a while it became part of the streetscape.

In the middle of the square stands the worn metal booth of a once-trendy fast-food counter, the first establishment to sell "American-type" food around the clock: hamburgers and hot dogs prepared with a few technical innovations but never admitted to be different from the original.[10] By now, the stand's monopoly has admittedly ceased, and it caters only to those who cannot afford the fare at the Burger King that is only "100 meters away," as the sign on the booth advertises its own competitor (Figure 5.3).

The place with tall arched windows where the Burger King has recently opened used to be the Honey Bear patisserie, until the last years of

Figure 5.3. This fast-food stand advertises its own competitor. Transylvanian laborers stand on the left. Photograph by author.

state socialism, when the windows were painted black and the space found a more profitable market niche as Eden Bar, a middlebrow strip joint and a new locus of prostitution. In 1993, Burger King remodeled the place completely and installed a gigantic neon sign on the roof of the building. Naturally, the renovation efforts stopped at the first level. This made the contrast between Burger King and the rest of the building even more striking. McDonald's could not be left out of the competition for presence in Moscow Square. It remodeled a two-story, turn-of-the-century building a few years after Burger King opened (see Figure 5.4).

For more than thirty years, a small, insignificant gray building has stood at the edge of the square with a sign that reads, "Budapest Transportation Company Dispatching and Technical Management, Buda Subcenter." Today, beside the text whose bite—the word *forbidden*—has been removed by an unknown citizen, leaving only "Wall posters are strictly . . . ," a much bigger billboard shows that in addition to the above services, "Boutique, Washed Imported Clothes, Ice Cream, Pepsi, Fruits, Vegetables and Discount in the Basement" are also offered.

Even the underground station bustles with commercial activities. Because the Budapest Transportation Company was given considerably more autonomy and proportionately less municipal money as a result of political

Figure 5.4. The McDonald's on Moscow Square. Photograph by author.

changes, the spirit of what is called in Hungary "entrepreneurialism" has taken hold in all subway stations as well. In the early stage of commercialization—which was over by 1995—newspaper and book stands mushroomed underground, absorbing the smell of the adjacent popcorn stalls. The not-too-roomy platforms managed to accommodate lonely and not officially sanctioned business initiatives as well: elderly ladies with their "very, very cheap pillows," a gentleman advertising the "Transylvanian writers' paper," and a young Ukrainian musician playing sad tunes on his balalaika accompanied by a tiny dog. An ominous presence for those hurrying to and from work, a newsboy decided to set up a "shop" in the station, advertising his paper: "Here is *The Job Seekers' Paper* with your weekly horoscope." Citing safety regulations, the Transportation Company ousted all underground vendors in February 1995. The old pillow woman, the Transylvanian writers' journal man, and the Ukrainian balalaika virtuoso, however, stayed; officially, they had never been there in the first place. With this move, the Transportation Company changed its "business" strategy: from then on it concentrated on selling the metro station's public space to corporate businesses and advertisers. On street level, inside the metro station, two stalls of a bakery have been squeezed between the escalators and the glass walls of the station on both sides, destroying the carefully designed visual effect of the modernist building and filling the air for passengers emerging from the world's deepest underground with the enticing aroma of freshly baked rolls and pastries. The media also went underground. Hungary's largest-circulation daily (owned by the second-largest German media conglomerate) is available free in limited numbers in the subway cars, along with practically unlimited copies of commercial leaflets. The maps of the city on the inside walls of the subway cars, although serving as the only official information indicating where one can travel underground, emphasize to the passengers the locations of all McDonald's restaurants, along with another five to ten different businesses in the city. Elevator music targets the ears and video screens entrap the eyes of those who cannot escape until the train pulls into the station. But escape is impossible, and the eyes have something to hang upon even in the subway car: commercial video clips are projected on the wall of the tunnel.

The informal economy and the spirit of exchange are manifested in yet another form in the square. Through the images of poverty and through their stories, participants in this economy "give" unofficial absolution, temporary relief of bad conscience. They are everywhere; they ask for charity "'for the love of God' as though each individual had the obligation of filling the holes of the order which God desired but has not fully implemented" (Simmel, 1971c: 152). The beggars of Moscow Square are well inserted into urban space: the less well-to-do and more environmentally conscious citizens of the neighboring prestigious areas traverse the "pit" daily. Aside from the crippled, the pseudocrippled, and the unfortunate with children and dogs, there is also a new kind of beggar who gives the good citizen an opportunity to believe that he or she is not giving charity but merely helping. Some stop passersby, chanting in monotonous voices that they came from Transylvania and lost their purses. They ask for train fare so that they can return, evoking ethnic comradeship while offering complete and immediate withdrawal from the donor's world. This social exchange has the air of efficiency and problem solving and removes the fear of what Simmel (1971c) refers to as moral induction, the duty on the part of the giver and the receiver to continue the first exchange.[11]

Intense, undisguised begging is certainly a new phenomenon in Budapest. Poverty is not new, but the wide-open perception of misery is, and inequalities are more striking than previously. Begging, usually considered an offense by the police, was not possible during the state socialist period: the fiction of full employment and security held so strongly in the days of "high" socialism that the motivators for giving—bad conscience or genuine empathy for displayed poverty—did not exist. While taking note of the striking and colorful crowd of beggars during his visit to Moscow in 1926–27,

Walter Benjamin (1986) observed that "one very seldom sees anyone to give. Begging has lost its strongest foundation, the bad social conscience, which opens purses so much wider than does pity" (106). Bad social conscience is back and it does open purses, but, due to the homogenization of neighborhoods and increasing motorization, not the purses of those whose conscience is supposed to be the worst: the wealthiest hardly ever encounter beggars. (Field evidence suggests that among those who have a choice, this is one reason for choosing to drive instead of using public transport.)

There are also vendors who almost never sell anything. They offer "antiques" ranging from half a bottle of ketchup to old things from their own lives whose only possible value is personal: an old, washed-out piece of embroidered lingerie, a used moustache press, a framed wedding photo of the vendor from thirty years ago, a socialist award, a badge, or a child's torn teddy bear. No one takes them; some do pay nevertheless.

The afternoon rush hour gives commercial life in the square its last boost; by early evening most vendors have gone home or relocated to drinking establishments, with the exception of the most persistent elderly ladies, who, repositioning themselves in the path of warm air flowing from the subway entrance, are still looking for people to buy their fading bouquets. In the young hours of the evening, the square's main function is that of a meeting place, where students wait for their sweethearts and friends. Some of these people can be seen again between 11:00 and 11:30 P.M. running for the last buses, trams, or subway trains. The departure of the last trams, buses, and trains has always been the final act in the life of the square, the moment when its transportation function overrules everything else. Hungarian writer Péter Lengyel (1993) chooses this particular moment to reflect on changes in the relationship between city dwellers and urban institutions that signal a diminishing concern for others:

> Ten years ago, when one wanted to take tram no. 6 in Moscow Square at eleven at night, and a bus was running instead of the tram that night because they were repairing the tracks, a uniformed employee of the Budapest Transportation Company was stationed at the stop. If he saw someone waiting for the tram, he would show the person where the substitute buses departed. This was a civilized and European arrangement. The uniformed man is not there anymore. The other day . . . the tracks were being repaired again. I was standing at the stop waiting for no. 6 together with other people; the tram did not come. I walked to the notice board, which indicated in fading print that buses were running instead of the trams. Passengers who know the custom will figure

this out sooner or later. But two people were chatting near the board in German. I told them to go over to the bus stop. The man thanked me and turned to the woman: "How marvelous these people are." Five minutes later he was still talking about this. He was wrong. Marvelous people would never have allowed one another and their guests to wait there at night. They would have directed us *institutionally.* (186; emphasis added)

Lengyel expresses a very complex sense of nostalgia that goes back to the civic virtues of modernity—a sense of *public* order maintained by functional institutional solutions and a transparent system of accountability—that was already in decline during the state socialist version of modernity and is even more so in the postsocialist period. The end of state socialism coincided with the advent of the new era of late modernity or postmodernity, deeply confusing all involved.

Along with its pivotal transportation function, Moscow Square has always been a small-scale commercial center. Suburbanization spreading from the square toward the hills in the northwest clearly held the possibility of converting the streets that line the square into a well-supplied, upscale shopping and service center catering to the suburban population. That "takeoff," however, has never happened. New times have not brought grand changes in this regard. The small-scale changes that have taken place are, nevertheless, very instructive.

While working on a plan for reviving Moscow Square, an architectural design company recorded all commercial activity in the area in 1990 (MATERV, 1991). This information enables us to account for changes that took place between the time of political change and 1995. The radical disappearance of small businesses and the emergence of new ones has been rare; to paraphrase David Stark (1996: 995), building *with* the ruins of old establishments has been more typical than building *on* those ruins.

One of the few visible changes is certainly linguistic. Signs in Hungarian describing services have frequently been replaced by signs in English. Shop or office names are often international, mostly written according to English spelling rules, sometimes vernacularized *(szuper)*, other times simply misspelled (Mayami for "Miami"). The city is flooded with "pubs," "centers" of "fitness" and of every other kind, "shops," and "supermarkets," which are usually called "Super," "Top," "American," "Crazy," or "Start."[12]

Among the institutions that completely disappeared from the landscape were two kindergartens. One gave way to the office of a foundation, the other to the "Roxy Party Pub." Keeping its longtime basement tenant—

a small tire-repair business—the old one-story building that houses the latter underwent complete renovation, which was financed by the pub's Dutch owner, who now rents the space from the local government. The pub's offerings, as posted on a billboard outside, include "Draught Beer, Food Specialities, Changing Programmes, Disco-Live Music," and its decor encompasses mirrors, some wilting palm trees in pots, and a dance floor. A naive visitor's initial enthusiasm to embrace these diversified services would have been sharply curtailed by the number of pit bulls and their extremely short-haired male owners who frequent the establishment.[13] The nearby laundry of a nationwide cleaning company also closed down only to make room for a more profitable use, the Nevada Gambling House, which has been operating around the clock.

Across the square a showroom ended its career, and a sign informs us that "Trespassing Is Over." The mycologist's office (Figure 5.5)—which served the nearby market and the urban dwellers who gather mushrooms in the Buda hills over the weekend—was taken over by the neighboring pub. FŐFOTÓ, a citywide photo shop chain, merely changed owner and name and became part of the Austrian FOTO PORST. The sweetshop abandoned its generic name and its old owner—a state-owned candy-making and -trading company—and assumed a new name, "Bonbon Hemingway," to boost its new owner, a Los Angeles-based businessman who has made spectacular inroads into the Budapest landscape with his chains of restaurants and shops.[14] (He bought fifty candy shops in Budapest, six of which were later turned into "L.A. Gear" stores; many others added "Dunkin' Donuts" to their product lines.)

Some offices closed simply because their raison d'être ceased, such as the district bureau of the former Hungarian Socialist Workers' Party. Catering to the needs of those spending their days in the square, the local headquarters of the Red Cross rented a large third-floor apartment with stained glass windows in an old building that smells of urine. In this office, the Red Cross collects and distributes charity food and clothes from corporate and private donors. In an out-of-the-way part of the square, a basement club came to be occupied by the Maltese Knights' Charity Service, which opened a heated public room for the needy during the day.[15]

Some businesses retained their old functions but adjusted their profiles slightly to take advantage of new possibilities. The new owner of the tiny former café called Gourmet Presso did not remove the modernist neon sign but simply painted the windows black, emblazoned the new name "Senator Poker Club" on the windows, and added an air conditioner. Another quiet drinking establishment—euphemistically called a café—

Figure 5.5. "Free mycological examination," around 1970. Photograph courtesy of the Kiscelli Múzeum, Budapest.

modernized itself by putting up new signs: "Holsten," "Coca-Cola," "Wrigley's." A small basement store that used to sell goldfish and small birds has now added cat and dog food to its offerings.[16] The neighboring tiny shop that has been buying and selling stamps for decades hung a new sign saying: "We also buy old letters and postcards." The demand for "antique" articles has increased as a result of tourism and economic mobility; in some families whose fortunes have recently been accumulated, antiques may be lacking.

The shoemaker expanded his focus of activity by establishing a real estate and land-surveying company, the second in the square following the new "Start Real Estate Agency." A small ordinary grocery store also rearranged its shelves and name and was born again as a health food store. The old Trumpeter Restaurant became a pub. Its beer garden has been reconstructed and turned into Trumpeter Pizza. An express shoe-repair shop and a small bakery have recently joined these two eating establishments. According to the owner and manager, this complex of four businesses has been the most successful venture in the square.

The owner of the Trumpeter has had a rather typical business career. Twenty years ago, when he set out to establish himself, "one had basically two choices: working at a gas station or going into catering." With a degree from the College of Food Industry, he chose the latter. After working a couple of years in a second-class downtown restaurant, he began to run the Trumpeter. The restaurant's patrons and profit peaked during the last years of state socialism. The Trumpeter specialized in a particular segment of consumers, the guests of so-called *gulyás* parties. A comprehensive form of cultural experience—huge meals, drinks, dancing, and Gypsy music until dawn—*gulyás* parties were very popular among West German and Austrian tourists and usually took place in the more rural settings of Buda. This institution still exists, but in a more subdued form: the isolated charm of communism and the kingly contrast between the prices of the "East" and the "West," which generated most of the attractiveness of the enterprise, have vanished. The manager no longer builds his hopes entirely on the restaurant. He owns a real estate agency next door, has some "dead capital"—a safety deposit of sorts—in a couple of small enterprises in the countryside, takes part in art auctions, and defines his job modestly as "selling and buying information." He walks around with a cellular phone and a dictaphone, and his businesses make use of three fax lines. He has a strong social conscience, blames politicians for their immorality, and claims: "All success stories are illegal in some way. If one does not want to fail, one cannot afford honesty. I am sick of this terrible *vulnerability.*"

The restaurateur is not alone in his sense of vulnerability and uncertainty.[17] These sentiments are defining features of the new times, tied to the decline of a specific type of low-risk economy, the mixed economy of state socialism.

Informality with Expanding Boundaries

Foreign laborers without documentation have certainly made their presence visible in Moscow Square. The construction worker from Transylvania who arrives in the spring and leaves in the fall is the main type. His path crosses Moscow Square—a point of entry for undocumented laborers who have no informal networks to rely on. Regularly commuting migrants usually do not return here: by the end of their first season, they have established sufficient networks (Hárs, 1995). Moscow Square acquired this special function for good reasons. The state has practically withdrawn from mass housing construction: construction of big housing estates stopped at the beginning of the 1980s. What has been built since then are family houses and small condominium buildings, primarily in the suburban areas of Buda and the outskirts of Pest. Because Moscow Square is the last patch of urban scene before the Buda suburbs, it is perfectly located to become the venue for procuring temporary labor for the most prestigious construction sites in the city.

In 1993, 16 percent of all Budapest housing construction took place in District II, which houses a mere 5 percent of the city's population but includes 30 percent of the new dwellings with at least four rooms (KSH, 1994a: 143–45).[18] This area has clearly been the site of a luxury construction boom. The creation of well-protected mansions with saunas and swimming pools is an enterprise undertaken by newly enriched businessmen to shape the most valuable spots of the city to their liking. The extent of this new construction would have been smaller and more exclusive without the undocumented, and therefore cheap, laborers who could be found in Moscow Square.

Reliance on informal labor was already widespread prior to the collapse of socialism. The proportion of the national income accounted for by the unregulated economy is conservatively estimated to have reached at least 15 percent by the mid-1980s (Sik, 1995: 15).[19] From 1977 to 1989, the most fundamental changes in countrywide housing construction were the steady decline of the role of the state as builder and the skyrocketing growth—doubling—of "self-help," which included domestic work, reciprocal labor exchange, and "black"—unreported wage—labor (Sik, 1995: 15). Income-earning strategies outside the regulated sphere were not limited to the poor or to small-scale farmers in the countryside. The proportion of unregistered income and expenditures compared with total income and expenditures of families is by far the highest in Budapest, and unregistered activities are quite common among families at all income levels, if not more so in higher-income groups.[20]

Yet the stereotypical figures of informal or illegal (a substitution that is easily made in these cases in Hungarian public parlance) wrongdoing are "Gypsies," the unemployed, and immigrants, among them the "Arabs" who exchange currency and the "Ukrainians" who supposedly run prostitution and get into trouble with organized crime. Very typical is the attitude of one small grocery store manager. He severely condemns people in the square who sell produce without permits, but he is vehemently opposed to the new regulation that requires him to give receipts to customers. His desire to maintain his previous "right" of not doing so, and thus avoiding taxation for part of his income, is so strong that it makes him practice double cash registering—registering purchases "on the side," in a second machine—even in front of his customers. In fact, it is hard to escape the conclusion that the continuity of informality is one of the defining characteristics of the post–state socialist transformation, and is bound to produce paradoxes of this kind. Even the most vehement advocates of market rationality, matter-of-fact business attitude, and contracts make allowances for themselves to "arrange things" through informal networks (see, among others, Böröcz, 1992, 1993; Sik, 1994). Although some illegality often invites an understanding and reinforcing wink, its marginalized practitioners are not treated so considerately. In a 1990 survey, 60 percent of the respondents thought that the problematic presence of "dubious elements" in Moscow Square should be "solved" through institutional deterrence: banning them from public spaces through violent police action, sending them to work camps, or administering physical abuse.[21]

Employing migrant labor is not a novelty internationally: it is new only in the east-central European context of previously relatively closed societies. More precisely, the scale and visibility of the phenomenon are new.[22] But the nature of manual labor migration to Hungary fits the global pattern. Laborers bring their assets to a particular niche in the labor market: skills, flexible adjustment to employers' needs, willingness to work harder and for less pay than locals would (e.g., Portes, 1978). Those who perform undocumented work mostly belong in this group. They tend to replace undocumented local labor or to take temporary jobs that local workers would not; by filling a special niche in the labor market, they do not literally take jobs away from Hungarian citizens (Hárs, 1995: 100). However, the initial warm acceptance seen in the 1980s, especially of ethnic Magyars from Romania (Portes and Böröcz, 1989), did not survive the test of increased refugee and temporary labor inflows, and, more important, that of increasing unemploy-

ment in Hungary. A curious type of xenophobia has emerged vis-à-vis ethnic Magyars from Romania: cultural and ethnic similarity has come to be
overshadowed by an exclusive "we-feeling" based on citizenship (Csepeli
and Sik, 1995). Compared with 1989, twice as many people in 1993 believed
that these immigrant laborers were "stealing" their jobs, and many fewer
thought that they deserved help (Csepeli and Sik, 1995). Clearly, the recep-
tion of immigrants has changed.

The composition of immigrant groups has changed too. Ethnic Hungarians arriving in the late 1980s were mostly professionals. They received
advantageous treatment and were prone to upward mobility and quick ab-
sorption. By contrast, the 1990s witnessed mostly a flow of manual laborers,
who started with a handicap in their new context and followed a less favorable path of secondary market incorporation. It is these immigrants, manual laborers outside of ethnic enclaves—unlike the Chinese, for example—
who are most visibly inserted in public space and who form the human
market of Moscow Square.

Great Expectations: Experiencing the Market through the Second Economy

It is not only immigrant laborers whose fate has become less favorable: the
market itself and the role it has played in people's livelihoods have changed.
The meaning of "market experience" was formed on the basis of the second
economy during eroding state socialism. Looking at contemporary social
changes, one increasingly comes to see the exceptionality of the state socialist market experience and to understand the unrealizably great expectations it had induced.

In Chapter 2, I discussed Polanyi's typology of forms of economic integration that inspired comparative strategies to describe state socialism.
As mentioned, following Polanyi, Szelényi defined state socialism as a social formation in which elements of redistribution and market exchange
were integrated under the overwhelming logic of state redistribution. In the
case of capitalism, market exchange is the dominant integrating force, and
redistribution plays a subordinate role. Chapter 3 examined how the two
systems thus defined made "mirrored comparison" possible. Although the
scheme is based precisely on the fundamental assumption that market elements function differently depending on whether they are dominant or
subordinate parts of the system, its implications have never been fully considered. A subordinate market can give us rather misleading impressions
regarding the nature of a market economy.[23]

Polanyi (1977) discusses the role of the market in the redistributive

economy of the polis.[24] The commercial section of the agora—the cooked
and raw food market—grew out of the city's responsibility for the livelihood
of its citizens, and it "played a key role in provisioning the populace" (166).
The agora operated under many restrictions: "rigid boundaries, specifica-
tions on who may and who may not trade, and with whom; official market
inspectors as well as municipal spies; commodities . . . sold directly by the
peasant either for money or in barter, such were the features of the ancient
agora" (187). Prices did not fluctuate greatly, although city administrators
tried to tie them to external prices (at the port of trade, or emporium), but
only as long as the latter remained "reasonable." Whenever the emporium
price rose sharply, the agora price did not follow. In spite of all these regulations, the agora was "crucial to the political constitution of polis democracy" (167) because it eliminated the bureaucracy from state distribution.

State socialism pictured in a Polanyian manner—as a redistributive
system that allowed the existence of market elements in the form of the
second economy—worked in a strikingly similar way. The second economy was crucial to fulfilling what the Communist Party called the government's "provisioning responsibility." It helped to satisfy the need for a
greater variety of consumer products and services—in the beginning mostly foodstuffs—which could not have been met by the more rigid system of
state redistribution.[25] Thus, in late state socialism, the second economy was
instrumental in maintaining the social and political peace, which explains
the often cordial relations that the redistributive socialist state was careful
enough to maintain with it (Portes and Böröcz, 1989). Ultimately, the second economy severed its symbiosis with the authoritarian, although car-
ing, redistributive economy. However, amid these rapid and fundamental
changes people were left with the impression of a subordinate market. The
idea that "market-based" economic relations might exert an entirely different effect on social relations without the constraining conditions of the
overarching socialist state was lost on both a large part of the populace and
reform-oriented economists and policy makers. The meaning of the "market" under the redistributive auspices of the socialist state differed from
the expanding and diversifying market(s) that followed, and this certainly
led to disenchantment among many. Insistence on the difference between
the two may explain occasionally uncritical market rhetoric on the part of
economic actors whose interests do not seem to justify it. This kind of
thinking is not necessarily the result of a fallacy that sees causality in the
coexistence of "market," "democracy," and "wealth" in the "West," nor is it a
product of some global ideology of market liberalism. Its *couleur locale* is

the history of state socialism and the understanding of the market that history had shaped.

Under state socialism, the dominant institutions were those of the first economy. These institutions regulated the space available to the market but also sheltered it. Although self-employment was accepted—even if it was ideologically discouraged—the proportion of those participating full-time in the private sector was only 3.8 percent of the Hungarian labor force in 1981; after the economic reform of 1982 expanded the private sector, the figure was only slightly higher—4.3 percent in 1986. Those who *combined* engagement in both sectors constituted one-third of the total labor force, however (Róna-Tas, 1997). Nearly everyone was employed at state institutions or enterprises, and many performed either the same or unrelated additional activities—farming small plots around the house was a popular choice—for extra income after hours. The boundaries between state and private, or first and second economy, were blurred even more with the establishment of Company Work Partnerships (VGMKs), which eliminated the spatial separation between "first" and "second" economies by allowing workers to perform the same jobs at the same places with the same tools as they did in their first jobs but to receive different wages as VGMK members on special projects.[26]

This change definitely played a part in transforming the meaning of the "second economy." As Ákos Róna-Tas (1997) describes it, the second economy was the "economy of the weak" during the 1970s; following the 1982 reforms, it became the "economy of the strong." Initially, when the major activity consisted of household farming, the second economy primarily offered the marginalized an opportunity to increase their meager income: due to its small scale and labor-intensive nature, it was equally accessible to all those willing to participate. In the 1980s it provided lucrative opportunities for those already more fortunate, those who were better educated and better paid in their socialist jobs. A study by József Böröcz and Caleb Southworth (1998) on income-earning strategies clearly shows that during the last years of state socialism the most rewarding strategy was not to exit from the state sector and engage only in private business but to work in both the state and the private sectors. The admission fees increased—involvement became more capital-intensive—and gradual differentiation took place in the second economy, but entry was still widely available.

As a result, involvement in the second economy was a low-risk strategy of economic autonomization. Participation in the first economy guaranteed low but regular income along with social security. A job of which one could be deprived only with difficulty and that did not require a lot in return allowed for flexible working arrangements and permitted the use of resources in one's private, alternative, or second economic life. In most cases this private economic life was very limited. It had no prospect of growth, and its returns could not be converted without restrictions into capital begetting further gain. However, a crucial, often-forgotten flip side of the phenomenon is that risk taking and the possible loss involved were even more limited. Demand for consumer products and services was practically guaranteed in a shortage economy. A widely documented characteristic of the second economy, vibrant informal networking,[27] provided, among other functions, a very efficient risk-reducing effect.

The experience of informal economic arrangements clearly showed that market activity could be beneficial for the laborer, but perhaps nowhere was this as true as in east-central Europe. Those who were part of the alternative economic space experienced expanding income-earning possibilities and a rising standard of living limited only by their capacity and willingness to work. In the political economy of late state socialism, the laborer was, as it were, forced to sell his or her labor power to the state in exchange for a quasi-lifetime membership of social security, but he or she was free to sell additional labor time. Doing so was so popular, and demand for participation was so high, that the minister of finance felt the need to point out in the unions' widely read national daily newspaper that "the right to labor [which was guaranteed by the constitution of the socialist state] does not mean the right to participation in Company Work Partnerships (VGMKs) or the right to overtime work" (Diósdi, 1983: 5).

The institution of the second economy, which provided an increased variety of products and services, benefited consumers as well. The institution of prices in state socialism turned out to play a trick on socialist consumers of second-economy products, however. Whenever there are prices and money used in the exchange, it is assumed that there is some sort of value equivalence. Except for education and health care, which were declared free, commodities and services had price tags attached. Many of these prices were—depending on the analyst's preferred terminology— "distorted," "subsidized," or simply "fixed." Whatever the nature of these prices, people were economically bound by them and made decisions based on them. The great trick of consumerism began with the gradual expansion of the second economy and the parallel existence of "free" services and privately priced ones. The gradual commercialization of services, especially of certain medical fields, such as dentistry and gynecology, gave consumers a certain false self-consciousness. They acted as if they had fully paid for the services, conveniently forgetting about the hidden subsidies factored into these relatively affordable prices. The quality of services thus obtained was usually somewhat better than what could have been provided in the free-of-charge, state-provided sphere.

As both laborers and consumers, people—mostly but not exclusively in the better-off segments of society—saw great potential in the expansion of the market. The sheltering institutions of the system either were taken for granted or their removal from the state-provider to the market appeared a viable and affordable solution. Through the simulated market prices embedded in state socialist redistribution, services looked accessible to a large part of the population, and the strengthening of their market character was to increase the efficiency, and even the fairness, of distribution.

The history of the second economy should be perceived as the best success story of marketization ever. Consumers—especially those with expanding income-earning opportunities—saw rising prices as part of a reasonable exchange for a greater variety and better quality of services. To its participants, the second economy embedded in socialist redistribution gave the impression that, on a small scale, human potential was realizable. Market activity was not curtailed by the fear of great loss; one could gain but could not lose everything. The lukewarm context of this low-risk economy, a moderate entrepreneurialism saturated by the petit bourgeois spirit of security so characteristic of the Kádár era, seemed to hold out a unique opportunity.[28] The bon mot "Second [income] is not secondary" (Kolosi, 1980: 5) certainly captured an element of collective sentiment behind the process of individual enrichment and the relative well-being of the Hungarian regime. The second may not have been secondary, but it could not become primary either, at least not without alterations in its meaning.[29]

Changing Scales: The New Face of the Market and the End of a Low-Risk Economy

The large-scale marketization that followed the collapse of state socialism has created a different situation. A new aspect of informality has emerged. The satisfaction individuals felt over unreported income and beating "the system"—a well-conditioned feeling from the time of the second economy—is diminished by the experience of being outside labor regulations concerning, among other things, work time and safety, and outside social security and collective rights. Economic activity has become riskier in its formal aspect as well. Formal employment cannot be taken for granted anymore. The level of nationwide unemployment was about 13 percent in 1993, but it varied greatly: in Budapest it was only 6 percent, but it reached 20 percent in more depressed parts of the country (KSH, 1994b: 260). Being fired is not

an unusual experience anymore, nor is the prospect of long-term temporary employment without social security. Former part-time engagement in
the second economy has become full-time informality for some, and it is
likely to result in increased inequalities (Sik, 1994). Some are forced to perform subsistence activities full-time in worse conditions; others may have
to deal with bigger profits but higher transaction costs, because entrepreneurial and especially informal or illegal business has become riskier.

The grim economic prospects encourage informal solutions. The current bifurcation between the informal and the formal segments of the
economy is an experience sharply different from the double income-earning
activity of state socialism. Even entrepreneurs who have matured and gradually taken off from their foundations in the state sector during the transition,
such as the restaurateur in Moscow Square, lament their increasing vulnerability and their riskier lives—riskier in the sense of the emergence of market
risks: demand for consumer goods, which had seemed bottomless, has become more diversified and more moderate, and competition is fierce between domestic and foreign products.

Uncertainty also prevails due to the lack of a social safety net. Not
only are there no more low-paid but guaranteed jobs to fall back on when
one's fortunes are reversed, but in a more commercialized web of existence,
the loss of regular income is a greater blow than before. The formerly relatively generous level of collective consumption, in which participation was
tied to nominal fees and "free riding" was a common practice, is in decline,
and its means are being privatized. Thus membership cannot be taken for
granted anymore. Although some basic services are still free of charge, auxiliary health and educational costs have risen enormously and their logic is
altered constantly, enhancing the vulnerability of those who have to or
want to rely on public services. The availability of public housing with low
rents has shrunk dramatically due to a series of housing privatization dri-
ves. Market rents and mortgages have gone up significantly, and the possibility of eviction, and homelessness, is not inconceivable anymore.

In general, uncertainty prevails largely due to the self-withdrawal of
the state. The east European "runaway state," as Ákos Szilágyi (1997) refers
to it, is escaping its former duties: it is dropping its external and internal redistributive burdens, driven by a severe fiscal crisis and political rhetoric.[30]
The state is escaping society and its consequent social obligations. It is a
commonplace that under state socialism society had been "statized." The
degree to which the state had also been permeated by society is much less
remembered today. The consequences of the state's speedily escaping the
confines of society and taking itself off the market were very difficult to

imagine, and the initial surprise at the fierceness of this act of disappearance is still felt in the societies of central and eastern Europe.

The transition from a low-risk to a high-risk economic and social existence as experienced by citizens of postsocialist Europe cannot be treated as independent from the widely noted transformation of the "West": the shift from Fordism to flexible accumulation, from industrial to postindustrial society, from organized to disorganized capitalism—in general, from the transformations assumed under the heading of late capitalism. The disintegration of "work society"—as standardized full employment is replaced by a "flexible" employment structure that systematically integrates mass unemployment into "pluralized underemployment with all the associated hazards and opportunities" (Beck, 1992: 143)—captures changes strikingly similar to those I have described.[31] What makes a difference is the history of the *embedded market* of state socialism and the more painful than expected process of its disembedding.

Hanging out too long in Moscow Square was politically somewhat risky during state socialism: one could be apprehended for vagrancy, which was considered an affront to the state that was to guarantee universal employment and thus constituted a "public threat," a police matter. In that particular logic, order meant, first of all, employment. Since then, the category of "vagrant" has gradually sunk into the broad concept of the "unemployed" or the "homeless." Being without a job does not entail political risks anymore, economic marginalization is a perfectly well tolerated accompaniment of a riskier economic existence and the polarization of market positions.[32] People who fill the men's market and the all-encompassing goods market in Moscow Square constitute one pole. Those who traverse the square on their way to the Buda hills come close to the other end.[33] The worlds of those who pass through and those who eke out a living by hanging out there hardly ever overlap. They encounter each other only in Moscow Square. Those hurrying downtown or to the suburbs would rather avoid this encounter; the people who live off the square do their best to ensure that it occurs.

This tension gives a bustling, seedy, and conflict-ridden quality to commercial and social life in Moscow Square. The brutally omnipresent forms of advertising, the sadly petty forms of commercial activity, and the mutually exploitative relations among "citizens" and "foreigners" of all kinds make the square "unsightly." New social problems—homelessness as well as under- and unemployment—are thrown out into public space and end up on top of old ones. The durability of the social fabric and of civic dignity is thus tested in the urban location of the square: the "first," "second," and "third worlds" of contemporary Hungary rub against one another in a new social synchretism, without any sense of collective responsibility.

The invigoration of a commercial spirit and the mushrooming of vendors in the square are not necessarily signs of expanding opportunities. Nor are they the expression of "man's propensity to truck, barter and exchange." Viewed from the experience of state socialism, the selling of labor power, lingerie, popcorn, vegetables, tunes on the balalaika, absolution from bad social conscience, or memorabilia of one's past is not an expression of the breakdown of regulations or of chaotic conditions. Such activities are not passing signs of a "transition" or the painful but necessary costs of adjustment. Rather, these phenomena are signals of a new order whose nakedly commercial premises are sanctioned by the runaway state. The new order is less orderly, and openly acknowledged uncertainty has become a normal condition of everyday existence.

Moscow Square has offered its own solution. Soon after the regime change, a small van appeared in the middle of a traffic island—in defiance of traffic safety regulations—with a billboard on top advertising security devices and displaying a sample door made of good-quality iron bars. Individualized solutions for individual misfortunes. The displayed door disappeared some time ago. In the beginning of 1998, a new phenomenon appeared at one of the intersections that border the square: when the traffic signal was red, beggars would approach the cars, forcing the drivers to face the social inequalities and asking them, in a chanting tone, to settle the imbalance immediately. In March 1998, one of the beggars was shot to death.[34]

6

Globalizing Art and Consumption

Art Movies and Shopping Malls

In November 1996, two items of cultural news stirred public opinion among Budapest's educated circles. An announcement of plans for the restructuring of Budapest's extremely successful and well-liked art movie theater network, in operation for six years at that time, came after several months of bitterness and resentment—a process seen by many as the beginning of the precipitous decline of the institution of art film distribution in Budapest. All this curiously coincided with the news that Budapest's first big shopping and entertainment center, the million-dollar, paradoxically named Pole Center opened on the outskirts of the city (see Figures 6.1 and 6.2). The first mall made a forceful debut, not just on the itineraries of the city's Christmas shoppers but also on the cultural scene. Even the traditional New Year's Eve cabaret of Kossuth Rádió, Hungary's public service national radio station–a show listened to by a very large audience throughout the country— was broadcast from the new mall. Featuring an American-style multiplex movie theater and several other spots of culture broadly conceived, it was bound to make a clear mark on the map of cultural consumption practices in Budapest.

Art movie theaters and malls are two genres of public space in Budapest that are new, institutionally. Shopping and cinemagoing had of course existed before, but not in these forms. They are similar in both being public spaces in which the copresence of urban strangers takes place under the auspices of attention focused on a shared object, rather than on one another. They are public spaces whose publics are primarily audiences. The difference is in the object of the gaze; in art movie theaters it is art, whereas in the shopping mall it is mostly a commercial object. This separation has a few twists, however. Art cinemas feature the "lowest" of high-art forms, the

Figure 6.1. Pólus Center. Photograph by author.

most popular high art. And cinema as such has, historically, shared a place with shopping in representing consumption and mass culture vis-à-vis art and refinement. From the early days of cinema, shopping and moviegoing have been closely associated. Rosalind Williams (1982) cites Louis Haugmard, who in his 1913 *Aesthetics of Cinema* links early moviegoing with shopping: "The passive solitude of the moviegoer resembles the behaviour of the department store shoppers who also submit to the reign of imagery with a strange combination of intellectual and physical passivity and emotional hyperactivity" (80). These passive but hyperactive pursuits of pleasure carried the danger of the loss of self-control and were quite unsettling for bourgeois self-restraint, a mode of life conduct still highly valued in the early twentieth century—all the more so because the majority of the audience in both cases were women. In their critique, bourgeois defenders of propriety and mass-culture-loathing intellectuals joined forces. Sharp analysts and critics of mass culture, thinkers of the Frankfurt school presented a feminized image of popular cultural forms that included moviegoing and commodification, even if not shopping directly (Huyssen, 1986; Nava, 1997). The status of cinema has risen selectively since the 1920s; although movies have never lost their mass appeal, filmmaking has made it into the arts. Art movies have come to be distinguished increasingly from commercial cinema. The new institution of the latter has taken the form of the multi-

Figure 6.2. Western City: thematic section of Pole Center mall. Photograph by author.

plex cinema that dispenses its product in the intimacy of the new temples of shopping, the mall.

This chapter examines art movie theaters and shopping malls as new institutions in Budapest. It is of course true that both emerged with the collapse of state socialism, but stating that fact in itself hardly does justice to the complexity of these institutions. More exciting is that their emergence is intimately linked to the process of globalization, but in very different ways. Their institutional histories tell us about the force of globalization and the possibility and limitation of creative strategies of its localization in the cultural and economic context of postsocialism.

In Defense of Diversity: The Art Movie Network

The network of art movie theaters emerged in 1989 following a series of organizational changes that started with the dissolution of the state-owned film company's monopoly on distribution in 1987. A company named Budapest Film was established to run all cinemas in Budapest. With the political changes in 1989, it became the property of the municipal government. Budapest Film became the legal successor of FŐMO, the capital city's state socialist monopoly film distribution and management company.[1] The idea of creating a separate art movie sphere was conceived as wide-scale marketization and privatization pervaded all areas of the economy, including the

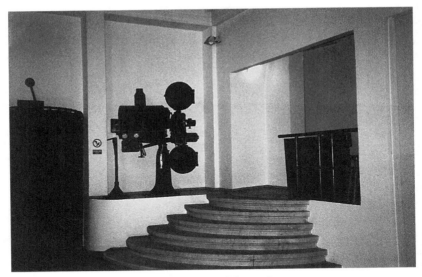

Figure 6.3. Toldi Studio Cinema. Photograph by author.

entertainment industry. The initiative came from people who, having worked at the state-owned film company—a state socialist monopoly—now moved to the reconfigured Budapest Film. As cultural bureaucrats and managers, they matured during the last mellow and gradually liberalizing years of state socialism. Some, including the general manager of the new company, also had brief experience with international distributors, having been involved in the creation of a joint-stock company by United International Pictures (UIP), the first foreign distributor to enter the Hungarian market—a company that was transformed into a fully foreign-owned subsidiary in 1992.

According to the recollections of Budapest Film's CEO, it was some managers' "professional conviction that a network of art movie theaters had to be created to provide the citizens of Budapest with an alternative cultural supply of quality art that should belong to the city in the same way as theaters or libraries do."[2] Relying on the financial and political support of the municipal government and the still-existing Film Authority at the Ministry of Culture, they started the gradual process of converting some of the city's small movie theaters into redesigned, technologically updated art cinemas. One of the progenitors of the Art Movie Network has explained: "We chose a few theaters from among those that only used to be referred to as the 'small and dirty' ones, those that could not have remained movies in a market competition and would have been converted into car showrooms or stores. We wanted to preserve them as cinemas, so we had to find a new function for them."[3]

The establishment of Budapest Film and its Art Movie Network in 1989 was possible because of two main factors: (1) the opening up of the movie market, which showed the sheer force of global competition, and (2) the personal informal network ties of the key actors of this institutional invention to all authorities involved—an asset they had accumulated, largely inadvertently, during their tenure as cultural managers and midlevel cultural bureaucrats during the last phase of state socialism. In this regard, Budapest Film is a clear example of one prominent type of institutional transformation isolated in the economic sociology of postsocialism, the form that relies on informal managerial asset structures.[4] This process is sometimes lamented, especially in the popular press, as a way in which structures of an uncanny past survive; the irony of the case of Budapest Film is that it also reveals a supreme sense of institutional creativity, resulting in a company whose activities are very much in line with the tastes and preferences of a large segment of the citizens of Budapest.

By 1990, the spectacular success of the art movie theaters became apparent. Not only did the number of visitors fail to drop because of the presence of for-profit commercial competition fortified by international capital, but attendance registered actual increases. With an audience that celebrated the enterprise as a form of lifestyle resistance to the increasing dominance of Hollywood movies consumed with popcorn, Budapest Film was also able to make some profit and took special pride in its art movie project.

The success of the Art Movie Network is especially remarkable in the context of the fading significance of moviegoing on the cultural landscape. Attendance at motion picture shows had been gradually declining in Hungary since the 1950s. It reached a moderate local maximum in 1985, only to drop quite sharply afterward (Figure 6.4). During the Stalinist period of the 1950s, films—products of what Lenin called in the early twenties "the most important art"—were screened in more than three hundred movie theaters in the city of fewer than two million. The cultural policy of high state socialism that aimed at complete provision in the city started to subside well before the collapse of the regime. During the 1960s, the state-run national television program took over many mass-entertainment functions previously provided by movie theaters. As cultural subsidies from the state became scarcer during the early eighties, many theaters with low attendance, especially those on the outskirts of the city, were shut down. It is not surprising, then, that following the radical expansion of the realm of the market in cul-

Visitors (thousands)

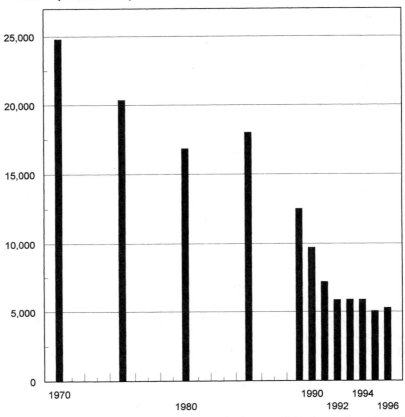

Figure 6.4. Annual number of visitors at movie theaters in Budapest for selected years, 1970–96. Sources: KSH (1980, 1997); *Népszabadság,* September 15, 1995.

tural goods in 1989, the number of Budapest's movie theaters shrank even more: whereas in 1989 fifty-eight theaters still operated, there were only thirty-five in 1996. The geographic distribution of this change shows further concentration in the inner-city areas (Figure 6.5). Considering these numbers, the very presence of twelve art movie theaters (more than one-third of the total) signals the curious strength of the Art Movie Network. This impressive position of art movies on the movie scene is unique, even for western and west-central Europe. (For instance, unified Berlin—a city more than twice the size of Budapest—does not have more functioning art cinemas, and those that do exist are typically in the dilapidated, low-prestige, low-rent parts of town.) Moviegoers in Budapest have a choice of more than

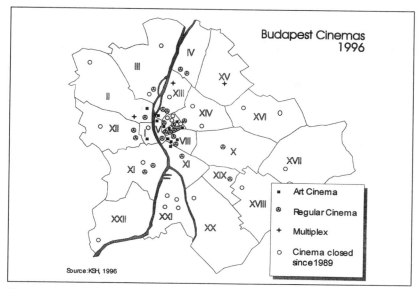

Figure 6.5. Budapest cinemas, 1996. Source: KSH (1997).

a hundred different films screened each week, the overwhelming majority of which are shown in the twelve cinemas of the Art Movie Network. (In Paris, with a population of more than nine million, the number of choices is approximately three hundred.)

The creation and operation of the Art Movie Network was a creative response to what had been conceived as the irresistible globalization and homogenization of the film market under the aegis of Hollywood. As the data in Table 6.1 suggest, the cultural diversity of new releases, which had been gradually declining for some time, shrank radically around 1989. This created a short period when the artistic poverty of the cinema scene and the power of the global market became concerns even for those who had never been outspoken advocates of the arts. The Art Movie Network has not stopped the overall shrinking of the diversity of new releases in Budapest (see Table 6.1 and Figure 6.6), but it is striking that the diversity that does exist is due almost entirely to the network. Art cinemas present a very broad selection of films. They do not show only locally produced films or only entirely "artsy" ones. They feature an emphatically multinational selection of "quality films," including U.S.-made ones. These art movie theaters represent resistance to cultural globalization without resorting to a nationalist countercode.

Table 6.1

New films released in Hungary by major countries of origin (annual %)

	1982	1985	1989	1992	1995
Hungary	16	16	14	13	6
United States	13	13	36	50	69
United Kingdom	1	3	5	5	4
France	5	6	9	12	8
Poland	4	3	3	0	1
(West) Germany	6	4	3	2	0
Italy	8	6	6	5	4
Romania	5	2	1	1	0
USSR (Russia)	17	16	4	2	1
Other	25	31	19	10	7
Total	192	201	236	190	143

Source: Népszabadság, July 5, 1996, 15.

To the contrast of local versus global—the apparent master distinction of the globalization universe—these small and midsize "art cinemas" of Budapest oppose a different contrast, rooted deeply in a practical reading of the Frankfurt school's aesthetic analysis. This distinction has been strongly present since at least the early 1960s due to the theory work of Georg Lukács and his disciples (known as the Budapest school of philosophy), the political code of socialist cultural policies, and the practical efforts of state socialist Hungary's vast network of cultural institutions (preserved in the minds, orientations, and professional habitus of their personnel): the distinction between kitsch and high art. The practical reading of this opposition, however, is not a crusader's mercilessness toward commercial entertainment; rather, it is a conviction that market volume is not the only valid measure of value, that there exists such a thing as artistic value, something that is conceptually independent from the value placed on an object by the exchange process. In this logic, high art also has a legitimate claim to be shown. The creation of the Art Movie Network signals an insistence on "quality" entertainment and high art in the name of diversity. The operation is explained not only by memories of critical theory, but by recollections of courses in marketing and a solid respect for the market.

With more than three hundred thousand people, or approximately 23 percent, of the city's population (KSH, 1997: 356), over twenty-five years of

number of films

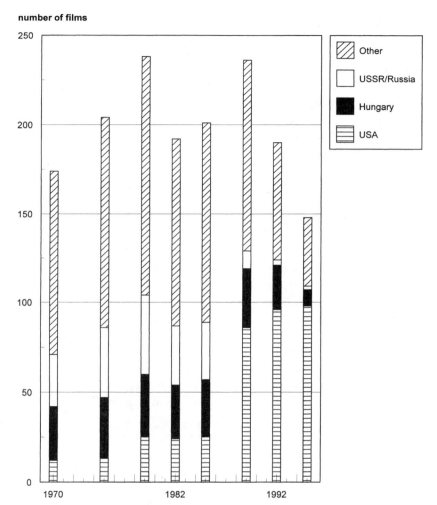

Figure 6.6. New films released in Hungary, by country of origin, for selected years, 1970–95. Sources: *Népszabadság,* July 5, 1996, 15; KSH (1980: Table 18).

age having graduated from institutions of tertiary education, the distinction between high and mass cultures is clearly well established in Budapest's social circles, quite beyond the narrow confines of cultural elites. With national and local television programming going ever more clearly for the Hollywood segment, and with the increasing takeover of the commercial cinema scene by Hollywood distributors and their staple, the Art Movie Network is understood to be an institutional niche where "quality" is preserved and provided to those interested. With ticket prices 30 to 50 percent *below* those of commercial movie theaters, the Art Movie Network is available to the most ardent and demanding section of the movie audience in Hungary: students in secondary schools and higher education. (Because of relaxed admissions policies, efforts to control unemployment, and certain demographic factors, the number of full-time students in tertiary education has increased by two-thirds in Budapest; the respective figures for secondary schools increased by more than 20 percent between 1990 and 1996; KSH, 1997: 204.) The image and marketing of art movie theaters follow a comprehensive understanding of cultural distinctions and their relationship to consumption. Art movie theaters constitute a genre that accommodates a certain idea of public space and its audience with the consumption of appropriate movies, internal designs, cafés, bookstores, reading rooms, even alternative designer clothing, all located in the cinema. The consumption element, however, is kept very low-key.

As an institution of resistance, the Art Movie Network would have been impossible without globalization: neither its current opportunity structure nor the pressure to use it would exist. Meanwhile, it has carved out its own space and identity by resisting "Hollywoodization." The Art Movie Network is an institutional development that insists on the diversity of the cultural process, creating a multidimensional representation of globalization. The institutional setup is a key to its success.

The Art Movie Network's theaters belong to Budapest Film. First it was a company of the municipality, managing theaters owned by the municipality, then it became a joint-stock company in 1993 to which the ownership of the theaters was added later. Budapest Film does not run all the theaters: it subcontracts most of them to entrepreneurs in contact with the company. The company has kept three of the twelve art movie theaters and has given almost complete independence to the managers of the individual theaters. Budapest Film looks for devoted people and institutions with professional interests in shaping theaters in their own image and interpretation of film culture. The pool of such partners includes film studios, workshops, the Hungarian Motion Picture Foundation, the National Film Archives, and even some previous theater managers. Each art movie theater has its own specialty area, series of films, interior design, and aura (see Figure 6.7).

The network's economic survival is ensured by a delicate financial scheme. Management of theaters that can be supported by ticket sales and auxiliary activities is only part of the story. Low rents are just as important: set around 10–20 percent of market rents, this form of subsidy has been kept so by cooperation between the municipal government and Budapest Film.

Figure 6.7. Art Cinema Szindbád (formerly Tanács [Council]). Photograph by author.

Further support comes from the company's distribution business. Most of the movies shown by the network are bought and distributed by Budapest Film. Although distributors are entitled to commissions of up to 43 percent of ticket revenues, art movie distribution is not a profitable business. Budapest Film distributes thirty to thirty-five art films and only a few commercial movies each year. This orientation translates into an annual loss of $250,000 to $300,000. The company that makes a big profit on running a few commercial theaters and leasing others to entrepreneurs sinks a considerable part of its profit into its art movie mission. The municipal government that had owned the buildings until recently "did not expect the company to realize huge profits, only to manage their assets and provide the citizens of Budapest with a cultural service without requesting further support from them," sums up the general manager of Budapest Film. The company as a whole is profitable, in spite of its system of cross-financing, whereby the losses from the art movie operation are offset by the profits from commercial sales.

The public service function and the economic rationality of the company produce a remarkably easy cohabitation that can be quite surprising to an outside observer. In interviews, the managers radiate a conviction that art and commercial theaters cater to two different segments of the market. The managers are not interested in taking sides in a debate on "art" as opposed to "commerce"; rather, they are concerned with the diversity that can be guaranteed only by this "self-subsidizing" scheme. Their managerial professional identity centers on "quality" films, foreign and Hungarian alike. They love movies of any kind that show signs of talent, but they are also businessmen who have a keen understanding of the market, to the extent that they try to think ahead. They are gifted survivors who have found a proper institutional form to capitalize on formerly public assets by bringing former state property into a company that was bound to be privatized eventually. They combine business and pleasure—a mix that leaves some personal element, quite unusual for a business of this size, in their operation. Budapest Film's CEO regularly sits around in the café of the network's new movie theater and watches the audiences while sipping his coffee.

The managers of Budapest Film are not worried about competition from newly emerging complex entertainment facilities—the malls that accommodate multiplex cinemas—because of their applied, almost Bourdieuian "sociology-of-culture" conviction regarding the split nature of the movie market: art movie friends do not go to shopping malls. Nevertheless, it was Budapest Film that opened the first multiplex cinema in Budapest—one that is not quite a multiplex, however. In 1995, the company sold some of its properties that could not have been run profitably to raise funds for the new enterprise. The $3 million project renovated and redesigned an old cinema on the margin of Budapest's movie strip, in a busy public transport hub with a subway station. The new theater, Corvin (Figure 6.8), has impressive high-tech features: the best available sound system in town and the best screens in all the six auditoriums.[5] Advertising for the theater builds on this image: great picture, hi-fi sound, and all-round comfort. There is more legroom in Corvin than in any other multiplex in Budapest—more even than in some I have measured in New Jersey. Its grand opening took place in 1996, and it was predicted at that time to repay investment in two to five years. "Corvin is not really a multiplex, it is only a multiplex type of a cinema," claim the owners. They have made this point also by naming it Corvin Budapest Film Palace. It exhibits many features of a multiplex; it has several auditoriums, high-tech projection facilities, popcorn and soda in three different sizes sold in the lobby, and first-run Hollywood movies and the paraphernalia that come with their effective marketing, such as papier-mâché Disney characters, in abundance. But this is encased in distinctly urban architecture and an interior space designed by a chic name designer that accommodates a small Rick's Café Americain and an art video rental place—another one of Budapest Film's ventures—and has an overall theme that speaks about the global history of cinema. Usually, one of the six movies

Figure 6.8. The tattered national flag, part of the 1956 memorial next to the entrance of the Corvin theater. Photograph by author.

playing at any given time is an art movie, and the "palace" also serves as home for current Hungarian cinematography. Corvin is a hybrid, as is the company that created it. "We wanted to transfer some of our art movie experience and create a sort of intimacy. Not to relegate it to some feeding-entertaining complex, but to elevate it to some communal space. It may be an illusion," explains the general manager of the company. But the elevated palace of a commercial cinema is doing fine.

The creativity of Budapest Film's response to the twin challenges of globalization and privatization is revealed in the recombinant institutional form (see Böröcz, 1993; Stark, 1996) it represents; it is neither completely private nor entirely public property, and it is an economically rationalizing actor with a cultural mission. Its internal system of cross-financing is something that annoys international auditing and accounting companies: it is uncommon and difficult to classify, in their logic. As such, it may turn out to be a disadvantage also when Budapest Film needs to apply for loans.

It is this constellation that seemed to end in 1996, generating intense media attention around Budapest Film and the Art Movie Network. In connection with its holding-type privatization, Budapest Film proposed to abolish its practice of cross-financing and make the Art Movie Network what it called "independent." The idea was to put aside a sum to establish an endowment whose annual interest earnings would be handed out to support art movie theaters in proportion to their art movie content. A board would determine what constitutes an art film. Budapest Film emphasized the financial independence and security it would give the network, which, thus, would not depend on the generosity and fortunes of the company. In exchange, Budapest Film would abolish rent subsidies and the theaters would pay much higher market rents. The company claimed that this would only be fair, because the new system would make the cinemas do better professional work and end abuses in the use of space, such as subletting parts of the theater to businesses whose profiles do not fit that of the cinema and charging them quasi-market rents. (Whereas it has been a general practice to accommodate auxiliary activities in the building, those activities should be in line with the main genre: small cafés, noncommercial book stores, video rentals, and so on; see Figure 6.9. Two art movie theaters that were located somewhat marginally violated this expectation by subletting space to a sports store, a travel agency, and even a currency exchange booth—an unfortunate practice that partly legitimated the "reorganization" rhetoric of the company.)

Disagreement came mostly from the partner institutions running the art theaters. Some movie managers are just as good economists as the managers of Budapest Film, although from a younger generation (thus having acquired practically their entire managerial experience after state socialism). Although the company was able to present convincing figures to those who worried about the endowment not covering increased market rents, the art movie managers pointed out just as convincingly that inflation—between 15 and 25 percent during the first nine years after the collapse of state socialism in Hungary—may diminish the promised financial security of the network. They saw the economic rationality of making rents compatible with the market, but argued bitterly that cultural production and consumption have a logic that is distinct from that of the generic notion of the market. The hybrid institutional form that worked for the company may not be applied to individual theaters.

One theater manager who most vehemently protested the proposal said: "You can't create your own image that takes a long time and run blockbusters and sublet space to a grocery store on the side. Those are incompatible." The theater managers pictured a stronger art movie market in Budapest with fewer cinemas, which would definitely include the three theaters run directly by Budapest Film that attract almost half the audience of the network (Szőnyei, 1996). The cultural consequence of this would be a shrinking of the diversity that makes the network so interesting now. "This will

Figure 6.9. Café of Art Cinema Müvész. Photograph by author.

mean the narrowing of culture, a closing of our playground," predict the young managers of the theater that is most committed to independent cinema and to hosting alternative film festivals.

In spite of the controversy this "reorganization for independence" proposal generated, it was unanimously accepted by the Art Movie Section of the National Cinema Association. There seemed to be a consensus on the overall necessity and direction of changes: "The network had to become more compatible with the logic of the market." And no one could come up with an alternative proposal better than that made by Budapest Film that was similarly "European-quality, market-conform, and sector-neutral." This rhetoric accords well with that of the general reorganization of the economy radiating from the political sphere. The fact that there are two art movie theaters that, being located on private property, are not protected from market-level rents and can still survive is fully used in the argument. It should be noted, however, that one of them is run by a promoter of the new institutional arrangement, also an employee of Budapest Film, who is therefore convinced that his theater is at a disadvantage now, and the other is a small dilapidated cinema that looks very marginal indeed—it is situated in a poorly ventilated basement. The story of these two small theaters can be used both for and against the rhetoric of restructuring; they can survive market rents, but very marginally. "We cannot provide a safety net for the network, especially not forever," argue the managers of Budapest Film.

But that is exactly what they have done so far, and with great success at that. The essence of the reorganization project is indeed creating a more market-compatible institutional form that will make the company a stronger economic actor. A new joint-stock company of Budapest Film would specialize in distribution, and another would handle all real estate of Budapest Film and charge art movie theaters higher rents; the theater managers could in turn apply for support from the Budapest Movie Endowment.[6]

This story is not only about a particular company. Until this proposal for restructuring, the economic and cultural policy of Budapest Film simulated the subsidy provisions of the redistributive state on a smaller, more transparent, scale. Now it also mimics the state—this time the east European runaway state (Szilágyi, 1997)—that is, escaping its former redistributive "duties," abandoning those activities that can be construed in a narrow-minded market logic as undue generosity. Times have changed. The municipal government is shifting from managerialism to entrepreneurialism (Harvey, 1989b) and Budapest Film is facing increased competition in the commercial market. The distributors' market has been sliced among fewer but stronger participants. In 1995, more than half of Hungary's film distribution revenues went to InterCom, a company directly linked to Hollywood studios. It buys Hollywood products exclusively. Another third belonged to UIP, and the rest came from three small distributors, including Budapest Film.

At the end of 1996, two multiplex cinemas opened in malls—$3 million projects financed largely by international capital.[7] Five or six further multiplexes are planned now, and Budapest Film intends to have a share in them. The company still cares about art movies and wants to preserve the network. It still supports diversity, but a kind that is more carefully and more narrowly circumscribed, more controlled and marketable, and one that costs Budapest Film less money. Although a doomsday scenario for the Art Movie Network would be but another typical cry of cultural pessimism, the new constellation will rearrange the moviescape. Some locations of the present cultural diversity may disappear or become effectively marginalized. Some art movie theaters may indeed turn into, or remain, "small and dirty" cinemas. This would be an outcome quite similar to those of the "alternative" art scenes in western Europe and North America, in spite of their different histories. The story of the network, however, is not over yet, and its existence remains important no matter what happens later. Those instrumental in conceiving and elaborating the scheme often give credit to themselves by claiming that "in Hungary, where things typically don't work, we managed to *preserve* something that is working." They may well deserve some credit, but they definitely misdefine what happened. The story of the network is not a story of preservation. Rather, it is about a creative reconfiguration of strategies of globalization and localization.

In Defense of Shopping: Secluding Public Space in the Mall

In terms of their aesthetics as well as their relationship to globalization, shopping malls are a counterpoint to art movie theaters. Instead of using commercial revenues to subsidize art (as Budapest Film has done), malls incorporate all manifestations of art into the overarching logic of commerce. Their spectacular spread is linked to global finance and culture quite directly, as the process is represented in public speech.

What is called in the Hungarian press a "European-quality shopping mall" was constructed in Budapest right next to a socialist-modernist "shopping center" in the middle of a large housing estate with outlets of the supermarket chain Kaiser's, the construction materials chain Bauwellt, and McDonald's. An "American-type" service center, for some reason called Europark Kispest—financed mostly by Austrian capital—has emerged on the outskirts of Pest at a major subway and train station whose aesthetic was already strikingly reminiscent of similar establishments on the working-class margins of Vienna. In 1995, a most grandiose and symbolically important project was conceived and begun, a combined "administrative-shopping-entertainment center for the family," the Pole Center. The $100 million establishment is housed in a redesigned former Soviet Army garrison in District XV. The progenitors and financiers of the enterprise are North American businessmen and Hungarian émigrés Peter Munk, Béla W. Fejér, Andrew Sarlos, and Otto Blau—the developer of the World Financial Center in New York—along with revered Hungarian entrepreneur Sándor Demján, who gained recognition and millions by establishing the East Bloc's first, cooperatively owned, supermarket in a busy traffic center of Budapest in the early 1980s.[8] The Pole Center was designed as the prototype for an additional twenty-five multifunctional centers to be erected all over eastern Europe. Following the success of Pole Center, the Pole Holding Company announced the opening of additional malls in twelve to fifteen Hungarian towns, "creating 700 new jobs" at each.[9]

The Pole Center is touted as a place that is all-around "American." The public has even been told that the separation of ownership and management "followed the American practice." The only "Hungarian feature" of the establishment is that it accommodates a traditional farmers' market.[10] Apart from its grand opening, Pole center has made it to the national news only once, precisely for its "American" character. The announcement that the center would be open on May Day—a national holiday—evoked strong sentiments from the public: the protests of unions and other interest groups were joined by criticism from the Ministry of Labor, which declared that working on a holiday is unlawful and that it would fine any stores that opened.[11]

The second major mall, Danube Plaza (Figure 6.10), is in a traditional industrial district of the city—a location chosen mostly because of the convenient availability of a major subway line and as a major contribution to the ongoing effort to "upgrade" that neighborhood into a minor commercial center. Another recently opened shopping mall, built by the same Israeli developers as Danube Plaza, has been named Csepel Plaza, after the district and island of Budapest where it is located; its name is synonymous with that of Csepel Iron- and Metal Works, the symbol of socialist industrialization (see chapter 4 for discussion of the transformations the plant has gone through). Apart from stores, Csepel Plaza includes a multiplex cinema and a video arcade.

Records are to be superseded, by definition. Hardly had the Pole Center opened as the number one site in Budapest before multinational and local capital and expertise realigned to promote the "construction of the century," the West End City Center, the scale of which is indeed unmatched since the fin de siècle. The U.S.$200 million project was launched by the cooperation of the same Sándor Demján and Peter Munk who had pooled resources for the Pole. The area, as suggested by the name, acquired its present layout with the construction of the wrought-iron structure of the Western Station—very much in line with the style of the Eiffel Tower, in fact, designed and erected by the company of Jean Eiffel in 1877. The station is an important switch point on the Pest side of the main ring whose transportation function was later supplemented and reinforced by a new subway line. The small square facing the iron-and-glass hall of the station gave place to a new department store in the 1980s that changed the character of the neighboring shopping streets. At that time the square was called Marx Square, and allegedly one entry in the competition to name the supermarket suggested "Karl Marx World Department Store." The store opened, but under a different name: Skála Metró. Its fame quickly declined with the status of the area, which in 1992 became revernacularized quite appropriately as Western Square. The new West End City Center, which involves the reconstruction of an area of 110,000 square meters, will not be simply another "town center"; the developers' ambition is to make it Budapest's new downtown (Szalai, 1998). The wide-open space that drives

Figure 6.10. Danube Plaza. Photograph by author.

constructions of this size to the outskirts of cities is created in this particular inner-city environment by covering the train tracks. Planned to debut at the turn of the millennium, the urban spectacle—"splendid as Piccadilly Circus but more exciting"—will offer a mixture of old and new themes: a main concourse wider than the Champs Elysées, wax figures in the manner of Madame Tussaud's, a scale replica of Niagara Falls, and a "world cinema" projecting life-size images from six cities of the world (Szalai, 1998). One of the developers—the largest in North America—who is building the new city claims, "Budapest is the most exciting investment site in Europe" (quoted in Szalai, 1998).

The new city is built in the form of shopping malls. Malls are a novelty in the local culture of shopping. They radiate a clearly Western, thus "more advanced," lifestyle and a general sense of abundance to consumers whose appetites had been whet for quite a long time by a socialist shortage economy. This partly explains the lack of popular resistance to malls, something that could lead through social and political conflicts to the emergence of more creative forms of shopping culture. Ironically, it is not the Hungarian press but the Western media that note the poverty of localization strategies. With respect to shopping malls and megastores in Budapest, even the *Financial Times,* overall hardly a bastion of resistance to the power of capital, observes:

> Budapest does not learn from western examples. . . . There are a lot
> of developers in the Hungarian capital today that could not work
> at home for reasons of environmental and urban planning consid-
> erations. Local municipalities short of resources are eager to sell
> off their real estate, thinking ahead for a mere 3 months, which
> could cost them a lot later.[12]

One of the few instances of registered resistance came from traditional market vendors, who occasionally protested the removal of their old market-
places: competition and higher stall fees tend to make their operation infeasible. Another genre of resistance has also been reported; an ecological
group went to court claiming that the increased traffic due to the construction of the new megastore of a French chain would reduce the quality of life
for two hundred thousand residents and pollute the environment. The lack
of support for the protest on the part of the local government took the steam
out of the initiative. The attitude of the local government was influenced by
the $5 million it received for the land sale; in an unconscious response to
pollution and health concerns, the government planned to invest it in a
new health center.[13] In February 1998, Budapest held its first conference on
shopping malls. Experts in attendance saw malls as an unambiguous result
of "the spread of global and multinational trends," noted the poverty of mall
architecture ("The outer look is not very sophisticated . . . and the interior
design is only slightly better"), and warned about the explosive contrast of
enormous consumption and poverty.[14]

For five years, the list of investments of more than $10 million in Bu-
dapest has included almost exclusively shopping, trade, or business centers
and, occasionally, housing parks. In other words, multifunctional service
centers (malls) fill the space for communal development projects. Such ambitions are captured in the straightforward language of the media, which
refer to them as "new town centers."[15] Malls are interesting not so much as
new shopping places, but as a new genre of public space that has made
a forceful appearance in Hungary. As such, they are becoming part of public culture. They figured very prominently in the narrative of a horrible
crime story for the first time as public places (where one goes for the sake of
company).

In late fall 1997, the Hungarian public was shaken by the brutal murder of a cab driver. What led to an uproar was not the murder itself but the
fact that it was committed by two fourteen-year-old schoolgirls who were
caught almost immediately and who told the shocked police that they did
it in order to get the driver's car (although they were hesitant whether the

new car, a Ford, was as good as the old one, a Mercedes, that he—the two girls' friend for a few weeks by then—replaced on the day of the murder) and show it off to their friends at Danube Plaza, where they hang out. In fact, they were caught while driving to Danube Plaza, in a routine traffic check. The only firsthand information released about the two perpetrators to the Hungarian public was an investigative reporter's interview with the two girls' friends, whom she found in front of the multiplex cinema at Danube Plaza. This narrative indicates how quickly the shopping mall as public space has been vernacularized by youth culture in a bundle of images intimately linked to cars. Although Danube Plaza is on a major subway line, it is mostly frequented by people who feel safe leaving their fancy cars in the mall's garage instead of on the streets, let alone taking the subway. This ghastly story also plays into the symbols used by conservative politicians who refer to the new, foreign-owned shopping malls as present-day equivalents of the Soviet tanks of 1956, stationed at the edge of Budapest.

The spread of malls in places like postsocialist Budapest is but another addition to a global cityscape. It is closely related to the well-documented decline of old city centers, the waning of hegemonic downtown shopping (Zukin, 1995), and the theming of cities (Gottdiener, 1997)—a vision of urbanity that has been on the defensive everywhere. Much has been said about the decline of public space (see, inter alia, Sorkin, 1992), its privatization and semiprivatization (Davis, 1992a), and more will be said in the next chapter. Here I explore this theme only in connection to malls. Instead of focusing on the decline of public space, optimists in the debate hold that old public spaces merely become empty and are reborn elsewhere. Witold Rybczynski (1995) writes in a chapter titled "The New Downtown" that, for the American citizen who flees the chaos and the challenges of downtown streets, the shopping mall takes over the function of the street:

> I think that what attracts people to malls is that they are perceived as public spaces where rules of personal conduct are enforced. In other words, they are more like public streets used to be before police indifference and overzealous protectors of individual rights effectively ensured that *any* behavior, no matter how antisocial, is tolerated. This is what malls offer: a reasonable (in most eyes) level of public order; the right not to be subjected to outlandish conduct, not to be assaulted and intimidated by boorish adolescents, noisy drunks, and aggressive panhandlers. It does not seem much to ask. (210)

Rybczynski's point is well-taken. Malls have certainly diversified, and now most of them provide many kinds of services. There is a high school counseling center in the West Edmonton Mall in Canada, as well as a synagogue, and the mall in Columbia, Maryland, has a designated booth for community services. The West Edmonton Mall even has a tiny homeless population of its own (Rybczynski, 1995: 210). There are some three hundred mall-themed weddings performed annually in the Mall of America. *Mall walking* has become a term in gerontology. A group of Baltimore Girl Scouts, after serious deliberation upon the nature of "traditional" public space around them, possibly motivated by the same fears as Rybczynski, decided to organize their annual outing in the Hunt Valley Mall.

Given that it is used as a public space, is the mall really the new downtown, *the* new public space? The dilemma took a legal turn early on: Should the principle of free expression apply to malls? In spite of the insistence of the American Civil Liberties Union that it should, Rybczynski recounts, the U.S. Court ruled in 1976 that the right to free speech is not relevant to shopping malls; they are privately owned spaces after all. Some state supreme courts, however, have ruled that malls must allow certain activities, such as the distribution of political leaflets.

Even if we think that—for lack of a better alternative—malls may eventually figure as public spaces, currently they are semipublic at best. There is more to this than merely their private ownership. In spite of their immense diversification and their tolerance for some traditional political activities, such as canvassing, malls constitute public spaces that are very different from the street. Of course, the public nature of city streets should not be idealized either; the pavement in front of the world's most elegant hotel–quietly but firmly controlled by liveried doormen and bouncers—is a very restricted public space indeed. That, however, is an exception rather than the rule, whereas in the case of shopping malls the logic is the reverse.

Streets are publicly owned, and although much of their excitement and potential for sociability come from the commercial spaces they accommodate, their main function is not commercial. Streets exist to provide, first of all, free movement, be that target oriented or just wandering. True, even the archetypical public space, the Greek agora, had a commercial section— a food market—but that was not what defined its nature. Shopping malls, in contrast, merely tolerate noncommercial activities—wandering and "hanging out"—motivated ultimately by commercial interests. A supporting character—a mall security guard—in a New Jersey independent film titled *Mall Rats* (directed by Kevin Smith, 1996) captures the spirit of the mall as a place when he states "I have no respect for people who don't do no shopping here . . . who just hang out." The commercial profile and the location effectively filter the public of malls. Rybczynski's argument about old downtowns and shopping malls mirrors the line of thinking that legitimates excessive suburbanization. Shopping malls can provide all the features Rybczynski lists—such as public order, cleanliness, proper maintenance—because the problems of "traditional" public space are removed from the consumers' horizon, they are left behind by the creation of a new frontier. Malls are inspired by the idea of radical ruptures, both with the past and with the environment.

By its size alone, the mall is not a simple insertion into the old fabric of the city; it always aspires to be a new "town center." Being surrounded by no-place parking lots and driveways, its edges imitate those of a town and its totality commands attention qualitatively different from that demanded by a department store. Hence the poverty of mall architecture: the exterior does not have to adjust to its environment. The immediacy and strict separation of inside and outside, characteristic of street shops, is modified already in the design of the department store, but the imitation of street exterior becomes complete in the interior of the mall. One does not just step into a shopping mall; consequently, one cannot easily escape its universe. There may be interior architectural variation, especially with thematic architecture representing various periods and styles, but the mall is ultimately unified architecturally, socially as well as aesthetically. This makes the mall unpleasant and even repulsive for some who see it as the largest immovable piece of middle-class taste. Unity on this scale can be oppressive, and escape is difficult for anyone who does not like it. Malls may be public spaces, but they also resemble, in some respects, total institutions.

Malls embody a new philosophy of public space: they are thoroughly regulated, protected, and confined commercial spaces for the "middle classes." Because there are neither resources nor political desires to design and maintain public spaces that can accommodate an increasingly diverse public, small and controlled islands of consumption *simulate* some functions of urban public space for those social groups that wish, and can afford, to transcend the fear and "inorderliness" that pervade other aspects of urban life.

The celebration of full-service malls as new public spaces signals a new twist on the fundamental question of public space that I discuss in the next chapter. The tension between the growing diversity of citizens, which today includes ever-wider social inequalities, and finding a common denominator for togetherness has been eroding public space everywhere. There may be several reactions to it; the creation of shopping malls as alternative public spaces is one such response. It is a defensive response. The defensible architecture and protected public spaces of the shopping mall grant shoppers and nonshoppers increased security to stroll around in a confined space with carefully prescribed aims that happen to be even more nakedly commercial than previously. The audience is filtered very crudely; those who live off public space informally—including beggars and the homeless—are excluded, and those without cars and those lacking appropriate financial means are discouraged from entering. The rest enjoy increased protection in a more narrowly circumscribed space than that of a shopping street. The gaps in the public are filled with the common pursuit of consumption.

This is not a novelty in the history of public space. The significance of the commercial element is often downplayed or dismissed as inauthentic. First, with increasing commercialization, the aestheticization of everyday life, and the popularization of high art, consumption is ever more difficult to separate from education or culturation (see, among others, Featherstone, 1991). Second, historically the advent and expansion of consumer culture had liberating effects: it bestowed a greater weight on women and marginal groups as consumers. The public appearance of respectable middle-class women was intimately tied to their identity as shoppers in the protected space of the nineteenth-century department store, where they could stroll unaccompanied, observe, be playful, and shop. As a side effect, feminist scholars emphasize, the commercial freedom of the department store also created other zones—restaurants, rest rooms, reading rooms—where women could go free of men's company (Wilson, 1992). The ambiguous role of consumerism and its relationship to citizenship figures prominently in debates on the democratization of the public sphere. "Minoritized subjects had few strategies open to them, but one was to carry their unrecuperated positivity into consumption," writes Michael Warner (1993: 241) in his critique of the bourgeois public sphere based on utopian self-abstraction that privileges unmarked identities. Consumer citizenship captures the virtuous aspect of the equalizing and differentiating tendencies of money and capital as their expansion liberates marginal groups—that is, treats them equally as consumers—but assigns them to different market niches determined by their consuming capacities.

Can we extend the same argument to the recent expansion of consumer culture in making shopping malls the new site of urbanity? Do malls provide small niches of freedom for any social group in particular? As consumers, women have been fully integrated into the system of consumption since the emergence of the first department stores. It would be equally difficult to argue for the liberating effect of the new shopping culture for ethnic minorities. However, the market still moves on. It seems to have extended its civilizing and liberating mission to the only members of society who still live under authority preventing them from becoming full-fledged consuming citizens: the young. They are torn between earlier physical and later emotional and financial maturation, and the protected space of the mall becomes the place where they hang out in between. They are transported there and back, and left to stroll around unaccompanied by adults and enjoy their limited commercial freedom (to be paid by their parents).

As I have noted, shopping malls are theoretically important, for they represent a characteristic global response to the tensions of urban restructuring. That response nevertheless can gain additional meanings place by place. In cities such as Budapest, the spread of malls is certainly a phenomenon with high global financial and cultural content. And referring to malls as the "new downtowns" resonates differently: in Budapest the urban spectacle is still very much alive within the city, unlike in some American cities or suburbs, where it either is lost already or has never existed. In Budapest, there are still alternatives at this stage; a few shopping malls may only add to the diversity of shopping culture—after all, malls can offer an effective and pleasant way of shopping. But there is much to be lost if the scale changes, if malls start figuring as new downtowns that contribute effectively to the elimination of alternatives. Their meaning changes precisely with the symbolic shift from "shopping center" to "new downtown"; it is then that, as total institutions, they become claustrophobic and suffocating. And, after all, town planning is too important a thing to be left only to international developers.

In this chapter, I have analyzed two genres of public space in Budapest that emerged in the postsocialist period. The shopping mall is different both conceptually and as a strategy of localization from the art movie theater, even though both are new and both are tied closely to the late-capitalist global nature of the transformation of Hungarian society. Cinemas that used to play art films were single-function public spaces through which audiences would pass quickly. Today's art movie theaters are open even when there are no shows; they are places where one can sit around, passing time instead of passing through. In this respect, they are more akin to early-twentieth-century cafés than to Hollywood-style cinemas. Their coherence is still created by the showing of films, and preferably good ones, but they are more comprehensive as public spaces, wishing to project and represent a lifestyle, a cultural identity. They are also more commercial than art movie theaters used to be, but their commercial logic serves the idea of screening good movies. The preservation of an old function took place partly through the creative reinterpretation of that old cultural position and the reconfiguration of a niche for the enterprise. Shopping malls are inspired more by the idea of radical rupture and constant expansion. Both draw from legacies of urban modernity, but whereas art movie theaters reach back to the traditions of observing and mingling in the urban spectacle under the aura of art, shopping malls restrict access through physical distance and rely on a commercial filter rather than an aesthetic one.

Art movie theaters and shopping malls represent two distinct strategies of globalization and localization in the postsocialist city.[16] Both hint that globalization and localization are intimately connected. They also reinforce the idea that global cultural flows do not lead to complete cultural homogenization. Cultural phenomena that emanate from global centers go through a process of indigenization in which they become our "own" (Appadurai, 1990). The same is true for economic institutions. The Art Movie Network is a thoroughly vernacularized version of global strategies for promoting high art. But the two institutional histories also reinforce strongly held notions concerning the force of global flows. Their direction is very apparent and well documented for shopping malls. However, the Art Movie Network itself is a strong indication of the hierarchical nature of the global landscape and of the limits of indigenization. Art movie theaters draw their selections from the same pool of films as most other theaters all over the world, but the timing of openings shows a rigid geographic distribution, in spite of local variations caused by Hungarian films and such curiosities as films by Hal Hartley that open in Budapest well ahead of their release in the United States. As a rule, most east European films travel to Budapest via western Europe or North America, in spite of their decades-long intensive presence in Hungarian distribution and film culture, and in spite of previously existing personal-professional networks and even such conjunctures as the excellent Russian-language skills of the general manager of Budapest Film. This flow of films is but another reiteration of the center-periphery relationship first addressed by world-system theory and then by the globalization literature (e.g., Wallerstein, 1974; Hannerz, 1996). Centers are not centers because everything originates there, but because they are places of exchange, switchboards of culture (Hannerz, 1996).

The two genres discussed above also show that there is quite substantial room for variations on the strategies of localization. The Art Movie Network subverts globalization on its own ground, by insisting on a more heterogeneous interpretation of it than mere "Hollywoodization." It disrupts the convenient association between globalization and mass culture that is entrenched among critical intellectuals and politicians. With the exception of overtly racist ideologies, any nationalist discourse makes this connection transparent by crusading against "foreign cultural trash." Institutions such as the Art Movie Network resist cultural homogenization by refraining from simplistic references to a nationalistic symbolism. They merge local and global under the aegis of "art" and "quality" while creating a new urban identity. Shopping malls unite global and local with less institutional creativity in a more plainly commercial spirit—contributing to the emergence of new urban identity of a different kind.

Urban Texture Unraveling

Fragmentation of the City

Mike Davis (1992a) connects his analysis of urban change in contemporary Los Angeles to my topic by observing that "as the walls have come down in eastern Europe, they are being erected all over Los Angeles" (228). True to a local tradition, he gives a noir account of how public space is extinguished, militarized, privatized, or semiprivatized in L.A.

For Charles Jencks (1993), who also writes about L.A., the recent vogue of "wallification" reveals ambiguity, sensuality, and playfulness as buildings and urban villages turn inward in "response to a hostile, polluted environment" (8). Jencks celebrates contemporary L.A. as it is becoming the first "self-conscious heteropolis" (8), a city that encourages heterogeneity in a unity that does not recognize any group as dominant. Whereas Davis presents prison-looking residential and public buildings whose aesthetic brutally excludes "others," Jencks notes, "Defensible architecture, however regrettable as a social tactic, also protects the rights of individuals and threatened groups" (93). Where Davis identifies the power elite(s), Jencks sees a mosaic of minorities that lacks any power structure. Davis envisions the ultimate fragmentation of the city and the possibility of a Beirut emerging; Jencks celebrates the pleasure of heterogeneity. Where Davis regrets the disappearance of public space, Jencks finds a new, fluid, and heterogeneous public space. These strikingly contrasting depictions of the same city aptly introduce the contested terrain of public space and the new concerns about the old tension in city life between heterogeneity and unity—problems whose full recognition is vital for urban planners and theoreticians alike.

Some—but not all—walls may have come down in eastern Europe, but others are being erected hastily, to paraphrase Mike Davis. Some walls may have come down between the "East" and the "West," but internal walls are almost universally being constructed in contemporary cities, regional geographies aside. Private enclosures are reinforced, and not only in Los Angeles; this global vogue is a marked feature of the contemporary east-central European urban transformation as well. Its importance goes beyond the problem of architectural design, and its emergence is embedded in the recent restructuring of cities. In this chapter I examine the relationships among the reinforcement of private enclosures, the polarization among city dwellers, the increasing heterogeneity of the urban public, and the challenges these phenomena pose to public space. I will address the limitations of an approach that sees urban public space as a physical and symbolic site for an undifferentiated celebration of difference and stress the importance of urban public space as a location of encounters.

Collective Paranoia

The advertising section of Budapest's real estate weekly *Ingatlanpiac* approaches the subject with remarkable, almost formulaic, clarity: "American family houses in four to five months; unmistakable American landscape at the end of Veresegyháza: air-conditioning and electric alarms!"[1] In the past ten years, middle- and upper-class housing standards have changed completely in Budapest. It is not only a quiet green neighborhood, southern exposure, abundant natural light, and brick walls, but also air-conditioning and sophisticated security devices as well as the quantity and quality of physically more imposing structures, such as gates, that define good homes for these groups. The "luxury" edition of these features—rustic ambience within the city limits—sells for at least Ft 150,000 (about U.S.$1,400 in 1994) per square meter, and those who sell it are quick to remark that "the domestic Hungarian buyer is a rare bird."[2] Local elites have their own houses built with no less sophisticated features. A young and very successful businessman proudly told me about the central alarm system he had installed for a million in his Ft 30 million (about U.S.$270,000) house for the protection of his family. In the event of an emergency (i.e., an attack), it shuts all the windows and makes a completely secluded bulletproof room. As Mike Davis (1992a) notes in his description of recent Los Angeles residential architecture, the architects working for exclusive clients who desire splendid and efficient isolation have found military technology useful in domestic life once again; the security techniques of American embassies and colonial posts could serve as models for comprehensive residential security systems. Inspiration is not limited to technology; the aesthetics of new architecture also draws on military style. The new Goldwyn Library in Holly-

wood reminds one of a fortress, and the downtown shopping mall looks like a prison. As an example of aesthetic consistency, Davis also notes that the new Metropolitan Detention Center in downtown Los Angeles is regularly mistaken for a hotel (257).

In Budapest, those who cannot afford to install sophisticated security devices individually are offered the choice of moving into guarded and gated "housing parks" (*lakópark*; Figure 7.1)—as they are euphemistically referred to in order to distinguish them unambiguously from housing estates *(lakótelep)*—on the outskirts of the city or in some nearby villages such as Telki and Veresegyháza. These designs are very much future oriented and may eventually generate some of the animosity against which they are armed. The spatial, aesthetic, and wealth-related separation of the project from the village, when conspicuously fortified, becomes so striking as to actually arouse suspicion. The climate of Hungary, especially of the countryside, does not make air-conditioning necessary. There are ways, however, to induce a need for air-conditioning; for example, when brick as a traditional building material is replaced by cheap wood and plaster, the insulation of buildings certainly suffers. Also, once the need emerges in collective forms of habitation, controlled climate becomes a standard that should be followed immediately; the free choice of not having it is severely limited by the disadvantages of opening the window and importing all the neighbors' noise. With electricity being exceedingly expensive, one must conclude that living in a controlled climate is a new status symbol: the newcomers do not even want to let the air of Telki into their homes unfiltered. It is not surprising, then, that the developer—the Glenn Eton family house constructing company from Canada—claims that "by this, it is not simply houses we offer but an entire life style."[3]

There are low-tech and more traditional security devices. Ten years ago no one would have thought that the notion of the "dense fence"—that is, a fence that is impenetrable by either the alien gaze or alien bodies—would become a key selling point in real estate in Budapest (Figure 7.2). Whoever can afford it withdraws into seclusion; the dwellers on the hillsides hide behind their concrete or brick fences, first-floor tenants decide to live behind iron bars—to the chagrin of the fire department—and pensioners install more locks on their doors. Parents show unusual understanding toward their children's desires and let dogs into their urban homes. The poorly paid and shabbily dressed cashiers and customers of Szuper grocery store are guarded by well-paid security men in black uniforms. This collective paranoia spreads around: it shows no mercy toward public or semipublic space either. Gates of apartment buildings became locked in a few years' time,

Figure 7.1. Gated community in a Buda suburb. Photograph by author.

and the only investment in most recently privatized apartment buildings has been the installation of entry-phone systems. In old tenement buildings, people whose doors open to the inner yard block the access of other tenants to the yard—including that of the representative of the condo owners' association—by supplementing the old secessionist French door with an iron gate that is locked day and night. Car alarms became a new standard overnight, fundamentally intruding on the sleeping habits of citizens in the inner city. Alarms are the most cunning and least sensible element of the auditory appropriation of urban public space, but the sanctity of private property has prevented the issue from being thematized at all.

Dogs and their traces are everywhere, and public scandals ensue when children and pensioners are injured by fighter dogs—a new phenomenon in the previously rather peaceful world of mixed types of the Hungarian dog universe—which prompts the owners to form the Fighter Dog Owners' Association in defense of their democratically granted rights to individual freedom and security.[4] Dogs are an undisputed success story in Budapest: in 1995 there were already 160,000 registered dogs in the city (one-twelfth of the population), and their number is growing by 25 percent each year. The number of veterinarians increased from twenty-seven in 1989 to two hundred by 1995, and the profession seems more respectable than ever.[5]

Figure 7.2. Dense fences in the Buda hills. Photograph by author.

Crime statistics indicate changes that coincide with political transformations. The number of delinquent acts, which had been growing very moderately since the end of the 1980s, displayed a 50 percent growth—the highest—in 1990, and after a peak in 1992, the figure seems to have stabilized. The quantified efficiency of the police was the lowest in 1990, when more than half of all delinquencies remained uncleared, and started to improve from then on (KSH, 1994b: 17). An overwhelming majority of these cases involve crimes committed against property: car thefts and burglaries rank the highest. The temporary loss of self-confidence among the police amid the debate about political cleansing and the hysteria connected to the unexperienced scale of crime urged citizens' action. There are twelve hundred voluntary civilian security guards on watch, driving in their own cars around the streets of Budapest at night.[6] A neighborhood watch group in District VI, formed in defense of small businesses in the area, was overpowered by emotions against disorderly living and decided to cleanse the Western Station of homeless people and passengers of all kinds without accommodation who were sleeping in the train cars. Security considerations have woven a tight net between "mine" and "yours," also between "us" and "them." The silent participants of this everyday collective paranoia try to keep not only "crime" out of their houses and neighborhoods but everything that is less known for those inside, thus strange, other, and threatening.

Space Eaters

Transportation connects localities but it also separates them: it reorganizes public space in a very effective manner. Depending on its type, the nature of space thus connected or disconnected can be more public or less so. In Hungary the number of cars grew by 15 percent in 1990. This is a uniquely high figure, but increases in the number of cars seem to have stabilized around 2–4 percent per year since then, with the total number of automobiles reaching more than two million in 1996. In other words, every second Hungarian household owned a car in 1996, and the number of cars in relation to population size was 50 percent higher in Budapest than in the rest of the country (KSH, 1997: 55). Mass transportation is clearly on the decline: in Budapest every branch transported fewer passengers in 1996 than in 1980 or 1990, except for the subway, whose passengers have reached the 1990 level again following a sharp decline in the early 1990s (KSH, 1997: 338). In brief, time-series data show that the importance of cars has increased spectacularly in short- and long-distance travel (KSH, 1997: 336, 338–39).

Individual motorization became a mass phenomenon during the petty entrepreneurial state socialism of the late 1970s through the early 1980s, when income generated in the second economy was consumed rather than reinvested in business and "Frigidaire socialism" had exhausted its possibilities in giving directions to consumers. Cars, along with small holiday houses and plots, emerged as the new mass status symbols in the 1980s. Behind the rearrangement of consumption patterns in favor of cars, the social change of the collapse of state socialism and its aftermath produced a curious movement favoring collectively wasteful individual solutions. Transportation policy, the fiscal crisis of the postsocialist state, the generic antistate rhetoric of the new political elites, and individual solutions to immediate everyday problems sought by millions of families coalesced in what is commonly described as the "rationalization" of those public services in which the state had been the main provider, creating a virtue, as it were, out of the municipal and national budget crises. Before the changes, west European social scientists had pointed out, one of the few concrete differences between "capitalist" and "socialist" cities that favored the latter was the advanced system of mass transportation of socialist cities, particularly the fact that mass transportation was widely available all over the cities and ran frequently outside rush hours and during the weekends (French and Hamilton, 1979). With the collapse of state socialism that observation of comparative difference had become an "anomaly" that postsocialist cities proceeded to correct. Measures to decrease the quantity and sink the quality of public transportation were backed by IMF and World Bank demands for "structural adjustment," including cuts in collective consumption in order to balance the national budget. As a result of the factors noted above, public transport fares have been raised and the quality of the service has declined across the board. Transportation lines have been "rationalized" away; service is less frequent, the hours of operation are shorter, there is no weekend service from some outer housing estates to the inner city, and travel time has become much longer due to increased car traffic and traffic jams.

As a result of the drops in both the quantity and the quality of service, the social composition of mass-transit ridership was bound to undergo rather profound changes. In Budapest, the first ones to leave public transport were the male heads of white-collar, and especially managerial, intellectual and upper-middle-class households. This change—making the personal car something of a symbol of social worth and success in the male breadwinner role—took place largely before the collapse of state socialism. Then the exodus continued with the city's yuppies, whose observance of the new business dress code suffers in the crowdedness of the subway car, which represents closer-than-desired physical proximity across social classes. The next groups to opt for the use of cars were middle- and upper-class mothers, who in Budapest's current gender division of labor continue to be entrusted with the task of making sure their children safely make the passage to and from school and to and from special language, music, and sports classes, as well as with providing their families with quality consumption, a geographically rather complicated task in Budapest. As a result of these departures, the social composition of Budapest's public transport system has become distinctly skewed toward the lower end of the city's social spectrum—a change that is hardly a prescription for increased elite pressures on the transport company or the municipal government to improve the quality of services.

The proliferation of cars reorganizes public space intensely: being one of the most individualistic forms of transportation, it fragments urban space and withdraws its users from the public.[7] It is obvious that the low-speed pedestrian's pavement is more exciting and conducive to social mixing than the road of the high-speed driver or the internal space of the car, for which the outer world becomes real only through an open window or an accident.[8] Through the filter of the windshield, the city is but another image on the television and intervenes only in the form of annoying transportation obstacles, such as traffic jams and road construction, that need to be avoided or overcome. Under the pretext of individual comfort, cars privatize urban space in a brutally straightforward manner. It would be foolish to assume that cars can, or should, be completely eliminated from contemporary cities. However, as Mumford (1961) argued forty years ago, alternatives are important, and they should be connected on the scale of the pedestrian. Alternatives not only make a good economics of space, they also provide a minimal base for encountering others, and, through the formation of the "multiple travel identities" of urban dwellers, they may prevent the ultimate fragmentation of space—a danger of monocultural transportation systems. Car traffic generates demands for new space exponentially: whereas one-third of Los Angeles is consumed by transportation facilities, as much as two-thirds of the city's center is occupied by streets, freeways, parking lots, and garages, Mumford recounts. This is, indeed, "space eating with a vengeance" (510).

The privatization of the means of transportation has been enormously consequential for urban public space. Historically, one of the most important themes of public space, especially that of the street, has been movement by masses of people, which even when it happened in the form of vehicular transportation involved walking and common switching points. The massification of individual car transportation does not make such reliance on streets necessary anymore, and the lessening of streets' function rearranges street life.

The Cynicism of Semiprivate Spaces

In July 1992, a new hotel opened in downtown Budapest: Grand Hotel Corvinus Kempinski. Great expectations preceded the event. The hotel, situated next to Vörösmarty Square (the heart of the downtown shopping district), the British embassy, and the Budapest police headquarters, was bound to become a symbol of the new inner city. It is part of the Kempinski hotel chain, which owns hotels all over the world, including a new one in Beijing.

The 376-room hotel is a grandiose production; its glittering high-tech features make it truly part of international postmodern architecture. Its guests are directly linked to global capital; Lufthansa Airlines guarantees the occupancy of most of its rooms regularly. Prices reinforce this link indirectly. Communication with the environment was nevertheless a great concern for both the architect and the owners in the building of the hotel. As one publication noted: "According to the business philosophy of the Kempinski hotel chain, a hotel should always be open to the citizens of the city which accommodates it. Thus, Budapest dwellers may use the garage of the hotel and the first three floors with all the communal service space."[9]

The Kempinski offers four conference rooms, a 400-square-meter ballroom, an art gallery, a bar, a restaurant, a swimming pool, a fitness center, and a handful of shops inside the building to establish the local link. Its architect, who also designed (aside from a dozen or so older works) one of Budapest's most elegant office buildings, the International Trade Center, and is planning to conclude his career with the gigantic West End City Center (see chapter 6), decided to follow his inclinations and the philosophy of his client in creating a building that communicates with the environment and is also properly enclosed. The latter endeavor turned out to be more successful than the former one. One side of the hotel is a windowless wall, designed so upon the request of officials at the neighboring Budapest police headquarters. In a development of some irony, the headquarters were soon relocated to a newly built, postmodern high-rise in an outer area, a building that entered local language as the Cop Palace *(Zsarupalota)*; the old site is being turned into yet another hotel. Kempinski's main entrance faces a dusty park that joins a bus terminal. In very obvious contrast to the exhaust fumes of the opposite square, the high-powered entrance of the hotel, with a dozen liveried footmen, is not very inviting for the public. The communicative function has clearly been assigned to the back of the building, which opens into a small pedestrian street. However, anyone who eventually enters the building from the back has to venture through the terrace of the café and an insignificant gray door only to reach a small hallway lined with extremely elegant shops. The shopping tour eventually takes one to the lobby, where high columns incorporate three levels. The side entrances are deliberately downplayed, almost hidden, as in the case of the Bonaventure Hotel in Los Angeles, which has served as an archetypical example of postmodern urban design (Jameson, 1984).

The connection between the shops of the hotel and the surrounding shopping streets, whose logical extension the hotel could have been, is broken by the hardly noticeable doors and the elevated hotel shops. The principle is similar to the new organization of some areas of downtown Los Angeles, where shops, bars, and restaurants are located underground and on terraces of different levels connected by fast-moving elevators, semiprivate hallways, and labyrinths—with fountains and intentionally user-unfriendly benches—that make these spaces contiguous but separate from the street. The Kempinski is inserted into urban space in a way that is characteristically different from its predecessors, the most elegant, most Western, most curious hotels of state socialism. Aesthete Péter György describes the different experience of Hotel Inter-Continental in the 1960s and Hotel Forum in the 1980s—both grand hotels of their time, located on the Danube embankment, and designed by the architect of the Kempinski. The hotels of state socialism radiated a sense of fortresslike seclusion from the everyday life of the city, which, argues György, was a completely adequate expression of the social situation of the times: they dominated the environment, but, as symbols of unlimited movement and consumption (by Western tourists), their interiors had to be hidden (György and Durkó, 1993).[10]

The Kempinski is supposedly open to any citizen; the architect and the corporation both have made a point about its openness. However, the users of the semiprivate space of the hotel are very homogeneous. No one ventures there except those for whom it was originally designed: those who are wealthy by global standards, be they locals or foreigners. In this respect, the cynical openness of the communal spaces of the hotel is as adequate a manifestation of social standing as the secrecy of state socialist hotels used to be. The rhetoric of communicative architecture is contradicted by every detail of the design, which radiates that the symbol of the new inner city does not wish to be part of the city. By reproducing the city's streets, nature, and climate in a filtered way, it is a replacement, a substitute for the city (Jameson, 1984). In spite of this, the Kempinski is still less savagely inserted into the surrounding city than L.A.'s Bonaventure (Davis, 1985), but that moderation is a merit of the surrounding city rather than of the design. The pedestrian scale of downtown Budapest and its consequent density make the hotel more easily accessible; it is less elevated from the street, and although in both hotels the misery of low ceilings in the residential section cannot but remind one of cost-efficiency amid luxury, the Kempinski at least has a main lobby that is less bunkerlike than the fragmented spaces of the Bonaventure and, not having a reflective glass surface, it looks more open to the city. Semipublic spaces of this kind are not rare in the inner city. The smart labyrinths and atria that accommodate high-priced commercial establishments protect their visitors not only from the swings of the weather but from the experience of encountering social otherness: they effectively homogenize their public instead of providing some common ground for a more inclusive togetherness in the same space.

Defending Public Space

Commercial public spaces can be controlled by delicate strategies of market segmentation, as the design of Hotel Kempinski suggests. Playgrounds constitute a different kind of public space. They feature free admission, usually without any pressure of consumption regulated by money or taste. Of course, their location may restrict access, and so may the presence or lack of seemingly unimportant communal establishments, such as public lavatories. Recently the playgrounds in Budapest's inner city have been acquiring a new architectural feature: fences. The Károlyi Garden, an old play-ground square in a somewhat hidden part of downtown's District V, has gained an imperial-looking railing, and the square is now open for visitors from 7:00 A.M. until sunset (Figure 7.3). Even though access is not limited during the day, this restriction obviously prevents people from sleeping in the park—a measure that at the time of the reconstruction of the park was largely preemptive. More popular reasoning argues for the necessity of sepa-rating the two main users of the park: children and dogs. There have al-ways been fights between the two uses, but no steps were taken until the number of dogs increased dramatically in the immediate area of the square as well as the overall city. Higher levels of danger and pollution by dogs ne-cessitated intervention. The fenced dog run built in the Károlyi Garden is the first solution of its kind. Fencing playgrounds is a way of privatizing public space, of restricting its use. Nevertheless, it may also be one of those instances Jencks (1993) had in mind when he argued that defensible archi-tecture "also protects the rights of individuals and threatened groups" (93)—in this case, the rights of children. Fencing has become a common practice in public parks, but unfortunately—unlike in the Károlyi Garden, which is small and where the playground takes up the majority of space—in larger parks the nature of defensible space becomes clearer and more prob-lematic even by its own premises. The smaller the park, the easier it is to control and clean; playgrounds have become small, concrete-covered con-finements within public parks, leaving the rest to dogs, their waste, and its smell. The last of these is, of course, very difficult to confine.

Fencing playgrounds is a form of defensible architecture that sepa-rates one type of public from another by imposing physical obstacles on ac-cess. For dogs at all times and for homeless people or couples in love at night, the fenced park is not a public space anymore. The common theme behind preventing people from sleeping in the park and dogs from per-forming their functions there is an insistence on separating public and pri-vate functions. The overflow of private life into the public realm can change the nature of public space. The lives of those who sleep, eat, wash, and so on regularly in public space shake our enlightened middle-class notion of pub-lic and private and provoke forceful associations with filth or dirt. Dirt, as Mary Douglas (1966) defines it, is matter out of place. Matter that should be private becomes dirt in public. Of course, the social battle is also fought on the frontier between private and public, for the "proper" location of the di-viding line. Fenced parks represent a characteristically mainstream, middle-class way of seeing and defending the proper use of public space. But ap-proaches of this kind will not solve the problem of the constant pressure of

Figure 7.3. Károlyi Garden, open from 7:00 A.M. until sunset, with a separate dog run. Photograph by author.

privatizing public space for lack of private homes and lavatories; they will merely relocate "dirt" to the streets, which are a degree more public than parks are and whose control may be the task of the municipal government rather than the district one.

Public space is increasingly conceived of as an expensive enterprise. The withdrawal of resources from collective consumption and the polarization of society do not encourage the creation of genuinely comprehensive public space. Even old commercial establishments fall prey to the pressure on district governments to economize with space. The leases of well-managed and popular coffeehouses are not renewed for the simple reason that municipal governments are unable to resist higher bidders with ambitions to open car salons, banks, or "coffeehouses" of a different kind, such as Kentucky Fried Chicken outlets.

Clearly, the municipal government is facing difficulties in fulfilling its provisioning responsibilities; the mere maintenance of the current level of services requires major efforts, and there has been a decline in almost every area, especially in the financing of schools, theaters, libraries, archives, and parks (Demszky, 1994). The municipal government is seeking to reduce its circle of responsibility; privatization is the main method. The method is not new, nor is it unique to the postsocialist context. We are currently living in the privatizing phase of what appears to be a global cycle. In the United States, state and municipal governments deliberate on privatizing their prisons, the New Jersey Turnpike, and parking-meter management in New York City (Adler, 1996). Privatization, however, also has its specific east European tone. It is a primary strategy of the postsocialist runaway state (for a definition of this term, see chapter 5).

In December 1995, following long debates, 46 percent of the Budapest Electric Company was sold to two German companies: RWE Energie and EV Schwabe Ag. A few days later, another German consortium—VEW Ruhrgas—bought 39 percent of the capital's Gas Works.[11] The problem with privatization of this kind, especially when a foreign company is involved, is not only that privatized services are not necessarily more efficient. The consequences of drastic price increases—which are "easy" ways to improve the level of services and profit margins—such as default on payment with the ensuing social tension, shutting off of services, eviction, and so on, are removed even from the provider's remote sphere of responsibility and become *public* issues. Before its partial privatization, the Electric Company had an outstanding balance amounting to Ft 2 billion, more than half of which resulted from nonpayment by 200,000 families.[12] The growing difficulties some people, especially pensioners and large families, face in covering their utilities and the parallel spread of air conditioners are but further signs of the increasing polarization of urban dwellers. And social polarization can be mapped more and more accurately.

The Segmented City

The territoriality of resources entails inequality in access to them. Inequality in one field can be balanced or mediated by better or worse access to other resources. Occurrences of spatial inequality become social when there is a systematic clustering of advantages in one area and disadvantages in another. Spatial inequality in Budapest is not a new phenomenon, but its growing rigidity certainly is. According to Hungary's City Law, earlier 50 percent and now 30 percent of the income tax collected by the central state apparatus goes to the district governments. In the "better" districts of Buda, the amount of income tax per district dweller is twice that in the outskirts of Pest and the two inner-city districts of Elizabethtown and Josephtown (Figure 7.4). As for other sources of income, there is even greater variation among the district governments. Revenues from housing privatization, real estate deals, and local taxes (building, land, and communal taxes) can be five to six times higher in some areas than in others (Demszky, 1994: 15).

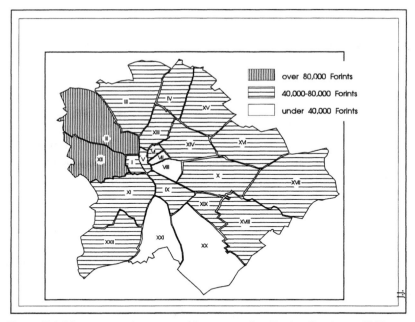

Figure 7.4. Mean per capita personal income tax by district, fiscal year 1994.
Source: Ministry of Finance, Hungary.

These differences are exacerbated by the range of the tasks and re-sponsibilities of the district governments: in some districts there are more public issues, such as homelessness and street prostitution, which may not occur in others. To mediate some of these differences, the law prescribes cost sharing between the city and the district governments and targets a more equal distribution of services by selectively adding centralized contri-bution to some areas, such as education and social policy.

Although this policy actually decreases the difference between the wealthiest and poorest districts in the areas it covers (Demszky, 1994: 15), territorial inequalities run rampant. On the one hand, in 1995, out of the city's eight soup kitchens, four operated in District VIII. On the other, in 1993 more than half of all day-care centers were privately run in District XII, closely followed by Districts V and II (KSH, 1994a: 173). The proportion of private kindergartens was uniquely high in District XII, whereas only public kindergartens existed in Csepel (District XXI), among other areas (KSH, 1994a: 186–87). These differences largely covary with housing prices by dis-tricts (see Figure 7.5).

An analysis of the variance in housing prices by districts is rather in-

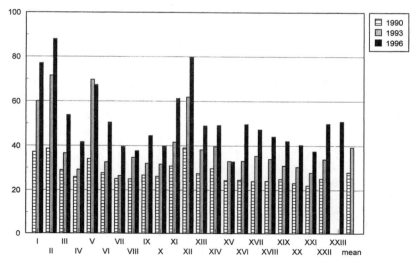

Figure 7.5. Mean housing sales prices, by Budapest district, 1990, 1993, and 1996, in current forints (thousands of forints per square meter).

structive. Variance tends to be smaller where the average price is lower (Districts IV, VII, VIII, IX, XV-XVII, XX–XXII) and the greatest in some high-priced areas (Districts V, XI, XII, XIII).[13] The degree of homogeneity of the city's districts also explains the distribution of costly private day-care centers and similar services: there are hardly any pockets of poverty in Districts XII and II, and the top level of wealth is located in these areas, causing a great deal of variation in housing prices and local services (shopping, day care, fitness, and catering). Internal differentiation within the city has been more significant than differentiation between the city and its surrounds. There has been a constant flight of citizens from the capital, which resulted in a negative migration balance in 1991, and that has only increased since then (see Table 7.1). Since the 1980s, about half of those who have left moved to the neighboring villages and towns in Pest County, and about a third of the in-migrants have come from there. What has changed since 1989 is that the capital started to lose population to an increasing degree to its surroundings (Table 7.1).[14] Although it looks like a classical pattern of sub-urbanization, this change does not pose a serious threat leading to the erosion of the tax base of the capital yet. Most of these families moved out of the city in reaction to the increasing dilapidation of certain inner-city neighborhoods and the corresponding reevaluation of the hillside districts. If one did not have the opportunity to settle for a lifetime in the green areas during the previous regime, one will not have a chance to do so now unless one

Table 7.1

Permanent migration to and from Budapest, 1975–93

	To Budapest	From Pest County	From Budapest	To Pest County	Balance Budapest	Balance Pest County
1975	21,137		12,946		8,191	
1980	21,566		14,006		7,560	
1981	22,140		12,799		9,341	
1982	22,977		13,577		9,400	
1983	22,987		12,981		10,006	
1984	25,520	8,475	14,384	6,705	11,136	1,770
1985	25,212		14,746		10,466	
1989	23,625	7,794	18,322	9,295	5,303	-1,501
1990	25,422		21,798		3,624	
1991	20,978		22,048		-1,070	
1992	22,455		26,057		-3,602	
1993	22,399	7,928	29,033	16,034	-6,634	-8,106

Source: Calculated from KSH (1985: 36–37; 1990: 29–30; 1994b: 41).

is a member of the new economic elite. Location sells more than any other feature of a house—a principle that has the power to overrule even the unpopularity of prefab buildings. Housing estates have always been ranked by newness, the proportion of state-owned flats to co-ops or condominiums (the fewer state-owned flats the better), and location. This has merely been extended and finalized: the always existing distance between Csepel and the Pók Street housing estate on the Buda side, stretching down to the best part of the river, has grown markedly (Figure 7.6), and the latter can be higher priced than better-quality housing in neighborhoods closer to the inner city. The general trend is nevertheless a decline in the status of housing estates. Their selective deterioration is tied closely to the fate of their inhabitants. The restructuring of the economy and the prevailing economic and moral depression exert more effects on the residents of the Csepel housing estate, the majority of whom work, or used to work, in the Csepel Iron- and Metal Works (an industrial establishment whose fate is discussed in chapter 5) than on the predominantly white-collar inhabitants of Pók Street.[15]

In spite of the degradation of life and the accompanying sense of social exclusion of the inhabitants of the older housing estates, the phenome-

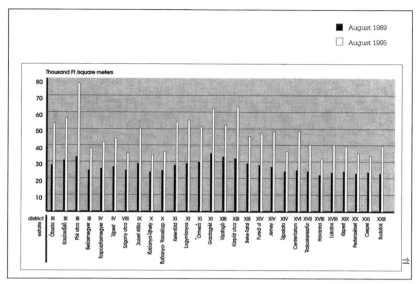

Figure 7.6. Mean housing prices at housing estates, Budapest, 1989 and 1995.
Source: *Ingatlanpiac.*

non of urban crisis that draws the attention of most Hungarian scholars is
the formation of a "ghetto"—as known from contemporary U.S. cities—in
inner Josephtown in District VIII. Partly because housing estates are not
located in the inner city, their hopelessness remains less visible. The other
reason inner-city segregation is more noticed is its ethnic component:
whereas the proportion of the population of Budapest that is Roma (Gypsy)
has doubled since the early 1970s, the proportion of Roma has tripled in
inner Pest, where there are schools in which every second child is Roma
(Ladányi and Szelényi, 1998). This constellation of poverty and ethnic difference prompted scholars and the media to identify the phenomenon as
the "ghettoization" of the inner city, and mention has even been made of the
emergence of an underclass. An Americanized nickname denoting poverty
had already been given to a slummy part of District VII, Csikágó (Magyar
phonetic spelling of Chicago), in the first half of the twentieth century, in
order to give appropriate expression to the higher-than-average crime rate
(and poverty level) in the area. The status of Csikágó has not improved, but
neighboring inner Josephtown—also marked as a "slum" on American
geographer Beynon's 1943 map of Budapest (reproduced in Figure 4.2)—
deteriorated even faster. And given that the name of Chicago had already
been taken, this area of newer marginality has recently begun to figure as a
"ghetto."

This particular trope of "Chicago"—representing a part of itself and being used to signal a constellation of spatially segregated poverty and ethnicity—is very powerful and widespread. Loïc Wacquant (1993), in his account of the *banlieues,* shows the stubbornness of ready-made identifications of the *banlieues* as "little Chicagos" or *cité-ghettos.* Wacquant quotes a police officer who found it necessary to remind journalists amid the uproar that this trope caused among the residents of one of the *banlieues,* "La Courneuve is not Chicago, let's not exaggerate" (369, n. 9). Wacquant's subsequent comparison of the ghetto and the *banlieue* suggests that this was one of those occasions when a policeman was right and showed remarkable social and intellectual sensitivity. As La Courneuve is not Chicago, inner Josephtown is not a ghetto either, nor is it La Courneuve. The reasons behind this seemingly elementary truth are similar to what Wacquant considers significant to mark off the *banlieue* from the ghetto. Although there is a distinct ethnic element in Josephtown, the extent of ethnic segregation does not even come close to that of the American urban underclass; there is still much social and ethnic mixing in these neighborhoods. Ethnic and territorial stigmatization do not overlap completely. Neighborhood and family ties seem to hold stronger, and the Budapest neighborhood is still more saturated by municipal and state institutions. This partly explains why the hopelessness of the American ghetto is more striking, and why it has become a more hostile and oppressive place for its residents.

Szelényi sees the formation of a Hungarian "underclass" as more of a rural phenomenon that has repercussions for an urban underclass (Ladányi and Szelényi, 1998). There is a chance that underurbanization—which had constituted a defining characteristic of state socialism—will turn out to have been merely delayed urbanization, and the peculiar spatial and occupational structure of the country will adjust to nonsocialist patterns, leading to an extreme migration of the present rural underclass—the Roma population of small settlements—into Budapest. The Roma would most probably move to the ghetto-suspect areas of the city, and that would give considerable momentum to the formation of an underclass in the inner city, especially if middle-class flight from the area continues along with the diminishing resources and will of public institutions. The housing estates may very well take a trajectory that will produce a kind of social and territorial marginalization close to that of the *banlieue.* In any case, there is a new type of polarization in the city, and the question remains whether the increasing fragmentation of the city will leave any common ground for its citizens. Social polarization certainly runs the risk of tearing public space apart or turning it into a set of more restrictive, defensible spaces. In all fairness, public space has historically accommodated greater inequalities, but the possibility of exit on a massive scale—not restricted to the upper classes— and a broadly conceived democratic system make the present challenge different.

Public Space versus Public Sphere

Public space is peculiar to cities. The copresence of many people in cities renders the emergence of an exhaustive, comprehensive network of personal communication impossible. It requires ways to deal with the tension between intense physical proximity and the lack of moral proximity (Simmel, 1971b). This is the source of the typical urban mentality that Simmel describes as a fundamental indifference to distinctions, to every instance of unfamiliarity or difference—the blasé attitude, as he calls it. Goffman (1963) accords a more specific social psychological meaning to fundamentally the same attitude and finds a more virtuous aspect of it by focusing on "civil inattention," which "makes possible co-presence without comingling, awareness without engrossment, courtesy without conversation" writes Lofland (1989: 462). Building on the work of both Simmel and Goffman, Lofland (1973) strikes a positive tone, claiming that the specificity of urban life is precisely that this type of social psychological situation and its main character, the stranger, create the very basis of public space where civility toward diversity rules.[16] Where people gather who represent different levels of wealth, come from different social backgrounds, have different features and bodies—look different—behave and dress differently, *strangely,* there has to be some common denominator to make copresence possible. Civility toward difference makes public space more accessible to citizens than do legal guarantees, should persons get together for a common pursuit, for public expression, or merely to pursue private activities in a public setting, such as private conversation in a coffeehouse that, if desired, can be expanded toward strangers.

"Public space" has become very elusive both physically and conceptually. Sometimes both the abstract notion of Habermasian public sphere and the figurative interpretation of public space are subsumed under a notion of public space. Public space is space to which anyone can have access. For commercial public space, admission fees and the explicit or implicit demand of purchase condition access. The public nature of noncommercial public spaces is similarly problematic. Public spaces, although defined as nonexclusive territory, cannot be designed for everybody: it is inevitable that they fit certain social groups more than others—a feature that may effectively discourage some groups. Public spaces have identities, and there is constant struggle about how these identities are defined and who the "others" are that are to be excluded. In nineteenth-century New York, for example, citizens could immediately sense the differences, and distinguish in their spatial practices, among Central Park, Washington Square Park, and Tompkins Square Park (Blackmar and Rosenzweig, 1992).[17] The same was true of various Budapest parks at the time. If public servants and soldiers gathered in great numbers in particular promenades or parks, the upper classes avoided those areas (Gyáni, 1994). However, in both New York and Budapest there was a strong feeling that public space should enable the democratic mixing of social classes, whether by luring them into the educating example of bourgeois pastimes or offering them opportunities to pursue activities in line with their own habitus. Central Park designer and superintendent Frederick Law Olmsted's philosophy was certainly an example of the first approach:

> No one who has closely observed the conduct of the people who visit [Central] Park, can doubt that it exercises a distinctly harmonizing and refining influence upon the most unfortunate and most lawless classes of the city—an influence favorable to courtesy, self-control, and temperance. (quoted in Davis, 1992b: 156)

After the first two decades, the character of Central Park changed and became more accommodating to the lower classes of the city by bringing the "tranquil retreat" closer to the city's commercial culture (Blackmar and Rosenzweig, 1992). The expansion of the public in the park took place along with the increasing commercialization of that public. The importance of this relationship goes beyond the history of Central Park; this point should be strikingly familiar to students of the public sphere who are well versed in Habermasian theory. Craig Calhoun (1992) makes it very explicit that in Habermas's analysis of the public sphere there is an emphasis on the strong correlation between the democratic expansion of the public sphere and its loss in "quality."

The public sphere in the Habermasian sense is "a forum in which the private people, come together, readied themselves to *compel* public authority to legitimize itself before public opinion" (Habermas, 1989: 25–26). In a historically less specific and less exclusive tone, Young (1987) distinguishes public space from public expression. Expression is public when others aside from those expressing themselves at the moment can respond and enter into discussion through institutions or the media. Young's definition of the political is also less exclusive: "Expression and discussion are political when they raise and address issues of the moral value or human desirability of an institution or practice whose decisions affect a large number of people" (73). This concept of the public is derived from aspects of the modern urban experience, writes Young, acknowledging the importance of urban public space in relation to a heterogeneous public life, but, correctly, keeping them separate.

The two are related, even in political theory. Geographers such as Howell celebrate Hannah Arendt's spatial imagination in analyses of public space and public sphere: in contrast to Habermas, by "public space" Arendt means space in the concrete sense as well. Howell (1993) does not say why: that it is the historical period that forms the basis of Arendt's public sphere that allows for her spatial imagination. In the polis, the designated place of politics and the most celebrated public space, the agora, had both a figurative and abstract meaning.[18] From Arendt to Habermas there has been a shift from an ocular to an auditory public, from a "space of appearance"—which the agora had been—to a desubstantialized public, a virtual community of readers, writers, and interpreters that the new publicity of the Enlightenment meant (Benhabib, 1996). The short cohabitation of urban sociability and political public in the public space of the agora has been replaced by the increasing divergence of urban public space and a public sphere that has neither a body nor a location in space anymore (Benhabib, 1996). With the tremendous expansion of the mass media it has become a truism that "going public today means going on the air" (Carpignano et al., 1993: 114). If this is so, the question is justly asked: Does urban public space and its widely lamented decline (most prominently by Sorkin, 1992) have any significance for a democratic political life?

Public space is more than a passive physicality. It implies, as I have noted, tolerance for difference and a certain degree of self-limitation, not necessarily of a political nature. The nature of any limitation—whether exercised by the self, other members of the public, or the authorities—is, however, strongly conditioned by culture and politics. The public gaze and visibility imply accountability and, ultimately, responsibility. The common denominator for the copresence of people—tolerance—can be encouraged institutionally. It can be a result of a precarious social and architectural design aside from the minimal legal definition of public access. If there is no convincing guarantee of free public appearance, then there emerges a fear of showing difference. People who have the most to fear—those who diverge most radically from the imagery of the ideal citizen of the public—and who can afford it start avoiding public spaces. They withdraw into privacy, and the delicate balance in the multilayered use of public space is offset. When this happens, some attempts at more exclusive appropriation of public space suddenly become successful. Urban public space is important: it is a place to encounter difference and to handle it properly.

This has a complex relevance for a democratic public life. One could of course argue that this kind of knowledge can also be gained through institutions that are not public, or from various media. Compared with mediated experience, urban public space has the uniqueness of physical proximity, which even in its most minimalist—and sometimes most annoying— form of the crowded bus can be more interactive, and richer in surprises, than other, despatialized (mediated) forms of learning about difference. True, the modern media offer interactive possibilities, but an interactive experience of difference through physical proximity involves a different degree of *responsibility* from that offered by any media, and this immediacy-cum-responsibility remains located in public space. Public space always carries the unexpected; the screenplay is never fully written, its actors are in constant search of a director and other characters.

The disappearance or appropriation of urban public space is a risky business. The accumulated lack of experience of social and racial otherness, especially when the two overlap, may reinforce the polarization of society by encouraging spatial segregation even more. The spatial segregation of different groups can always be increased. However, it can never become complete, and it breeds fear and phobic reactions. Whenever "accidents" take place, they tend to be severe and violent. Where there is a lack of a common language or any previous experience in handling encounters of a strange kind, ensuing hysterical communication may result in violence.[19] Nonminimalist views of the city and its public spaces attempt to defuse the potential for violence entailed in encounters of otherness, and they do so *not* by minimizing encounters through spatial distance. Public space does not have to be pleasant, encountering difference can be rather disturbing, and its normal working can even be intimidating for "improper" behavior. The public realm has always been and perhaps should be gritty, as Sennett (1990) demonstrates, using subjects ranging from Baudelaire to his own *flâneurie* in New York. The fearless use of public space does not exclude the possibility of becoming frightened, but one should not be conditioned to enter it with fear. Public space very rarely emerges from the free congregation of people: it is usually designed, created, and constantly transformed. In any case, it needs the quiet background routine of public investment, maintenance, and the constant involvement of citizens in the public sphere.

Communal investment or planning does not figure very often in the vocabulary of either postmodern or postsocialist urbanism. Both seem to be afraid of the universalist rhetoric of politicians and urban planners and the dominant position that rhetoric—combined with an impressive concentration of resources—has created. The hypocrisy or, in a more positive light, the extreme naïveté, of all-encompassing claims has been duly challenged in both urban design (most uncompromisingly by Jane Jacobs, 1961) and democratic political life.

City Life and the Celebration of Difference

The impersonal and tolerant diversity of city life, which is manifested in its purest form in urban public space, shows a strong affinity with the ideals of democratic politics. Young (1990) makes the city the locus and model for her politics of difference. Following predictions concerning the disappearance of the boundary between city and countryside—where communities prevailed—the city again becomes counterposed to community. Communities value and enforce homogeneity, claims Young. They do so as they are based on the exclusion of others and nostalgia. As opposed to this, the ideal of city life is a "vision of social relations affirming group difference" (227). Young thus gets rid of the specter of community that has been haunting certain forms of alternative thinking. Idealizing face-to-face immediacy, locales, and a sense of community in politics is naive, and this naïveté leaves important questions unanswered that go beyond the community. The idea of a democratic politics whose several versions have been criticized on grounds of exclusivity (inter alia, see Robbins, 1993) cannot be based on the idea of a utopian community that is, meanwhile, defined by exclusion. Young argues for a nonessentialist view of difference as the basis for a heterogeneous public. Such a conception of difference makes groups nonexclusive; if differences within the group are acknowledged, "different groups are always similar in some respects, and always potentially share some attributes, experiences, and goals" (171). A normative ideal of city life is "the being together of strangers" that encourages the differentiation of social groups but prevents exclusive identification with one group. "In the unoppressive city people are open to unassimilated otherness" (241). The questions of whether unassimilated otherness is possible and whether a multitude of unassimilated others can coexist, and if their coexistence makes them a city, inevitably arise. Young does not address them.

Charles Jencks's (1993) new model of the city and democratic politics—Heteropolis—is constructed along lines similar to those developed by Young. In Jencks's model, public space is defined "in such a way that different people can enter into fluid social situations" (124). In the language of Jencks's new, hetero-architecture, the public should be able to "identify momentarily with new images of otherness" (103) in an architectural piece that is inclusive without being condescending.

Difference is a precondition for identity formation that originates from the "us and them" relationship. The two sides cannot exist without each other, but one is not the other, so an element of exclusion is always there. True, we can dissolve exclusiveness theoretically by making the boundaries more porous, opening up both sides into clusters of differences, which will result in the recognition of shared parts. However, that recognition assumes the unlimited multiplication, or fragmentation, of identities. Chantal Mouffe's (1995) warning concerning the extreme fragmentation of the social is valid:

> Such a view leaves us with a multiplicity of identities without any common denominator and makes it impossible to distinguish between differences that exist but should not exist and differences that do not exist and should exist. In other words, by putting an exclusive emphasis on heterogeneity and incommensurability, it impedes us to recognize how certain differences are constructed as relations of subordination and should therefore be challenged by a radical democratic politics. (262)

Under the category of difference, Young and most other theorists of difference usually list race, ethnicity, sexual orientation, physical ability, and age. Their "difference" does not include class difference; shared attributes are more difficult to identify, and they should belong to differences to "be challenged by democratic politics." Young is aware of the problem; exploitation is one of the five faces of oppression she sets up. These are to be resolved through "institutional change." But how is institutional change to come about if the "business community" and employees cannot find any shared identity that is *relevant* to the question to be resolved?

The undifferentiated celebration of difference runs the danger of becoming almost as utopian as universalist ideas of a homogeneous public. Along the same lines, what would ensure the communication between the unassimilated otherness of a suburb with high-tech employment opportunities and that of a decaying inner city whose "public" space for the suburbanites is a display of layers of social problems into which they would not insert themselves very willingly? Young proposes to solve this problem by redrawing boundaries: regional governments would include both city and suburb. The new "urban" form, however, whose purest expression is to be found in Orange County, California, would not produce diversity even under regional governments. Cyburbia (Sorkin, 1992) is a minimalist settlement made possible by technological development, especially in communications. It provides the fundamental material functions of the city—it has high-rises, shopping malls, even industrial sites and a lot of family houses—with no connections among them. It is an "ageographical place" that could be anywhere (Sorkin, 1992), a suburb without its *urbs*.

Fixing the diversity and heterogeneous public of cities makes sense only in relation to "communities" that are similarly fixed in their homogeneity and exclusiveness. The celebrated attributes of urban life cannot be taken for granted. Public space can become empty; heterogeneous voices can withdraw from it. That can also happen, to return to Rybczynski's (1995) point noted earlier, if public space is not taken care of, if none of those voices feels secure and some are given the possibility of exit. In this sense, some streets in the Bronx, for example, are not public, as they are not democratically accessible to "strangers"—the quintessential actors of urban public space—nor do they belong to the people who live there. Certain differences in public space have to be challenged; "antisocial" activities can be defined based on a full consideration of group differences along the line of highest tolerance, and laws against those activities should be enforced. This is a truly political issue that connects public space to a democratic public sphere—a question that we cannot avoid by abandoning and relocating public space. What holds public space together is not only the diversity of voices at the same place but a certain degree of homogeneity that makes all that possible. One gives up certain things to be seen in public and to see others there. The individual who joins a group gains something in exchange for bracketing his or her difference from the group in some respect, as Craig Calhoun (1994) reminds us in his discussion of an often understated side of the politics of difference. Along what lines this minimal homogenization should be encouraged and by what means, again, are truly political questions. It would be a mistake to blame the emptying out of old public spaces and their relocation into malls on "police indifference" or the "overzealous protectors of individual rights," following Rybczynski. Nevertheless, it is important to remember that the nature of public space is linked to the dilemmas of a democratic public sphere. Public space may easily dissolve in public debates. It is one of the reasons recent genres of public space tend to be privately owned. Instead of publicly defining and enforcing certain rules of conduct, the task is passed on to less ambitious but—within their own limits—more legitimate private actors. A safe public space, however, one that encourages the diversity of social interactions and is "inclusive without being condescending," is an expensive, collective, and *public* enterprise—a political and social endeavor.

Public space is where the consequences of increasing social polarization, growing heterogeneity, and the reinforcement of private enclosures around the home and the car become magnified. If the idea of democratic public space is simply abandoned under the pretext or the real pressures of the fiscal crisis of the state, especially of the postsocialist state, and of the unpopularity of higher-than-local-level solutions, the last links connecting groups whose spatial and social boundaries are becoming less permeable are severed. The city whose texture unravels is not a city anymore in the sense of being a collective enterprise of its citizens.

Conclusion

In his book on central Europe, in which he uses the river Danube as the poetic focus, Italian essayist Claudio Magris (1989) writes about fin de siècle Budapest:

> The enterprising new middle-class, it has been said, wished to build itself a heraldic past. It wished to disguise the feverish metamorphosis and tumultuous industrial expansion of the city—which led to the Seventh District being called Chicago—behind an appearance of frothy lightness, and to flaunt Magyar culture at all cost, and the more so since capitalist development was tearing its traditions up by the root. (262–63)

At the end of the century whose beginning Magris depicts, again a new city was being constructed as rapidly as a century before. Magris's description succinctly captures the tension of the development of Budapest into a metropolis—a process that was characterized because of its speed as the "American pattern of growth" (Bender and Schorske, 1994: 3). In contrast to a hundred years ago, the current transformation of the city is occurring after the conclusion of a high-modernist and eagerly modernizing epoch—that of state socialism—which, along with the city's decaying infrastructure remaining from an earlier era, provides the building blocks with which the current construction is taking place.

The scale of the current urban transformation is, on the other hand, clearly more moderate and less ambitious than that of a hundred years ago. It is not a growth or expansion of "American proportions" but a rearrangement of economic and social layers, a "restructuring." The present metamorphosis of urban life, in spite of the active presence of an "enterprising new middle class," does not share the optimism and lightheartedness that accompanied the transformation of Budapest into a modern metropolis a century ago. There are strong ambitions to rearrange economic and social positions, but perhaps less illusion of a general growth that can benefit all.

Today's process can be seen as "Americanizing" in a different sense: the symbolic structure of the transformation is thoroughly saturated with objects and linguistic formulas borrowed from the mass culture of North American capitalism. The picture emerging from this is a very selective kind of cultural influence under the blanket of globalization. Fast-food restaurants are present, but part of their cultural baggage is lost en route: once in place, they cease functioning as locations marked for lower-class consumption, and their cultural message, just like the food they serve, is digested in a different context. The study of postsocialist east-central European cities clearly presents new challenges to global analysis; the only way we can meet them is through a multidimensional, not only economics- but also culture- and politics-sensitive historical-comparative account of the active localization of global economic, cultural, and political processes.

In Budapest, the collapse of state socialism has brought sea changes in property relations and reorganized the basic principles of the use of urban space. In this book I have identified the privatization of formerly public goods—most important, housing and public space in the urban context—as a major underlying theme of the city's current transformation. The fiscal crisis of the state and of local governments acts in the direction of shifting—along with ownership rights—the burdens of economic, social, and environmental risks to more individual levels, thereby actively, although sometimes perhaps quite unintentionally, supporting a rampant "free market" rhetoric. The restructuring of the economy, with its twin processes of globalization and marketization, influences both privatization and the role of the state. Large-scale property change, the fiscal crisis of the "runaway state," and the restructuring of the economy create a situation that opens up new possibilities in a riskier web of existence as well as the possibility of converting redistributive privileges into market advantages and, eventually, accelerates the accumulation of advantages and disadvantages.

The popularity of the "free market" rhetoric—something that is also responsible for preventing collective responses to the privatization of urban space—is not simply an alien external product of ideological globalization. State socialism individualized and atomized actors quite substantially (Rév, 1987) and served, in this sense, as an engine of radical social modernization. It also created curiosity and desire for commercial variety and destroyed the possibility of collective defense strategies against the market—at least for now.

The analysis of the postsocialist urban transformation gives us a new perspective on the widely discussed otherness of state socialist cities. Even if one can say in retrospect, countering Lefebvre (1991), that state socialism did not really "create its own space," it surely made a large number of small differences in the lives of urban dwellers. State socialism produced under-urbanization, curtailed the urbanity of cities, filtered their marginality, and used urban space, from the perspective of capital, strictly speaking, in a wasteful manner (Szelényi, 1993, 1996). This, however, does not necessarily imply that its use of space was wasteful, and only wasteful, in a more complex social sense. Against the backdrop of the socialist logic of the use of urban space that mixed market efficiency, non-market-type economic considerations, unmediated political power, widely practiced strategies of informal collective and individual resistance, and very elaborate symbolism, the simple force of the market is striking. It has accelerated the rate of change in the city. Yet principles other than the market are still vital in organizing the complexity of urban life, and the consequences of this new constellation are not elementary. Any description of the social world of post-socialist Budapest as a manifestation of the market logic and nothing else is inadequate. The urban transformation of postsocialist Europe is embedded in the path-dependent transformation of the region "that is shaped by cross-nationally (and sub-nationally) variant historical legacies and current conjunctures," says Michael Harloe (1996: 10), who voices a consensual opinion among the institutional economic sociologist contributors to the volume *Cities after Socialism* (Andrusz, Harloe, and Szelényi, 1996). Path dependence, I should emphasize, refers not only to the survival of the legacy of state socialism—as it is often presented as the only factor that introduces variation into an overwhelming market scheme—but to a different type of modernity, a process that is not a simple "survival" in a historically deterministic manner at all. Rather, postsocialist social change should be seen as a dynamic process that mixes elements that are familiar to nonpostsocialist contemporary advanced and less-advanced cities as well—more to some than to others.

The parallel processes of in-group homogenization and the emergence of more-pronounced between-group boundaries give the impression that dimensions of social existence have slid on top of each other and almost overlap in their new constellation. There are fewer and fewer "un-accountable" incidents, socially startling events that bring together and contrast "inconsistent" social and spatial features. Some aspects of city life offer fewer surprises, things and people out of place. Many elements of the new city are not new; what is new about them is the increased rigidity of their spatial boundaries. Formerly suppressed complex differences have unfolded and expanded, becoming literally easier to map, especially at the top and bottom of society. The twin processes of the social and spatial polarization of urban dwellers and homogenization within their groups shape the cityscape. In a similar vein, there is growing tension between the increasing diversity of the city and a vigorous tendency toward social and, to a lesser extent, ethnic unmixing. This tension with a decreasing emphasis on the means of collective consumption has serious implications for the nature of public space. The decline of public space through the establishment of private enclosures in turn reinforces the processes noted above and increases pressures toward the fragmentation of urban space.

The present transformation of the postsocialist city is not adequately described as an unstoppable, inevitable process of privatization and fragmentation. This book should not be read as making that claim. Rather, I have discussed here some common tensions of urban life and have sought to illuminate the relationship between the public of the city and its public spaces, urban life in its private and collective forms. There are, in this contemporary remapping of Budapest, plenty of countervailing forces as well. The fragmentation of urban space is not as excessive as it is in other, "nonadvanced" cities or in the United States. This is the result partly of some particular features of east-central European semiperipheral development and partly of the background work, especially in the sphere of collective consumption and informality, that state socialism had done. Wise use of some elements of the legacy of state socialism—something that can be seen as less alienating if understood as part of European modernity—can be a retaining force against the polarization and fragmentation of the city.

One lesson of arguably the most thorough, large-scale modernization project of our time, state socialism, in east-central Europe is that all-encompassing emancipatory projects of its kind run the risk of becoming exclusive. There is, however, another, much more rarely drawn, lesson in east-central Europe's recent history and current state. This suggests that certain institutional elements of the collective projects included in that vast social transformation have indeed made some, often quite profound, difference. How such elements can be extricated and used in a different (postsocialist) context is a crucial question worthy of further analysis by social scientists—it is also likely the most important political issue in east-central Europe today.

Diversity in urban unity can, and should, be designed. So should the complex infrastructure of surprises, encounters, and small niches of urban freedom. The opportunity for globalizing semiperipheral cities, it seems, lies in the full recognition and creative recycling of the manifold possibilities that their multilayeredness, including the remnants of the "premature" welfare state of state socialism, offers.

That in Budapest the legacy of the past is more than just ruins—of socialism or the many undeniable social ills that came before—and that the loss of that past is more than a simple move to "catch up" with an unambiguous civilizational pattern is a sense that emanates from a large number of Budapest's ordinary and creatively expressive citizens alike. In the image of the new Budapest they also see the fading contours of a slower and less glitzy urban modernity. Theater and literary critic Péter Molnár Gál's 1995 obituary for Iván Mándy, perhaps the most important Hungarian writer of the Budapest urban experience of the past three decades, captures this sentiment eloquently. Molnár Gál's farewell to Mándy, as it were, closes an urban epoch, as he notes the disappearance of the many public and yet so intimate spaces serving and protecting the ordinary people of the city, without any nostalgia for any particular previous period:

> Well, I'll never . . . They shut down his espresso-universe. His small cafés became peep shows. They set up banks in his large cafés. Where could he spread his papers on a table, where could he listen patiently to the waitresses' lot before writing his daily norm, one concerned sentence? . . . No wonder he has moved away.[1]

Appendix

Models of Housing Privatization

The predictor variables included the number of persons in the household, the gender of the head of the household, and his or her educational attainment (measured by whether he or she finished primary school, secondary school, or college or university). Two additional dummy variables were created, one that indicated full-time employment and another for signaling the household head's top managerial position, which was expected to produce an additional effect beyond other socioeconomic indicators. Age was introduced as a quadratic function. Total family income was entered in the next step as an intervening variable.

The quality and value of housing was approximated by five variables. (Although respondents were asked to assess the value of their units, the results could not be used even with corrections. The number of missing cases exceeded that of valid ones and the standard deviation of the mean of Ft 1.83 million was as large as Ft 1.43 million. This should not diminish confidence in the survey: all other variables worked vastly better.) KOMFORT (the variable name is from the Hungarian term used in real estate parlance to describe the level of amenities in a unit) distinguished between units equipped with full amenities and those not so equipped (the latter constituting 15 percent of the sample). Size (FLSPACE) was measured by floor space expressed in square meters.

The overall condition of the unit (INSIDE) and that of the building (OUTSIDE) were ranked on a five-point scale by the interviewer after a series of detailed inquiries concerning the construction conditions and the history of repair work in the building. Respondents were also asked to rank their apartments and buildings on the same scale, but because the answers tended to produce less variation and systematically underestimated

quality—their rankings contradicted information obtained about the con-
stituent parts of quality throughout the questionnaire—the interviewer's
judgments were used.

Table A.1

Variables in the analysis and their univariate distribution (N = 871)

Dichotomous variable	Variable name	Yes (1) %
Respondent's apartment privatized by January 1992	PRIVAT7	18
Respondent's apartment is being privatized but not complete yet	PRIVAT67	23
Respondent has not considered privatization or does not want to	PRIVAT2	38
Gender of the head of the household	FEMALE	35
Top manager	TOPMGR	3
Respondent is employed full-time	FULLTIME	49
Respondent finished elementary school	BASICED	41
Respondent finished high school	HS	27
College degree	COLLEGE	11
University degree	UNIV	13
Housing unit is equipped with full amenities	KOMFORT	85

Variable	Variable name	Mean	Standard deviation	Minimum	Maximum
Respondent's age	AGE	38.94	16.29	3.00	72.00
Age squared	AGE2	1,781.37	1,273.16	9.00	5,184.00
Total monthly family income in forints	FAMINC	22,266.50	15,311.67	3,500.00	264,000.00
Number of persons in household	PERSONS	2.58	1.31	1.00	9.00
Interior condition of unit	INSIDE Q	3.25	.88	1	5
Very bad (1)					
Bad (2)					
Medium (3)					
Good (4)					
Very good (5)					
Condition of building	OUTSIDE Q	2.72	.88	1	5
Floor space in square meters	FLSPACE	54.69	22.27	10	180
Location: mean apartment price by district (thousands of forints per square meter)		32.57	6.22	25	51

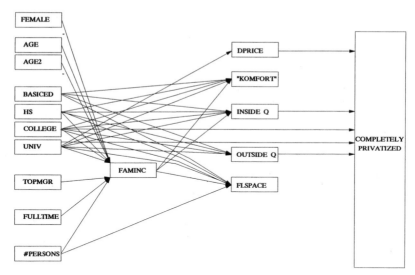

Figure A.1a. Path model of log likelihood of housing privatization in Budapest between 1990 and 1992. Significant paths ($p < .05$). Unit of analysis: flats. Dependent variable: privatization complete by 1992.

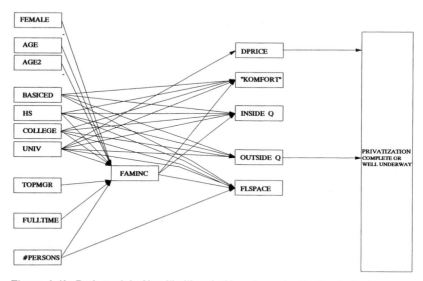

Figure A.1b. Path model of log likelihood of housing privatization in Budapest between 1990 and 1992. Significant paths ($p < .05$). Unit of analysis: flats. Dependent variable: privatization complete or approved.

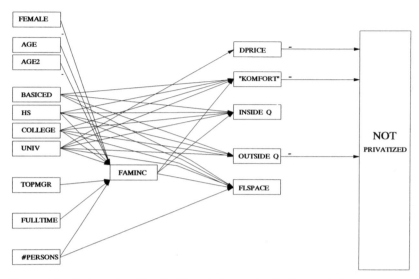

Figure A.1c. Path model of log likelihood of nonprivatization in Budapest
between 1990 and 1992. Significant paths ($p < .05$). Unit of analysis: flats.
Dependent variable: no desire or ability to privatize.

Notes

1. Posted

1. There reigns daunting terminological chaos regarding the region in which my subject matter is located. Cutting through thickets of heavily ideological—Orientalist and counter-Orientalist—discourses of identity politics, I will refer to *east-central Europe*, with a lowercase adjective. This denotes the historical area of the eastern half of what used to be the Habsburg lands, with the westernmost reaches of the former Ottoman Empire and the area of historical contention between the great powers of Germany and Russia. Far from a homogenizing concept, it is intended as mere, admittedly imprecise, shorthand for the following list of countries: Poland, Czechoslovakia, Hungary, Yugoslavia, Romania, and Bulgaria for the state socialist period and their successor states after the collapse.

2. About this, see also Friesen (1997) and Birmingham (1998).

3. In 1989, revenues of the European socialist states averaged about 43 percent of the GDP, or about 5 percent higher than in the OECD countries (Campbell, 1996).

4. For details and references, see chapter 2.

5. *The Compact Edition of the Oxford English Dictionary* (Oxford: Oxford University Press, 1971), 859.

6. Ibid.

2. Constructing Difference

1. Along the lines of Miliutin's (1974) constructivist vision of the socialist city, the little morphological dissimilarity that was to be found between socialist and capitalist cities was largely assumed to be a consequence of the blueprints drafted by socialist planners and enforced by the all-powerful socialist states.

2. Had that been the case, the habit of desperately trying to "read between the lines" of party documents, public statements, policy analyses, and literature by the populace and political actors themselves would not have gained such widespread importance.

3. In a discussion of the theoretical puzzle socialist cities pose to urban studies,

Szelényi (1993) describes the ecological perspective without any contemporary example; he refers only to the classics of the tradition.

4. Even if this sort of argumentation is used to make a daring political statement against Communist rule, the point is always made: communism is not indigenous but a bad influence coming from the east of "us." The famous speech by then young dissident politician Viktor Orbán—currently prime minister of Hungary—delivered on the occasion of the reburial of Imre Nagy in 1989 is a prime example of this rhetoric; communism figured as "Asiatic barbarism."

5. I am grateful to Michael Kennedy for pointing this out.

6. More precisely, underurbanization is a European state socialist phenomenon. Non-European socialist countries have exhibited either significantly lower underurbanization or urban development defined more accurately as deurbanization (Forbes and Thrift, 1987).

7. I thank Jiří Musil for pointing out some of these variations.

8. *Less urban* here refers to less diversity, less density in the inner city, and less marginality, following largely Wirth's model of urbanism (Szelényi, 1993).

9. In Budapest, the few years of political freeze after the extinguished revolution of 1956 represent a noticeable exception to this rule. In other cities, it varied slightly.

10. There is also evidence that is directly contrary to the above. Hungarian writer Péter Lengyel (1993) recalls that Ernest Hemingway, for instance, insisted on naming Budapest—along with Paris and Havana—as one of the three most exciting cities he had visited: "Paris—where, as we know, he had lived, had been happy, in love and a writer—Havana—where, as we know, he had been happy . . . etc.—and Budapest which he had only visited—well, I said, an objective person who talks facts" (186).

11. In the case of Hungary, the linguistic distance of Magyar from the Indo-European group—which makes it virtually inaccessible to "Western" visitors—should also be taken into account in any evaluation of such disparaging judgments.

12. Uniformity of housing construction can create remarkable class homogeneity if coupled with a very differentiated price and rent system. Planning social homogeneity and strict segregation on the level of the whole settlement can be very successful in rapidly built new communities, a good example of which is Irvine, California, where most housing was constructed in a period of ten to fifteen years, designed and built by the same company, with very little variation in visual experience, use value, and rent level.

13. See Weber (1978) on the distinction between *class* and *status (estate)*. Although, as Weber says, "Estate situation [can] express itself through connubium and commensality" (305), it does not contradict the mingling of different social groups otherwise—that is, residentially.

14. The origins of this type of architecture can be traced back to Vienna almost a century earlier *(Wohnhaus),* and such buildings were to be found in other central European cities of the time, but nowhere did they reach the sort of popularity they did in Budapest (Hanák, 1984; Schorske, 1981).

15. The regulatory function of rents was rather minimal, and the redistributive state did not function as a substitute for the market in this regard.

16. The importance of this three-dimensional comparative field may vary depending on the research problem and the applied methods. Analyses of urban pri-

macy, for example, may arrive at more consensual statements than studies of spatial segregation; they may need to line up an ideologically less charged theoretical apparatus and lesser historical analyses, and their conclusions may be interpreted more easily on a fairly general level. So, by simply measuring urban primacy and comparing it to other regions in the world-system, one may conclude that one of the characteristics of state socialist urbanization relative to other noncore regions is its significantly lower level. Even then, the conclusion needs to be preceded by a specifically historical explanation of Hungary's exceptional degree of urban primacy. Hungary's current urban primacy is, to some extent, an artifact of the peace treaties signed after World War I, which cut off two-thirds of the country's territory, including many relatively important medium-sized cities on the peripheries along with the nonradial transportation connections among them.

3. "He That Hath to Him Shall Be Given"

1. Market transition theory has grown into a debate, and the institutionalization of the concept is signified by the fact that a 1995 conference was organized under that title ("The Market Transition Debate," held at the Center for Social Theory and Comparative History at the University of California, Los Angeles).

2. Róna-Tas (1994) does this by relying on institutionalist economist Douglass C. North (1993). This state-centered institutionalist understanding is one possible way of defining the starting point of the transition. No doubt, the state usually assumes immediate responsibility for institutional-legal changes, but there are economic or political reasons that the state may act so, such as the expansion of the second economy, the loosening of party control, political movements, or even the severe indebtedness of the state to international finance.

3. Peter Marcuse (1996) presents a good social analysis of the complexity of property rights concerning land and housing in state socialist countries that should prevent us from treating privatization as a mere transfer of ownership from the state to individuals.

4. In some cases restrictions applied to buildings for which the ownership was unclear; that is, they were legitimately claimed by their prenationalization owners as part the restitution process. In other cases, the local governments only used their newly achieved freedom not to sell out the bases of their public housing policy.

5. The districts of Budapest are denoted by Roman numerals. For a contour map of the city showing the current district boundaries, see Figure 4.4.

6. A distinctive feature of state socialist housing was the extent of the quasi–property rights tenants enjoyed. Children could legally inherit tenancies, which they could exchange for other public units or "sell" upon leaving the public sector through either the legal or the "gray" market, depending on the buyer and the circumstances.

7. Some tenants were not allowed to purchase their homes, mostly because some local governments put a halt to privatization, for lack of a better strategy, while they awaited new legal regulations.

8. By 1993, the exchange rate was different.

9. Beginning in 1990, Hungary's first postsocialist government launched a major program providing compensation for property confiscated by the early socialist state more than four decades before. Its purpose was partly political appeasement

of the victims of the socialist state's economic violence and partly the creation of new group of small property owners in the great scheme of the transition from state socialism (for an extensive overview of such complex procedures, see Böröcz, 1993). Compensation claims were filed by the millions. They were individually assessed, and vouchers were issued to claimants or their surviving families in amounts roughly proportionate to, but never even approximating the monetary value of, the original losses. The vouchers could be used, among other things, as cash substitutes in acquiring housing property in state-related privatization, with the restriction that only the claimant's own subsidized rental unit could be purchased (a general restriction in housing privatization). Soon the market value of the vouchers dropped significantly (by 1994, to approximately 60 percent of the nominal value), but the district governments were required by law to accept them at a rate indexed for inflation (by 1994, approximately 140 percent of the nominal value) at the point of payment in the process of housing privatization. Local governments could in turn participate in complex trading with compensation vouchers (a very sluggish market indeed) or redeem the vouchers' countervalue at a deeply discounted level from the central government.

10. 57/1994. (XI.17.) *Magyar Közlöny,* 1994/113.

11. This happens partly under pressure from potential buyers, but, more important, especially in the initial stage, it is the legacy of the state socialist simulation of market price. Consumers are not used to the entirely monetary expression of differences and can hardly conceive of great variation in prices.

12. I calculated the rate of privatization—the rate of exit from the public sphere—by dividing the number of privatized apartments in the given year by the number of units constituting the complete public housing sector at the beginning of the year. It should be noted that the Buda outskirts area of District XXII, with its speedy privatization, may not be a very typical example, for it has had by far the lowest proportion of state ownership in housing.

13. The latter is calculated on the basis of the entire housing sector, including private housing.

14. This is reflected in the Pearson's correlation rates, which drop precipitously from an initial $r = .7996$ in 1990 through $r = .6830$ in 1991 to a mere $r = .2917$ in 1992. These Pearson's correlations were computed for 22 data points (districts) for each year (so that d.f. = 20).

15. Note that these were not the areas with the highest average rent in 1991 (KSH, 1992).

16. See the appendix to this volume for the list of variables and their univariate distribution.

17. The survey did not contain other variables that could inform us completely about the reasons for the lack of property change. Nevertheless, some evidence suggests that it was not related to administrative constraints; that is, people did not elect to privatize because the local government had decided not to sell the building where their apartment was located or because the number of potential buyers did not reach half of the households in the building. Only 20 percent of the sample claimed to be aware of any administrative obstacle to privatizing their units, but probably this is not the group constituting the most passive category—those who had not even taken a mental step toward privatization—because one has to bring the issue up and usually start the procedure in order to learn about administrative restrictions.

Therefore, it seemed reasonable to assume that negative decisions were driven by either miserable housing conditions or the financial vulnerability of the family, or both.

18. I compiled these figures from data presented in the 1993 issues of the biweekly *Ingatlanpiac* (Real estate market).

19. This path may suggest that state allocation of housing did in fact fulfill some of its social policy aim of benefiting large families. However, I cannot substantiate this claim because family size may have changed since the time of the original allocation of the apartment. Furthermore, tenants may have used nonstate channels to exchange their initial units for others. Having controlled for how the present apartment was obtained, my further analysis showed that direct state allocation—in the strict sense—did favor large families; however, in the entire public sector, larger families lived in more spacious units despite state involvement.

20. It would be misleading, however, to see a simple conversion of political capital into "housing capital" or rent and interpret it as derivative of a general conversion of power that suggests the old cadres take advantage of their formerly formal—now mostly informal—position in acquiring state property (Staniszkis, 1991). I do not have data to show whether former cadres benefited from housing privatization, and I think that, as we move away from the collapse of the institutional structures that gave power to the old-regime bureaucracy, time is overruling the relevance of that question. Besides, there have always been finer mediations in the process, such as formal and informal social network ties shown to be meaningful predictors of income (Böröcz and Southworth, 1998) *as well as housing inequalities* (Bodnár and Böröcz, 1998). State socialist allocation of housing certainly favored the intellectuals as a whole (Szelényi, 1983; Szelényi and Konrád, 1969), both in the formal and the informal dimensions of educational "capital" (Böröcz and Southworth, 1996). If cadre status carried any non-cultural-capital- and non-social-network-related advantage, by the time of the housing privatization it had vanished or was overtaken by other factors. In their examination of the transformation with respect to not housing-related but managerial status-related inequalities, Böröcz and Róna-Tas (1996) found that former cadre status carries no additional advantage over and above simple former membership in the Communist Party.

4. Inner City Doubly Renewed

1. Luděk Sýkora (1994) poses similar questions based on the experience of Prague. His answer is that Prague is becoming a "standard western city" shaped by the forces of global capitalism, and the postsocialist transition is only a radicalized version of general restructuring. Although I have no quarrel with that assessment, I abstain from assuming the existence of a single path for modernity. On that metatheoretical basis, I seek to emphasize variation *as well as* uniformity.

2. Hamnett (1991) provides a very good analysis of the main lines of the gentrification debate and the popularity of gentrification research.

3. Even if one can identify all the details of the process, translating the English name of the phenomenon "gentrification" into Hungarian as *dzsentrifikáció* is more severe a mistake than catches the ear of a linguist who is a devoted advocate of vernacularization. Although the term *gentry* historically refers to the middle segment of the nobility, it connotes the déclassé elements of the nobility, who, ridden of their base of former seigneurial existence (in which they often took an active role by

compulsively playing cards or betting on horses and losing), parasitically attached themselves to state offices that their class background predisposed them to take. The central European concept of the *dzsentri* is clearly not equipped to signify the entry of upwardly mobile professionals. The resolution of this naming awkwardness belongs really to local analysts, and it should not prevent one from situating Budapest in the gentrification debate.

4. Population density of dwellings was also high in the outer industrial districts, such as X and XIII. District XIII may seem partially contradictory to the argument, but administrative boundaries being different at the time, they did not include the wealthy neighborhood of New Leopoldtown, now part of the district.

5. For a similar analysis concerning Prague, see Musil (1987).

6. Unless otherwise noted, all translations are my own.

7. The average rent in Budapest was also about 5–6 percent of family income in 1981 (KSH, 1982).

8. All quotations from tenants and from local government officials are taken from interviews I conducted with them in October 1993, unless otherwise noted.

9. In order to draw a parallel between housing privatization in Budapest and tenure conversion in London, I will highlight some of the features of housing privatization again that I address explicitly in chapter 3.

10. The play of urban powers around centralization and decentralization produced such paradoxical situations as the mayor of Budapest's declaring homelessness a district-level problem. This proposition, also inspired by the spirit of decentralization, was flatly rejected by the local governments, which cited the interests of their constituencies in asserting that there would be no homeless shelters in their districts.

11. Business manager of the local government, interview, October 1993.

12. The building was completed by the mid-1990s.

13. The capital city's receiving a disproportionately great share of foreign investment is not unique to Hungary, nor is it very extreme in Hungary's case: among other capitals, Lisbon received 85 percent of all foreign investment to Portugal in 1992 (Barta, 1994: 15).

14. Aside from the ideologically motivated bias of the socialist regime toward the mining sector, its size may account for its still outstandingly high wages: only 0.2 percent of the labor force of Budapest is employed in mining.

15. Interview, summer 1993.

16. The East-West Center is a joint venture; more than half of it is owned by Skanska, a Swedish construction company of European significance.

17. *Ingatlanpiac,* August 24, 1995, 3.

18. For example, it is quite unlikely that Hungarian elites would use deutsche marks in the way described anymore: the forint has been made convertible through the government's successful efforts to keep the exchange rate extremely low, making the use of forints more advantageous for those who have access to business opportunities abroad. The reference to "the vulgate" calls to mind the fellow Romance language Romanian, which can be seen as relating to French (historically the preferred Western language of the educated, wealthy elites in Romania) as a "vulgate" to a sophisticated, literary language—a relationship that is entirely absent between Magyar and English.

19. The visitor's surprise is only greater upon seeing its Moscow equivalent, the lifestyle of the "new Russians."

20. Duke and Grime's (1997) research supports these observations for other postsocialist cities as well.

21. *Uniform money* was the term used to describe a special allowance—occupying a position between monetary payment and benefit in kind—paid to workers in jobs that required uniforms. This category, which included teachers, was quite large.

22. The similarity to the "functional aesthetics" of Fordism (Aglietta, 1987) is not accidental.

5. Assembling the Square

1. *Magyar Narancs,* December 1, 1994.

2. A monograph on the city written at the time the regime changed still depicts Moscow Square in a matter-of-fact way, mentioning its "many uses": its transportation function, its weekday users going to work, and its crowds on their way to the hills on weekends (Enyedi and Szirmai, 1992). The emotional overtones that were to accompany later references to the square had not yet appeared.

3. Although citizens were critical of the widening inequalities that were a consequence of increasing market opportunities (see, among others, Hann, 1990), and the fact that uneducated vegetable vendors were making several times more than engineers hurt people's sense of propriety, many attributed these problems to the incompleteness of market conditions rather than to market exchange per se.

4. Stalin's name crossed the Danube in 1946 and, for seven years, settled downtown on the former Elizabeth Square. For years this square was considered the possible locus of a real socialist square modeled after Moscow's Red Square. The grand plan did not materialize: the name giver's direct political significance shrank, together with available resources. In 1953, in a cautious return to the classics, the square became Engels Square; after the collapse, the name Elizabeth was reinstated.

5. Except where otherwise indicated, the following description is based on fieldwork data obtained through participant observation. I carried out the bulk of the research in the summer of 1995, but I revisited the site in 1996 and 1997 and have adjusted some of the descriptions accordingly. Thus, although the exact physical time of the snapshot is 1995, my description operates in an extended time frame, in "postsocialist" time.

6. Note the distinction between the terms *Magyar,* which refers to ethnicity, and *Hungarians,* which denotes citizenship.

7. *Füstösképű* in Hungarian.

8. I have elected to use the term *Roma* rather than *Gypsy,* as some consider it less derogatory.

9. The Vietnamese element is made up of people who arrived as students and remained after their higher education was completed. When they graduated, the obligation to repay the cost of their education to the Vietnamese state if they refused to return to Vietnam pushed them toward entrepreneurial efforts. An apocryphal story tells of a young polytechnic student who supported himself so successfully selling cigarettes that he established his own "business," becoming his own supplier. With these business profits, he bought a year for himself at Harvard Business School.

10. The technology of the hot dog—an American invention—has its local version in the Hungarian fast-food cuisine. Hot dogs have never been available in their original American form. Hot dog technology came to Hungary from France, where a roasted frankfurter is stuffed into a piece of fresh baguette with some Dijon mustard. The bread is pulled over a heated aluminum stick to create a hole inside for the sausage. The French equipment was adjusted to suit local Hungarian ways and ingredients. The frankfurter was boiled, the mustard was minimized, and the baguette was replaced by half of a giant, crescent-shaped salt stick, a typical central European bread.

11. In a similar vein, perhaps the most efficient method of acquiring personal donations is that of African immigrants sitting in the streets of German cities with purses and signs saying, "For going back home."

12. In the discussion that follows, names and signs that appear in English in the Hungarian context are enclosed in quotation marks.

13. The building has recently received another face-lift. The billboard has been removed, red lanterns have been placed in all the windows, and the Chinese restaurant that has replaced the pub is frequented by quite another type of clientele: Chinese families, local couples, and mid-echelon office workers from the international corporate community.

14. Many people in staunchly cosmopolitan and well-read Budapest also wonder why Ernest Hemingway came to be associated with the most popular candy shops in the city.

15. The room is open from 9:00 A.M. to 12:00 A.M., except on Sundays, when the needy and their caregivers are supposed to be in church.

16. The need for pet food has been created entirely by foreign companies' efficient advertising. From one day to the next, grocery stores, so pressed for space that they had to pile up toilet paper in their windows, installed separate shelves designed and provided by companies producing pet food.

17. Chris Hann (1995) presents stories that demonstrate citizens' mixed sentiments concerning privatization and free markets, and their nostalgia for the security of the old regime.

18. District II starts at Moscow Square and includes Rose Hill, a few older inner-Buda suburbs, and the most rapidly growing new suburbs on the outskirts.

19. It is little surprise, then, that more extensive informal social network ties produced advantages in both incomes and the quality of housing (see Bodnár and Böröcz, 1998; Böröcz and Southworth, 1998).

20. Sik (1995) presents data for 1992 and 1993 that reveal a monotonic decrease in the proportion of unregistered work from the lowest income decile—in which it is around 50 percent—to the highest decile. Even in the highest decile, however, it is still 30 percent. Using a different methodology, Sik also offers estimates that conclude with significantly lower numbers and a reversed relationship by income, suggesting that in fact the proportion of unregistered work correlates positively with income. Regardless of the discrepancies in the estimates, the point can still safely be made that unregistered activities are not limited to the poor.

21. The survey included three groups of Budapest citizens: those from areas surrounding Moscow Square, those who live further away on the outskirts but travel through the square, and a general control group from the rest of the city (MATERV, 1991).

22. State socialist economies also had guest worker arrangements, but these individuals were few and hardly visible (e.g., Hungarian machine tool operators working in East Germany, Cuban women textile workers in Budapest, or the Polish construction workers who used to work only in the basement of Budapest's Karl Marx University); they worked and lived together, and mixing with the locals was not encouraged.

23. Needless to say, one should avoid positing markets and redistributive systems with impermeable boundaries and their subordinate elements as incomparably different from each other. Calculative behavior, even if pertaining to a smaller sphere of things, was a defining characteristic of the second economy of state socialism. The differences between market and Market are subtle.

24. He does this in a way that suggests the analytic subtext of state socialism.

25. The political importance of this policy can be seen in the fact that, partly due to the second economy, there was no food shortage in Hungary. In fact, Hungary enjoyed a food surplus, making the food industry and agriculture a net contributor to the gross national product—a rare occurrence in today's world market of highly subsidized agribusiness and food production regimes. By contrast, in Poland, a worse-than-usual shortage of food was one reason for the 1980 strikes—which led to the emergence of the Solidarity movement.

26. Members of the police, military, and judiciary were excluded from these activities, along with those employed in health care, child care, most educational and legal services, wholesale trade, and advertising (Róna-Tas, 1997). Membership was based on work participation—investment did not make one a partner.

27. Such informal networking is the main terrain of wide-ranging reciprocity that is usually forgotten in the dualism of "mirrored comparisons."

28. I refer to this spirit of security as petit bourgeois not necessarily in a derogatory sense but mostly because of its scale. Striving for security is not unknown for higher groups of the bourgeoisie, but it may be accompanied by more leverage and playfulness.

29. Elemér Hankiss's (1990) discussion of the "first" and the "second society" captures a similar tension. After registering initial surprise that "the 'second society' had failed to develop into an autonomous sphere of social existence, an alternative society governed by organizational principles different from those of the 'first society,'" Hankiss notes that they were intertwined in a parasitic way, implying the radicalness of their separation (107).

30. The typical model of the runaway state in Szilágyi's (1997: 13) analysis is the current, post-Soviet Russian state, which has had, indeed, many external burdens to drop: Afghanistan, Cuba, Ethiopia, the "Eastern Bloc," the world's communist parties, the non-Russian former Soviet republics, the costs of the arms race, and so on.

31. Beck's (1992) notion of "risk society" as a successor to "industrial society" is inspiring in a general metaphorical sense. Much of Beck's concrete discussion of risk society focuses on global ecological hazards—a level different from the kind of risk exposure and risk taking my material discloses. He coined the phrase but has not fully exploited it, thus an unmarked reference to his notion of risk may be misleading. Beck's ultimately "supra-national, non-class-specific, global" risk production incorporates at places a rather more class-specific aspect of risk, for example, in the

description of the privatization of physical and mental health risks of work that accompany spatial flexibilization (143).

32. Multicolored has become black and white, writes Sik (1994) on the experience of the transformation of a "first"/"second" economy into a "formal" "informal" one. He is right in emphasizing the polarization of possibilities. The metaphor of black and white captures only part of the truth, however. The process does not entail any loss of complexity; polarization is taking place along with wild diversification.

33. The really wealthy live, of course, in the isolation of their villas and cars and rarely interact with the population of Moscow Square. Theirs is almost a nonpresence insofar as public space is concerned, more so now than ever before. Their attention and wallets are caught elsewhere, in the semipublic spaces of malls and clubs of all kinds.

34. *Magyar Hírlap,* March 19, 1998, 15.

6. Globalizing Art and Consumption

An earlier version of this chapter was published in *Proceedings of an International Symposium: City Space + Globalization,* College of Architecture and Urban Planning, University of Michigan, 1998. Pp. 183–93. Edited by Hemalata C. Dandekar.

1. The Hungarian acronym FŐMO stands for Fővárosi Mozgóképüzemi Vállalat (Capital City Motion Picture Management Company).

2. All quotations from people affiliated with the Art Movie Network and Budapest Film and from various theater owners are taken from interviews I conducted with them in December 1996 and January 1997.

3. The institution referred to here as the Art Movie Network has a name that is partly in English, partly in Hungarian: Art Mozi Hálózat. *Art* is not a Hungarian word, but has become part of the urban vocabulary as a borrowing from English. Noteworthy is its use in the name in spite of an available Hungarian equivalent, *művészmozi*—a word that was used during late state socialism to denote movie theaters featuring films aimed at audiences with more demanding tastes.

4. See Böröcz (1993), Sik (1994), Böröcz and Róna-Tas (1995), Stark (1996), and Eyal, Szelényi, and Townsley (1997).

5. Corvin is a highly marked location in Hungarian culture, especially political culture. The area immediately surrounding the theater was one of the three main hubs of armed, predominantly blue-collar resistance to the Soviet invasion in 1956. (Figure 6.8 shows the corner with the 1956 memorial, which attracts a public separate from the moviegoers.) The choice of the Corvin cinema as the flagship of Budapest Film's network thus invokes the heroic image of national resistance and uses a political notion—a decisive break with the past (as recognition of the heritage of 1956 was one of the socialist regime's taboos)—to fix the newly redesigned cinema in the minds of the Budapest public. As a symbolic reinforcement of this imagery, László Rajk Jr.—the son of László Rajk, the most prominent victim of the Stalinist mock trials, and himself a well-known member of the democratic opposition to Hungary's late-socialist regime—was commissioned to design the building's new interior.

6. Since the new scheme went into effect, two art theaters and two small commercial theaters have closed. In March 2000, "friends of the cinema" demonstrated in defense of small movie theaters. *Magyar Nemzet Online,* March 24, 2000.

7. The stronger competitor, located in an upscale mall that is closer to both the inner city and the wealthiest suburbs, is a joint venture of InterCom and the Australian Village Roadshow International, owned by Hollywood producer Andy Vajna.

8. *Ingatlanpiac,* August 24, 1995, 13.

9. *Ingatlanpiac,* June 5, 1997.

10. *Ingatlanpiac,* August 24, 1995.

11. *Világgazdaság,* April 29, 1997.

12. Quoted in *Népszabadság,* October 21, 1996.

13. *Ingatlanpiac,* June 5, 1997.

14. *Népszabadság,* February 23, 1998, 1, 8.

15. *Népszabadság,* August 28, 1998.

16. I define localization as the creation of local identity, the harmonization of physical and moral proximity in a context in which responsibility becomes even more elusive.

7. Urban Texture Unraveling

1. *Ingatlanpiac,* February 10, 1994, 15.

2. *Ingatlanpiac,* July 21, 1992, 5.

3. Quoted in *Ingatlanpiac,* September 8, 1994, 7.

4. *Népszabadság,* July 1, 1996.

5. *Népszabadság,* January 24, 1995.

6. *Népszabadság,* January 25, 1995.

7. The bicycle is more individualistic than the car. It is, however, a much more open form, making the bicycle rider's relationship to the other users of space more humble.

8. In her classic analysis of American cities, Jane Jacobs (1961) discusses the importance of pavements and their environments for urbanity and social control.

9. *Ingatlanpiac,* July 23, 1992, 3.

10. The strict closure of the international hotels has been mediated by the ice cream parlor of Hotel Forum, which opens to the walking strip on the Danube embankment, and, in the case of the Inter-Continental, by the curious habit of local foreign-language learners who would go to the hotel without being harassed to buy Western newspapers and magazines–a rather expensive hobby indeed—which they would then cherish and read from cover to cover until the next payday.

11. *Népszabadság,* December 29, 1995.

12. Ibid. Considering a mean family size of three persons, this amounts to roughly one-third of the population in the city of two million inhabitants. Families had been accumulating debt for a long time–a practice clearly understandable given the lack of punitive measures for nonpayment under the state socialist regime. Even after the regime change, feeble attempts by the service providers—now more profit oriented than before—to shut off services broke down on local solidarity. Although units received separate utility bills, energy could not be shut off in individual apartments in most prefab housing estates; only entire blocks could be shut off. Thus neighbors made sure that at least one family in each block of flats paid the bill on time each month in order to avoid the disruption of services.

13. *Ingatlanpiac,* July 21, 1992.

14. A real estate agent I interviewed in January 1995 put it this way: "Nowadays

places like Nagykovácsi or Szentendre [neighboring towns] have their own intelligence coefficients."

15. In 1993, 68 percent of the unemployed were manual laborers, whereas their proportion within the entire labor force was only 51 percent (KSH, 1994a).

16. For more on this topic, see a whole range of work by Richard Sennett (e.g., 1970, 1974, 1990).

17. On recent struggles for the appropriation of Tompkins Square Park, the complicated symbolism of which often results in physical spatial struggles, see Smith (1992) and Harvey (1992).

18. All the usual restrictions of Greek politics apply: foreigners, slaves, women, and minors were excluded from the "public" space and the politics of the agora. Their exclusion did not include the commercial section of the agora.

19. An example of this is found in Tom Wolfe's celebrated novel *The Bonfire of the Vanities* (1987). The book's plot is propelled by an unexpected and unwanted encounter between a white Wall Street financier and two black youths on an abandoned street in the Bronx at night, the result of which is an accident whereby one of the young men is hit by the financier's car and later dies. Before the accident, no one attacks the passengers of the car—there is no clash between them and the two men. The reader does not know, nor does the financier, what the black youths may have been up to. They themselves probably had not quite made up their minds. The hurried escape that causes a death is the result of fear prompted by assumptions formed on the basis of limited life-world experiences.

Conclusion

1. Mondhatom. Becsukták eszpresszó-univerzumát. Peep-show lett kiskávézóiból. Bankokat gründoltak nagykávézóiban. Hol rakhatná ki az asztalra papírjait, hol hallgathatná türelemmel a pincérlányok sorsát addig is, amíg le nem írja napi penzumát, egyetlen aggályos mondatot? . . . Csoda, hogy elköltözött?"

Works Cited

Abu-Lughod, Janet. 1965. "A Tale of Two Cities: The Origins of Modern Cairo." *Comparative Studies in Society and History* 7: 429–57.

Adler, Moshe. 1996. "In City Services, Privatize and Beware." *New York Times*, April 7, F9.

Aglietta, Michel. 1987. *A Theory of Capitalist Regulation: The US Experience*. London: Verso.

Andrusz, Gregory, Michael Harloe, and Iván Szelényi, eds. 1996. *Cities after Socialism: Urban and Regional Change and Conflict in Post-Socialist Societies*. Oxford: Blackwell.

Appadurai, Arjun. 1990. "Disjuncture and Difference in the Global Cultural Economy." *Theory, Culture & Society* 7: 295–310.

———. 1996. *Modernity at Large: Cultural Dimensions of Globalization*. Minneapolis: University of Minnesota Press.

Balás, Fruzsina, and József Hegedűs. 1990. "Budapest VII. ker. 15-ös tömb rehabilitációjának tapasztalatai a lakossági vélemények tükrében." Unpublished research report, Városkutatás Kft., Budapest.

Banerjee, Tridib. 1993. "Transitional Urbanism Reconsidered: Post-Colonial Development of Calcutta and Shanghai." In Greg Guldin and Aidan Southall (eds.), *Urban Anthropology in China*. Leiden, Netherlands: E. J. Brill.

Barta, Györgyi. 1994. "The Change of Budapest's Role in Industrial (Economic) Control." Paper presented at the international conference "Villes, entreprise et société à la veille du XXIe siècle," Lille, France.

Bartók, Miklós, János Pomsár, and Judit Cs. Falk. 1993. "Az erzsébetvárosi rehabilitációról a Madách sétány kapcsán. Tervező: Pomsár János." *Magyar Építőművészet* 2/3: 24–25.

Beck, Ulrich. 1992. *Risk Society: Towards a New Modernity*. Trans. Mark Ritter. London: Sage.

Beilharz, Peter. 1994. *Postmodern Socialism: Romanticism, City and State*. Carlton, Victoria: Melbourne University Press.

Bender, Thomas, and Carl E. Schorske, eds. 1994. *Budapest and New York: Studies in Metropolitan Transformation, 1810–1930*. New York: Russell Sage.

Benhabib, Seyla. 1996. *The Reluctant Modernism of Hannah Arendt*. Thousand Oaks, Calif.: Sage.

Benjamin, Walter. 1986 [1927]. "Moscow." Pp. 97–130 in Walter Benjamin, *Reflections*. Ed. Peter Demetz. New York: Schocken.

Berend, Iván T. 1971. "Fordulópont és ellentmondások az urbanizációban." *Valóság* 12: 10–18.

Berend, Iván T., and Ránki, György. 1974. *Economic Development in East-Central Europe in the 19th and 20th Centuries*. New York: Columbia University Press.

Beynon, E. D. 1943. "Budapest: An Ecological Study." *Geographical Review* 3: 255–75.

Birmingham, Elizabeth. 1998. "Reframing the Ruins: Pruitt-Igoe, Structural Racism, and African American Rhetoric as a Space for Cultural Critique." *Positionen* 2 (June). (Available on-line at http://www.theo.tu-cottbus.de/Wolke/X-positionen/Birmingham/birmingham.html)

Blackmar, Elizabeth, and Roy Rosenzweig. 1992. *The Park and the People: A History of Central Park*. Ithaca, N.Y.: Cornell University Press.

Bodnár, Judit, and József Böröcz. 1998. "Housing Advantages for the Better-Connected? Institutional Segmentation, Settlement Type and Social Network Effects in Late State-Socialist Housing Inequalities." *Social Forces* 76, no. 4: 1275–1304.

Böröcz, József. 1992. "Dual Dependency and the Informalization of External Linkages: The Case of Hungary." *Research in Social Movements, Conflicts and Change* 14: 189–209.

———. 1993. "Simulating the Great Transformation: Property Change Under Prolonged Informality in Hungary." *Archives européennes de sociologie/Europäisches Archiv für Soziologie/European Journal of Sociology* 34: 81–107.

———. 1996. *Leisure Migration: A Sociological Study on Tourism*. Oxford: Pergamon.

———. 1997. "Stand Reconstructed: Contingent Closure and Institutional Change." *Sociological Theory* 15, no. 3: 215–48.

———. 1999. "From Comprador State to Auctioneer State: Property Change, Realignment and Peripheralization in Post-State-Socialist Central Europe." Pp. 193–209 in David A. Smith, Dorothy Solinger, and Steven Topik (eds.), *States and Sovereignty in the Global Economy*. New York: Routledge.

Böröcz, József, and Ákos Róna-Tas. 1995. "Small Leap Forward: Emergence of New Economic Elites." *Theory and Society* 24: 751–81.

———. 1996. "Musical Chairs: Economic Elite Selection under Managerial Hegemony in Four Post-State-Socialist Societies." Paper presented at the annual meeting of the European Studies Association, March 14–16, Chicago.

Böröcz, József, and Caleb Southworth. 1996. "Decomposing the Intellectuals' Class Power: Conversion of Cultural Capital to Income, Hungary, 1986." *Social Forces* 74, no. 3: 797–821.

———. 1998. "'Who You Know . . .': Earnings Effects of Formal Informal Social Network Resources under Late State Socialism, Hungary, 1986–87." *Journal of Socio-economics* 27, no. 3: 401–25.

Bourdieu, Pierre. 1984 [1979]. *Distinction: A Social Critique of the Judgement of Taste*. Trans. Richard Nice. Cambridge: Harvard University Press.

Braun, Róbert, Klára Czike, and Erika Lencsés. 1993. "Madách sétány: Ellent-mondások, dilemmák." *Kritika* 8: 22–24.

Calhoun, Craig, ed. 1992. *Habermas and the Public Sphere.* Cambridge: MIT Press.

———. 1994. *Social Theory and the Politics of Identity.* Oxford: Blackwell.

Campbell, John. 1996. "An Institutional Analysis of Fiscal Reform in Postcommunist Europe." *Theory and Society* 25: 45–84.

Carpenter, Juliet, and Loretta Lees. 1995. "Gentrification in New York, London and Paris: An International Comparison." *International Journal of Urban and Regional Studies* 19, no. 2: 286–303.

Carpignano, Paolo, Robin Andersen, Stanley Aronowitz, and William DiFazio. 1993. "Chatter in the Age of Electronic Reproduction: Talk Television and the Public Mind." Pp. 93–120 in Bruce Robbins (ed.), *The Phantom Public Sphere.* Minne-apolis: University of Minnesota Press.

Castells, Manuel. 1976. "Theory and Ideology in Urban Sociology." Pp. 60–84 in C. G. Pickvance (ed.), *Urban Sociology: Critical Essays.* London: Tavistock.

———. 1978 [1972]. *City, Class and Power.* London: Macmillan.

———. 1979 [1972]. *The Urban Question.* Cambridge: MIT Press.

Chase-Dunn, Christopher. 1981. "Interstate System and Capitalist World-Economy: One Logic or Two?" In W. Ladd Hollist and James N. Rosenau (eds.), *World Systems Structure: Continuity and Change.* Beverly Hills, Calif.: Sage.

———, ed. 1982. *Socialist States in the World-System.* Beverly Hills, Calif.: Sage.

Church, Gordon. 1979. "Bucharest: Revolution in the Townscape Art." In R. A. French and Ian Hamilton (eds.), *The Socialist City: Spatial Structure and Urban Policy.* Chichester: John Wiley.

Codrescu, Andrei. 1994. *Zombification.* New York: St. Martin's.

Csanádi, Gábor, and János Ladányi. 1987. "Budapest—a városszerkezet történetének és a különböző társadalmi csoportok városszerkezeti elhelyezkedésének vizs-gálata." In *Szociológiai Műhelytanulmányok.* Budapest: Marx Károly Közgazdaságtudományi Egyetem.

Cséfalvay, Zoltán. 1995. "Budapest, a minikapitalisták városa." *Valóság* 8: 77–92.

Cséfalvay, Zoltán, and István Pomázi. 1990. "Some Problems of Innercity Revitaliza-tion (A Case Study of Budapest)." *Területi Kutatások-Regional Researches* 9: 27–37.

Csepeli, György, and Endre Sik. 1995. "Changing Content of Political Xenophobia in Hungary: Is the Growth of Xenophobia Inevitable?" In M. Fullerton, Endre Sik, and J. Tóth (eds.), *Refugees and Migrants: Hungary at a Crossroads.* Budapest: Institute for Political Science.

Daniell, J., and R. Struyk. 1994. "Housing Privatization in Moscow: Who Privatizes and Why." *International Journal of Urban and Regional Research* 18, no. 3: 510–25.

Davis, Mike. 1985. "Urban Renaissance and the Spirit of Postmodernism." *New Left Review* 151: 106–13.

———. 1992a. *City of Quartz: Excavating the Future in Los Angeles.* New York: Vintage.

———. 1992b. "Fortress Los Angeles: The Militarization of Urban Space." Pp. 154–180 in Michael Sorkin (ed.), *Variations on a Theme Park: The New American City and the End of Public Space.* New York: Farrar, Straus & Giroux.

Demszky, Gábor. 1994. *Budapest jövője. Várospolitika 2000–ig.* Budapest: Vánosháza.

Diósdi, László. 1983. "Szakszervezeti tagok kérdezik: Hogyan lehet ugyanazért a munkáért a költségek terhére többet fizetni, mint a bérgazdálkodás keretei között?" *Népszava*, March 12.

Douglas, Mary. 1966. *Purity and Danger.* London: Routledge.

Duke, Vic, and Keith Grime. 1997. "Inequality in Post-communism." *Regional Studies* 31, no. 9: 883–90.

Enyedi, György. 1988. *A városnövekedés szakaszai.* Budapest: Akadémiai Kiadó.

———. 1992. "Urbanisation in East-Central Europe: Social Processes and Societal Responses in the State Socialist Systems." *Urban Studies* 29, no. 6: 869–80.

Enyedi, György, and Viktória Szirmai. 1992. *Budapest: A Central European Capital.* Trans. Vera Gáthy. London: Belhaven.

Erdei, Ferenc. 1974 [1939]. *A magyar város.* Budapest: Akadémiai Kiadó.

Eyal, Gil, Iván Szelényi, and Eleanor Townsley. 1997. "The Theory of Post-Communist Managerialism." *New Left Review* 222 (March-April): 60–92.

Featherstone, Mike. 1991. *Consumer Culture and Postmodernism.* London: Sage.

Forbes, Dean, and Nigel Thrift, eds. 1987. *The Socialist Third World: Urban Development and Territorial Planning.* Oxford: Blackwell.

French, R. A., and Ian Hamilton. 1979. "Is There a Socialist City?" In R. A. French and Ian Hamilton (eds.), *The Socialist City: Spatial Structure and Urban Policy.* Chichester: John Wiley.

Friesen, Hans. 1997. "Von der Moderne zur Postmoderne. Zur Genealogie der Architektur im 20. Jahrhundert." *Positionen* 2 (November). (Available on-line at http://www.theo.tu-cottbus.de/Wolke/X-positionen/Friesen/friesen.html)

Fucskó, Hajnal. 1995. "'Emberpiac' a Moszkva téren." *Magyar Nemzet,* April 27.

Fullerton, M., Endre Sik, and J. Tóth, eds. 1995. *Refugees and Migrants: Hungary at a Crossroads.* Budapest: Institute for Political Science.

Gale, Dennis E. 1984. *Neighborhood Revitalization and the Postindustrial City: A Multinational Perspective.* Lexington, Mass.: Lexington.

Gerő Péter, and Cs. Pecze. 1994. "A Belvárosi Irodaház Kft. elemzése a budapesti irodaházakról." *Ingatlanpiac,* September 18.

Glass, Ruth. 1964. "Introduction." In Ruth Glass, *London: Aspects of Change* (Centre for Urban Studies Report 3). London: MacGibbon & Kee.

Goffman, Erving. 1963. *Behavior in Public Spaces.* New York: Free Press.

Gottdiener, Mark. 1997. *The Theming of America: Dreams, Visions, and Commercial Spaces.* Boulder, Colo.: Westview.

Gottdiener, Mark, and Joe R. Feagin. 1988. "The Paradigm Shift in Urban Sociology." *Urban Affairs Quarterly* 24, no. 2: 163–87.

Gyáni, Gábor. 1983. *Család, háztartás és a városi cselédség.* Budapest: Magvető.

———. 1994. "Uses and Misuses of Public Space in Budapest: 1873–1914." In Thomas Bender and Carl E. Schorske (eds.), *Budapest and New York: Studies in Metropolitan Transformation: 1870–1930.* New York: Russell Sage.

György, Péter, and Zsolt Durkó Jr. 1993. *Utánzatok városa—Budapest.* Budapest: Cserépfalvi.

Habermas, Jürgen. 1989 [1962]. *The Structural Transformation of the Public Sphere.* Cambridge: MIT Press.

Hamilton, Ian. 1979. "Spatial Structure in East European Cities." In R. A. French and

Ian Hamilton (eds.), *The Socialist City: Spatial Structure and Urban Policy.* Chichester: John Wiley.

Hamilton, Ian, and A. Burnett. 1979. "Social Processes and Residential Structure." In R. A. French and Ian Hamilton (eds.), *The Socialist City: Spatial Structure and Urban Policy.* Chichester: John Wiley.

Hamnett, Chris. 1991. "The Blind Men and the Elephant: The Explanation of Gentrification." Pp. 30–51 in Jan van Weesep and Sako Musterd (eds.), *Urban Housing for the Better-Off: Gentrification in Europe.* Utrecht, Netherlands: Stedelijke Netwerken.

Hamnett, Chris, and Bill Randolph. 1986. "Tenurial Transformation and Flat Break-Up in London: The British Condo Experience." Pp. 121–52 in Neil Smith and Peter Williams (eds.), *Gentrification of the City.* Boston: Unwin Hyman.

Hanák, Péter. 1984. "Polgárosodás és urbanizáció (Polgári lakáskultúra Budapesten a 19. században)." *Történelmi Szemle* 1–2: 123–44.

Hankiss, Elemér. 1990. *East European Alternatives.* Oxford: Oxford University Press.

Hann, Chris M., ed. 1990. *Market Economy and Civil Society in Hungary.* London: F. Cass.

———. 1995. *The Skeleton at the Feast: Contributions to East European Anthropology.* Canterbury: University of Kent.

Hannerz, Ulf. 1980. *Exploring the City: Inquiries toward an Urban Anthropology.* New York: Columbia University Press.

———. 1996. *Transnational Connections: Culture, People, Places.* London: Routledge.

Harloe, Michael. 1996. "Cities in the Transition." Pp. 1–29 in Gregory Andrusz, Michael Harloe, and Iván Szelényi (eds.), *Cities after Socialism: Urban and Regional Change and Conflict in Post-Socialist Societies.* Oxford: Blackwell.

Hárs, Ágnes. 1995. "Migration and the Labour Market." In M. Fullerton, Endre Sik, and J. Tóth (eds.), *Refugees and Migrants: Hungary at a Crossroads.* Budapest: Institute for Political Science.

Harvey, David. 1973. *Social Justice and the City.* Baltimore: Johns Hopkins University Press.

———. 1978. "The Urban Process under Capitalism: A Framework for Analysis." *International Journal of Urban and Regional Research* 2, no. 1: 101–31.

———. 1987. "Flexible Accumulation through Urbanization: Reflections on 'Postmodernism' in the American City." *Antipode* 19, no. 3: 260–86.

———. 1989a. *The Condition of Postmodernity: An Enquiry into the Origins of Cultural Change.* Oxford: Basil Blackwell.

———. 1989b. "From Managerialism to Entrepreneurialism: The Transformation in Urban Governance in Late Capitalism." *Geografiska Annaler* 71: 3–17.

———. 1989c. *The Urban Experience.* Baltimore: Johns Hopkins University Press.

———. 1992. "Social Justice, Postmodernism and the City." *International Journal of Urban and Regional Research* 16, no. 4: 588–601.

Hegedűs, József. 1987. "Reconsidering the Roles of the State and the Market in Socialist Housing Systems." *International Journal of Urban and Regional Research* 11, no. 1: 79–97.

Hegedűs, József, K. Mark, R. Struyk, and Iván Tosics. 1993. "Privatizációs dilemma a budapesti bérlakásszektorban." *Szociológiai Szemle* 1993, no. 2: 45–69.

Hegedűs, József, and Iván Tosics. 1991. "Gentrification in Eastern Europe: The Case of Budapest." In Jan van Weesep and Sako Musterd (eds.), *Urban Housing for the Better-Off: Gentrification in Europe*. Utrecht, Netherlands: Stedelijke Netwerken.
———. 1994. "Privatisation and Rehabilitation in the Budapest Inner Districts." *Housing Studies* 9, no. 1: 39–54.

Heinritz, Günter, and Elisabeth Lichtenberger, eds. 1986. *The Take-Off of Suburbia and the Crisis of the Central City*. Stuttgart: Steiner Verlag Wiesbaden.

Howell, P. 1993. "Public Space and Public Sphere: Political Theory and the Historical Geography of Modernity." *Environment and Planning D: Society and Space* 11: 303–22.

Huyssen, Andreas. 1986. "Mass Culture as Woman: Modernism's Other." Pp. 44–64 in Andreas Huyssen, *After the Great Divide: Modernism, Mass Culture and Post-modernism*. Basingstoke: Macmillan.

Illyefalvy, Lajos, ed. 1941. *Budapest Székesfőváros Statisztikai Zsebkönyve*. Budapest: Budapest Székesfőváros Statisztikai Hivatala,.

Jackson, Kenneth T. 1985. *Crabgrass Frontier: The Suburbanization of the United States*. Oxford: Oxford University Press.

Jacobs, Jane. 1961. *The Death and Life of Great American Cities*. New York: Vintage.

Jager, Michael. 1986. "Class Definition and the Esthetics of Gentrification: Victoriana in Melbourne." Pp. 78–91 in Neil Smith and Peter Williams (eds.), *Gentrification of the City*. Boston: Unwin Hyman.

Jameson, Fredric. 1984. "Postmodernism, or the Cultural Logic of Late Capitalism." *New Left Review* 146 (July-August): 53–92.

Jencks, Charles. 1984. *The Language of Post-Modern Architecture*. New York: Rizzoli.
———. 1993. *Heteropolis: Los Angeles: The Riots and the Strange Beauty of Hetero-Architecture*. London: Academy Editions.

Kane, Robert S. 1968. *Eastern Europe, A to Z*. New York: Doubleday.

Kennedy, Michael, and David A. Smith. 1989. "East-Central European Urbanization: A Political Economy of the World-System Perspective." *International Journal of Urban and Regional Research* 13, no. 4: 597–624.

King, Anthony. 1990. *Global Cities: Post-Imperialism and the Internationalisation of London*. London: Routledge.

Knight, Richard, and Gary Gappert, eds. 1989. *Cities in a Global Society*. Newbury Park, Calif.: Sage.

Kolosi, Tamás. 1980. "A 'mellékes' nem mellékes." *Élet és Irodalom*, March 29, 5.

Konrád, György, and Iván Szelényi. 1977. "Social Conflicts of Underurbanization." In Michael Harloe (ed.), *Captive Cities: Studies in the Political Economy of Cities and Regions*. London: John Wiley.
———. 1979 [1974]. *The Intellectuals on the Road to Class Power*. Trans. by Andrew Arato and Richard E. Allen. New York: Harcourt Brace Jovanovich.

Koptiuch, Kristin. 1991. "Third-Worlding at Home." *Social Text* 28: 87–99.

Kornai, János. 1997. "Editorial: Reforming the Welfare State in Postsocialist Societies." *World Development* 25: 1183–86.

Kovács, Zoltán. 1990. "Rich and Poor in the Budapest Housing Market." In Chris M. Hann (ed.), *Market Economy and Civil Society in Hungary*. London: F. Cass.
———. 1994. "A City at the Crossroads: Social and Economic Transformation in

Budapest." *International Journal of Urban and Regional Research* 31, no. 7: 1097–1115.

KSH. 1980. *Budapest statisztikai zsebkönyve, 1980.* Budapest: KSH.

———. 1982. *Budapest statisztikai évkönyve, 1981.* Budapest: KSH.

———. 1985. *Magyar statisztikai évkönyv, 1984.* Budapest: KSH.

———. 1990. *Magyar statisztikai évkönyv, 1989.* Budapest: KSH.

———. 1992. *Budapest statisztikai évkönyve.* Budapest: KSH.

———. 1993. *Az önkormányzati bérlakásban élők lakásviszonyai.* Budapest: KSH.

———. 1994a. *Budapest statisztikai évkönyve, 1993.* Budapest: KSH.

———. 1994b. *Statistical Yearbook of Hungary, 1993.* Budapest: KSH.

———. 1997. *Budapest statisztikai évkönyve, 1996/Statistical Yearbook of Budapest, 1996.* Budapest: KSH.

Ladányi, János, and Iván Szelényi. 1998. "Class, Ethnicity and Urban Restructuring in Postcommunist Hungary." Pp. 67–86 in György Enyedi (ed.), *Social Change and Urban Restructuring in Central Europe.* Budapest: Akadémiai Kiadó.

Lees, Loretta. 1994. "Gentrification in London and New York: An Atlantic Gap?" *Housing Studies* 9, no. 2: 199–217.

Lefebvre, Henri. 1972. *Le droit à la ville.* Paris: Editions Anthropos.

Lefebvre, Henri. 1991 [1974]. *The Production of Space.* Trans. Donald Nicholson-Smith. Oxford: Blackwell.

Lengyel, Péter. 1993. "Belső európai tájon" (interview by Zsófia Mihancsik). *Budapesti Negyed* 1, no. 2: 180–88.

Lofland, Lyn. 1973. *A World of Strangers: Order and Action in Urban Public Space.* New York: Basic Books.

———. 1989. "Social Life in the Public Realm." *Journal of Contemporary Ethnography* 17, no. 4: 453–82.

Lukacs, John. 1988. *Budapest 1900: A Historical Portrait of a City and Its Culture.* New York: Weidenfeld & Nicolson.

Magris, Claudio. 1989 [1986]. *Danube.* Trans. Patrick Creagh. New York: Farrar, Straus & Giroux.

Manchin, Róbert, and Iván Szelényi. 1987. "Social Policy under State Socialism." In Gosta Esping-Andersen, Lee Rainwater, and Martin Rein (eds.), *Stagnation and Renewal in Social Policy.* Armonk, N.Y.: M. E. Sharpe.

Marcuse, Peter. 1996. "Privatization and Its Discontents: Property Rights in Land and Housing in the Transition in Eastern Europe." Pp. 119–91 in Gregory Andrusz, Michael Harloe, and Iván Szelényi (eds.), *Cities after Socialism: Urban and Regional Change and Conflict in Post-Socialist Societies.* Oxford: Blackwell.

Margolis, Jon. 1995. "Reopening the Frontier." *New York Times Magazine,* October 15.

Márkus, István. 1971. *Kifelé a feudalizmusból.* Budapest: Szépirodalmi Könyvkiadó.

Massey, Doreen. 1988. "A New Class of Geography." *Marxism Today,* May, 12–15.

MATERV. 1991. *Moszkva tér. Részletes rendezési terv.* Budapest: MATERV.

Mészáros, István. 1995. *Beyond Capital: Towards a Theory of Transition.* London: Merlin.

Miliutin, Nikolai Aleksandrovich. 1974. *Sotsgorod: The Problem of Building Socialist Cities.* Trans. Arthur Sprague. Cambridge: MIT Press.

Mills, C. Wright. 1959. *The Sociological Imagination.* London: Oxford University Press.

Mollenkopf, John Hull, and Manuel Castells. 1991. *Dual City: Restructuring New York.* New York: Russell Sage.

Molnár Gál, Péter. 1995. "Mándy Iván elköltözött." *Népszabadság,* October 7.

Mouffe, Chantal. 1995. "Post-Marxism: Democracy and Identity." *Environment and Planning D: Society and Space* 13: 259–65.

Mumford, Lewis. 1961. *The City in History: Its Origins, Its Transformation, and Its Prospects.* New York: Harcourt, Brace & World.

Murie, Alan. 1991. "Tenure Conversion and Social Change: New Elements in British Cities." In Jan van Weesep and Sako Musterd (eds.), *Urban Housing for the Better-Off: Gentrification in Europe.* Utrecht, Netherlands: Stedelijke Netwerken.

Musil, Jiří. 1980. *Urbanization in Socialist Countries.* Armonk, New York: M. E. Sharpe.

———. 1987. "Housing Policy and the Sociospatial Structure of Cities in a Socialist Country: The Example of Prague." *International Journal of Urban and Regional Research* 11, no. 1: 27–36.

———. 1995. "The Czech Housing System in the Middle of Transition." *International Journal of Urban and Regional Research* 32, no. 10: 1679–1684.

Nava, Mica. 1997. "Modernity's Disavowal: Women, the City and the Department Store." Pp. 56–91 in Pasi Falk and Colin Campbell (eds.), *The Shopping Experience.* London: Sage.

Nee, Victor. 1989. "A Theory of Market Transition: From Redistribution to Markets in State Socialism." *American Sociological Review* 54: 663–81.

———. 1991. "Social Inequalities in Reforming State Socialism: Between Redistribution and Markets in China." *American Sociological Review* 56: 267–82.

Nguyên, duc Nhuân. 1984. "Do the Urban and Regional Management Policies of Socialist Vietnam Reflect the Patterns of the Ancient Mandarin Bureaucracy?" *International Journal of Urban and Regional Research* 8, no. 1: 73–89.

North, Douglass C. 1993. "Institutions and Credible Commitment." *Journal of Institutional and Theoretical Economics* 149, no. 1: 11–23.

Pahl, Ray. 1977. "Managers, Technical Experts and the State: Forms of Mediation, Manipulation and Dominance in Urban and Regional Development." In Michael Harloe (ed.), *Captive Cities: Studies in the Political Economy of Cities and Regions.* London: John Wiley.

Peacock, James. 1986. *The Anthropological Lens: Harsh Light, Soft Focus.* Cambridge: Cambridge University Press.

Perlez, Jane. 1993. "Gentrifiers March on, to the Danube Banks." *New York Times,* August 18.

Pichler-Milanovich, Natasha. 1994. "The Role of Housing Policy in the Transformation Process of Central-East European Cities." *Urban Studies* 31, no. 7: 1097–1115.

Pickvance, C. G. 1994. "Housing Privatization and Housing Protest in the Transition from State Socialism: A Comparative Study of Budapest and Moscow." *International Journal of Urban and Regional Research* 18, no. 3: 433–50.

Pietz, William. 1988. "The 'Post-Colonialism' of Cold War Discourse." *Social Text* 19–20 (fall): 55–83.

Pogány, Sára. 1990. "Madách sétány '90, avagy lesz-e magyar Bond Street?" *Beszélő,* September 15, 15.

Polanyi, Karl. 1944. *The great transformation.* New York: Farrar & Rinehart.

———. 1957. "The Economy as Instituted Process." In Karl Polanyi, Conrad M.

Arensberg, and Harry Pearson (eds.), *Trade and Markets in the Early Empires: Economies in History and Theory.* Glencoe, Ill.: Free Press.

———. 1977. *The Livelihood of Man.* Ed. Harry W. Pearson, New York: Academic Press.

Portes, Alejandro. 1974. "Modernity and Development: A Critique." *Studies in Comparative International Development* 9 (spring): 247–79.

———. 1978. "Toward a Structural Analysis of Illegal (Undocumented) Immigration." *International Migration Review* 44, no. 12: 469–84.

Portes, Alejandro, and József Böröcz. 1989. "Contemparary Immigration: Theoretical Perspectives on Its Determinants and Modes of Incorporation." *International Migration Review* 87, no. 23: 606–30.

Rév, István. 1984. "Local Autonomy or Centralism—When Was the Original Sin Committed?" *International Journal of Urban and Regional Research* 8, no. 1: 38–63.

———. 1987. "The Advantages of Being Atomized: How Hungarian Peasants Coped with Collectivization." *Dissent* (summer): 335–50.

Robbins, Bruce, ed. 1993. *The Phantom Public Sphere.* Minneapolis: University of Minnesota Press.

Róna-Tas, Ákos. 1994. "The First Shall Be Last? Entrepreneurship and Communist Cadres in the Transition from Socialism." *American Journal of Sociology* 100, no. 1: 40–69.

———. 1997. *The Grand Surprise of the Small Transformation: The Demise of Communism and the Rise of the Private Sector in Hungary.* Ann Arbor: University of Michigan Press.

Rutherford, Jonathan. 1990. "A Place Called Home: Identity and the Cultural Politics of Difference." In Jonathan Rutherford (ed.), *Identity. Community, Culture, Difference.* London: Lawrence & Wishart.

Rybczynski, Witold. 1995. *City Life: Urban Expectations in a New World.* New York: Scribner.

Sassen, Saskia. 1990. "Economic Restructuring and the American City." *Annual Review of Sociology* 16: 465–90.

———. 1991. *The Global City: New York, London, Tokyo.* Princeton, N.J.: Princeton University Press.

Schorske, Carl. 1981. *Fin-de-Siècle Vienna: Politics and Culture.* New York: Vintage.

Sennett, Richard. 1970. *Uses of Disorder.* Harmondsworth: Penguin.

———. 1974. *The Fall of Public Man.* New York: W. W. Norton.

———. 1990. *The Conscience of the Eye: The Design and Social Life of Cities.* New York: W. W. Norton.

Sik, Endre. 1994. "From the Multicoloured to the Black and White Economy: The Hungarian Second Economy and the Transformation." *International Journal of Urban and Regional Research* 18, no. 1: 46–70.

———. 1995. "Measuring the Unregistered Economy in Post-Communist Transformation." In *Eurosocial Report,* vol. 52. Vienna: European Centre.

Simmel, Georg. 1971a [1904]. "Fashion." Pp. 294–323 in Georg Simmel, *Georg Simmel on Individuality and Social Forms: Selected Writings.* Ed. Donald Levine. Chicago: University of Chicago Press.

———. 1971b [1903]. "The Metropolis and Mental Life." Pp. 324–39 in Georg Simmel, *Georg Simmel on Individuality and Social Forms: Selected Writings.* Ed. Donald Levine. Chicago: University of Chicago Press.

———. 1971c [1908]. "The Poor." Pp. 150–78 in Georg Simmel, *Georg Simmel on Individuality and Social Forms: Selected Writings.* Ed. Donald Levine. Chicago: University of Chicago Press.

Smith, Neil. 1986. "Gentrification, the Frontier, and the Restructuring of Urban Space." Pp. 15–34 in Neil Smith and Peter Williams (eds.), *Gentrification of the City.* Boston: Unwin Hyman.

———. 1987. "Of Yuppies and Housing: Gentrification, Social Restructuring, and the Urban Dream." *Environment and Planning D: Society and Space* 5: 151–72.

———. 1992. "New City, New Frontier: The Lower East Side as Wild, Wild West." In Michael Sorkin (ed.), *Variations on a Theme Park: The New American City and the End of Public Space.* New York: Farrar, Straus & Giroux.

———. 1996. *The New Urban Frontier: Gentrification and the Revanchist City.* London: Routledge.

Smith, Neil, and Peter Williams, eds. 1986. *Gentrification of the City.* Boston: Unwin Hyman.

Sommer, Robert. 1969. *Personal Space: The Behavioral Basis of Design.* Englewood Cliffs, N.J.: Prentice Hall.

Sorkin, Michael, ed. 1992. *Variations on a Theme Park: The New American City and the End of Public Space.* New York: Farrar, Straus & Giroux.

Staniszkis, Jadwiga. 1991. *The Dynamics of Breakthrough in Eastern Europe: The Polish Experience.* Berkeley: University of California Press.

Stark, David. 1986. "Rethinking Internal Labor Markets: New Insights from a Comparative Perspective." *American Sociological Review* 51: 492–504.

———. 1992. "Path Dependence and Privatization Strategies in East Central Europe." *East European Politics and Societies* 4, no. 1: 17–54.

———. 1996. "Recombinant Property in East European Capitalism." *American Journal of Sociology* 101, no. 4: 993–1027.

Sudjic, Deyan. 1993 [1991]. *The 100 Mile City.* London: Flamingo.

Sýkora, Luděk. 1994. "Local Urban Restructuring as a Mirror of Globalisation Processes: Prague in the 1990s." *Urban Studies* 31, no. 7: 1149–1166.

Sz., A. 1995. "Csepel: egy gyáróriás tündöklése és bukása." *Népszabadság,* August 15, VIII.

Szalai, Anna. 1998. "Az évszázad építkezése a Nyugatinál." *Népszabadság,* October 28.

Szalai, Erzsébet. 1993. "Technokraták, kliensek, yuppie-k." *Kritika* (September): 10–12. (Reprinted in *Útelágazás. Hatalom és értelmiség az államszocializmus után.* Budapest: Pesti Szalon és Savaria University Press, 1994.)

Szelényi, Iván. 1978. "Social Inequalities in State Socialist Redistributive Economies." *International Journal of Comparative Sociology* 19, nos. 1–2: 63–87.

———. 1981. "Urban Development and Regional Management in Eastern Europe." *Theory and Society* 10: 169–205.

———. 1983. *Urban Social Inequalities under State Socialism.* London: Oxford University Press.

———. 1988. *Socialist Entrepreneurs: Embourgeoisement in Rural Hungary.* Madison: University of Wisconsin Press.

———. 1993. "East European Socialist Cities: How Different Are They?" In Greg Guldin and Aidan Southall (eds.), *Urban Anthropology in China.* Leiden, Netherlands: E. J. Brill.

————. 1996. "Cities under Socialism—and After." Pp. 286–317 in Gregory Andrusz, Michael Harloe, and Iván Szelényi (eds.), *Cities after Socialism: Urban and Regional Change and Conflict in Post-Socialist Societies*. Oxford: Blackwell.

Szelényi, Iván, and George Konrád. 1969. *Az új lakótelepek szociológiai problémái*. Budapest: Akadémiai.

Szilágyi, Ákos. 1997. "A kelet-európai szökőállam." *2000* 9 (October): 12–24.

Szőnyei, Tamás. 1996. "Bérszomj." *Magyar Narancs*, November 7, 12–14.

Texier, Edmond. 1852. *Tableau de Paris*. Paris: Inter-Livres.

Tosics, Iván. 1987. "Privatization in Housing Policy: The Case of the Western Countries and That of Hungary." *International Journal of Urban and Regional Research* 11, no. 1: 61–78.

Tóth, Zoltán. 1991. "A rendi norma és a 'keresztyén polgárisodás.'" *Századvég* 2–3: 75–130.

Városkutatás Kft. 1992. *Passage Madách* (survey). October.

Wacquant, Loïc. 1993. "Urban Outcasts: Stigma and Division in the Black American Ghetto and the French Urban Periphery." *International Journal of Urban and Regional Research* 17, no. 3: 366–83.

Wallerstein, Immanuel. 1974. *The Modern World-System*. New York: Academic Press.

————. 1999. "Social Science and the Communist Interlude, or Interpretations of Contemporary History." Pp. 7–18 in Immanuel Wallerstein, *The End of the World as We Know It: Social Science for the Twenty-First Century*. Minneapolis: University of Minnesota Press.

Warner, Michael. 1993. "The Mass Public and the Mass Subject." Pp. 234–56 in Bruce Robbins (ed.), *The Phantom Public Sphere*. Minneapolis: University of Minnesota Press.

Weber, Max. 1978 [1920]. *Economy and Society: An Outline of Interpretive Sociology*. Eds. Guenther Roth and Claus Wittich. Berkeley: University of California Press.

Weclawowicz, Grzegorz. 1996. *Contemporary Poland: Space and Society*. London: UCL.

Weesep, Jan van, and Sako Musterd, eds. 1991. *Urban Housing for the Better-Off: Gentrification in Europe*. Utrecht, Netherlands: Stedelijke Netwerken.

Williams, Peter. 1984. "Gentrification in Britain and Europe." In Bruce London and John Palen (eds.), *Gentrification, Displacement, and Neighborhood Revitalization*. Albany: State University of New York Press.

————. 1986. "Class Constitution through Spatial Reconstruction? A Re-evaluation of Gentrification in Australia, Britain, and the United States." In Neil Smith and Peter Williams (eds.), *Gentrification of the City*. Boston: Unwin Hyman.

Williams, Rosalind. 1982. *Dream Worlds: Mass Consumption in Late-Nineteenth-Century France*. Berkeley: University of California Press.

Wilson, Elizabeth. 1992. *The Sphinx in the City: Urban Life, the Control of Disorder, and Women*. Berkeley: University of California Press.

Wirth, Louis. 1938. "Urbanism as a Way of Life" *American Journal of Sociology* 44, no. 1: 1–24.

Wolfe, Tom. 1987. *The Bonfire of the Vanities*. New York: Farrar, Straus & Giroux.

Young, Iris Marion. 1987. "Impartiality and the Civic Public: Some Implications of Feminist Critiques of Moral and Political Theory." In Seyla Benhabib and Drucilla Cornell (eds.), *Feminism as Critique: On the Politics of Gender*. Minneapolis: University of Minnesota Press.

————. 1990. *Justice and the Politics of Difference*. Princeton, N.J.: Princeton University Press.

Zolnay, János. 1993. "Lakásprivatizáció, városfejlesztés, helyi politizálás Erzsébetvárosban." *Esély* 1: 5–32.

Zukin, Sharon. 1982. *Loft Living: Culture and Capital in Urban Change*. Baltimore: Johns Hopkins University Press.

————. 1995. *The Cultures of Cities*. Cambridge: Blackwell.

Index

Accumulation (of capital): flexible, 62, 127; original, 2

Agora, 122, 150, 177

Agricultural town *(mezőváros)*, 27–28

American (-type), 110, 145, 184; housing, 158; "pattern of growth," 183

Architecture: communicative, 166; defensible, 152, 157, 167; European urban, 69, 196 n.14; hetero-, 179–80; mall, 148, 151; postmodern, 63–64, 93, 158–59, 164–65; socialist, 3, 30

Arendt, Hannah, 177

Autos. *See* Cars

Banlieue, 27, 174

Beggars (begging), 113–14, 128

Block 15 rehabilitation, 73–77

Bonaventure Hotel, 165, 166

Budapest Film, 131–33, 138–44, 154

Capitalist city, 9; versus socialist city, 20, 162

Cars, 149, 162, 164; alarms, 160; and public space, 163

Central Park (New York), 176

Chicago, 173–74

China, 36, 37

Cinema, 153; art (Art Movie Network), 129, 131–45, 153–55; attendance at, 133–34; multiplex, 131, 140, 144, 149

Collective consumption, 2, 9, 126, 168, 186; the city as site of, 17; the state in, 20

Colonial city, 4

Commercialization, 30, 62, 112, 152

Community, 177, 179, 181

Comparative strategy, 6, 14, 23, 24; implicitly, 8; mirrored comparison, 34, 38, 56

Compensation vouchers, 43–44, 197–98 n.9

Consumerism, 60; and citizenship, 152; socialist *(see* Frigidaire socialism)

Consumption: collective *(see* Collective consumption); cultural, 129, 138, 142, 151, 152

Conversion of buildings: functional, 60, 63, 89; tenure, 63, 67, 77–79

Corvin (Budapest Film Palace), 140–41, 204 n.5

Crime, 161, 173

Csepel, 87–89, 146, 170, 172

Csikágó. *See* Chicago

Defensible architecture, 152, 157, 167

Democratization: and fragmentation. *(see* Fragmentation); of public sphere, 152

Dense fence, 159, 161

Difference, 6; capitalist-socialist

219

Judit Bodnár is a research fellow in the Center for Russian, Central, and East European Studies at Rutgers University and a member of the Trans-Plan(e)t Research Group for Comparative-Historical Cross-Border Studies in Budapest. She has taught at the Eötvös Loránd University in Budapest, the Budapest University of Economics, and the University of California at Irvine. She has published on cities, public space, and social change.